Echoes
from the
Battlefield

"We have come here, not for things that die, but for things that cannot die... For human history is not a Dead Sea, it is a flowing river."

—Major General Joshua Lawrence Chamberlain at a monument dedication in Gorham, Maine, October 1866

Echoes
from the
Battlefield

First-Person Accounts
of Civil War Past Lives

Barbara Lane

ASSOCIATION FOR
RESEARCH AND
ENLIGHTENMENT

A.R.E. Press • Virginia Beach • Virginia

A.R.E. Press
Sixty-Eighth & Atlantic Avenue
P.O. Box 656
Virginia Beach, VA 23451-0656

Library of Congress Cataloging-in-Publication Data
Lane, Barbara, 1947-
    Echoes from the battlefield: first-person accounts of Civil War past lives / by Barbara Lane.
        p.   cm.
    Includes bibliographical references.
    ISBN 0-87604-355-4
    1. Hypnosis—Case studies. 2. Reincarnation—Case studies. 3. United States—History—Civil War, 1861-1865—Personal narratives. I. Title.
BF1156.R45L36   1996
133.9'01'3—dc20   95-44539

Cover design by Richard Boyle

Dedication

This book is dedicated to my loving parents, John and Kathleen Lane, to all those touched by the Civil War that they might be healed, to my fellow light workers, and to my partners, Robert E. Lee and Edgar Cayce, who assisted in this work from the other side.

"We are not enemies, but friends. We must not be enemies. Though passion may have strained, it must not break our bonds of affection. The mystic chords of memory, stretching from every battlefield, and patriot grave, to every living heart and hearthstone, all over this broad land, will yet swell the chorus of the Union, when again touched, as surely they will be, by the better angels of our nature."

The conclusion of President Lincoln's
First Inaugural Address

Contents

Acknowledgments ....*xiii*

Foreword ....*xv*

1 • Echoes in the Mist 1

2. • Do We Live Again? 15

3. • A Short Course in Reenacting and Civil War
Buzz Words 32

4. • *Steve:* The Soldier Returns 45

5. • *Alan:* Beginner's Luck 59

6. • *Dave:* Strange Coincidences 69

7. • *Rob:* Out of the Mouths of Babes 85

8. • *Buddy:* Heart Problems 106

9. • *MaryLynne:* A Hoop Skirt for a Gun 118

10. • *Dale:* Richmond Burning 128

11. • *Ed:* Food for the Soul 149

12. • *Tom:* An Officer and a Gentleman 159

13. • *David:* Living Death 174

14. • *Paul:* Home to Alexandria 183

15. • *Brian:* A Historian's Heart 193

16. • Echoes Revisited 217

Endnotes *227*

Bibliography *237*

For Further Reading *243*

Reenactment Events and Involvement *245*

Acknowledgments

With joy and gratitude in my heart, I thank all those who supported my research and writing, particularly the staffs at the National Archives in Washington, D. C., and the Lloyd House in Alexandria, Virginia; Tracey Hormuth of the Prince William County Park Authority; Don Steiner of Fort Washington, Maryland; Captain Albert Fuerst, Company D, 1st U.S. Artillery; and especially historian Brian Pohanka for assisting me with Civil War research.

I would also like to thank Dr. Albert Lock for his organizational abilities and scientific approach; Jon Robertson of A.R.E. Press for his gentle guidance and enthusiasm for my project; my friend, Dodie Henson, and my mother, Kathleen Lane, for their joyful editing. I am grateful to my parents, John and Kathleen Lane, who unwittingly laid the groundwork for my passion for metaphysics, Barry Woods for taking this Civil War journey with me, Marie Sisk whose Civil War attire transformed me into an elegant nineteenth-century lady, and the reenactors in my study for their delightful cooperation and their insatiable appetite for the Civil War.

Foreword

Heavy rain created monumental ruts and puddles in the field that had been used to film the movie *Gettysburg*. Only the heartiest reenactors and spectators were trudging through ankle-deep mud to commemorate the 132nd anniversary of the battle. On Saturday, July 2, 1995, fifteen months after I had completed a study on Civil War reenactors, I found myself one of them. I was learning how many bones there are in a hoop skirt, how to sit (semi-gracefully), and how to keep my light pink dress out of the mud. I was wearing the complete authentic ensemble from snood to stockings.

Meanwhile, my friend Barry Woods had been outfitted in a butternut uniform that was authentic, right down to the brogans that were a size too small. By the time of the battle, he had been drilled in the use of two manuals of arms, in the shooting of his rifle, and in preparing his own cartridges. He could even explain to spectators why his Confederate uniform was butternut colored.

The transition to my involvement with Civil War reenacting had been interesting—first as a spectator, then as a researcher, and finally as a participant.

How did this unusual situation come about? After talking to various reenactors at several reenactments and living history events, I was impressed with the serious enthusiasm they exuded—so much so that their involvement in "the hobby," as they call it, appeared to be more of an obsession. The fervor and sincerity of the participants led me to ask: Could this passion be a result of the remembrance of a lifetime in the Civil War period? And if so, could I, in my capacity as a past-life regression therapist, help them to recall their past life-times?

This precipitated my study into the idea. I located twelve subjects, all reenactors, who were willing to try the experiment. They had several things in common: Most were sticklers for facts. Nearly all were perfectionists when it came to reenactment of Civil War themes.

And most of these Civil War enthusiasts had skepticism about reincarnation. Even so, under hypnosis, all twelve recalled memories of a past life in the Civil War era.

As a clinical hypnotherapist using standard past-life regression hypnosis techniques, I was able to eavesdrop into their minds as they were actually reliving their experiences in the Civil War. No longer was the war something from old history books. It was alive in my living room. From their lips, piece after piece of astonishing information unfolded: details about their uniforms; camp life; being wounded, even dying.

The results of their past-life regressions, which I carried out between late 1993 and early 1994, were as varied as the people themselves, who were a mix of social classes, gender, geographic origin, and occupations.

This book, then, is the first-person account of twelve past lives that took place during the Civil War. I originally carried out this work as part of my dissertation for a Ph.D. in metaphysical sciences from Westbrook University in New Mexico, but became so excited by the material's broader implications and interest for a larger audience that I began to assemble the material in book form.

In addition to the regression interviews themselves, I invested hundreds of hours doing historical research and fact-checking on the data that came out of the regressions. The search led to cemeteries, battlefields, archivists, and historians. I found myself sifting through original Civil War muster rolls and felt as if I were exhuming the soldiers and infusing life back into them as I dusted off the National Archives's musty file folders that held their war records. Not only were most of my subjects' historical facts accurate, but I was able to find eleven matches of twelve that had some conformity to the recalled lifetimes.

Author's note: With the exception of Paul Jones, all the reenactor regression subjects have given permission for me to use their real names. The actual text of the regression narratives has been, in places, condensed and edited to enhance readability.

1

Echoes in the Mist

Light rain beat down on the windshield, as my friend Barry Woods and I drove through the streets of Old Town, Alexandria, where iron lamp posts light up two-story eighteenth- and nineteenth-century restored rowhouses.

We had been debating if the weather would allow us to continue with our plans—a torchlit tour of Fort Washington, just across the Potomac River in Maryland. The fort has been historically preserved and on special occasions, like that evening, living historians would dress as Civil War soldiers and re-create the way life was at the fort during the Civil War.

We decided to take a chance and go despite the weather.

Once across the Potomac, the visibility was poor. Through the darkness and the drizzle, the steamy June evening mixed with the rain which caused vapors to rise from the warm ground, creating a surrealistic feeling. The forests surrounding Fort Washington seemed to shroud it from the twentieth century. After wondering if we were lost, we approached a small gate house. We were becoming disoriented. A winding road left us confused as to the location of the parking lot. Finally finding it, we jumped out of the car. As we began walking, we distinguished Fort Washington's masonry looming out of the mist.

We hastened to the stone drawbridge but, instead of seeing friendly faces, a serious duty guard in a Union Civil War uniform, already in character, challenged us. He looked at our passes, discovering that one had not been signed by the adjutant. This made for a delay. He eyed us suspiciously after determining that we had just come from Alexandria. For all he knew, we might be spies or we might have come to sell liquor to the soldiers. After all, not just anybody can walk into a military garrison.

While we waited for the adjutant's approval, he told us the latest gossip and politics in the capital. Although it usually took a few days for news to reach the fort, he was quite current on the happenings of June 9, 1861. Never stepping out of character, he described for us the edginess of the soldiers. The firing on Fort Sumter had only been seven weeks earlier, and it was just a fortnight since the Union occupation of Alexandria. Relaxing a bit, he said the soldiers were all in a twitter about a recent balloon ascension in Washington City that had been visible from the fort.

The smell of a wood fire wafted from his guard room. Through the door, I could see two bunk beds. They were wide ones, and he told us that, in winter, the men doubled up to keep warm. There were two wooden crates on top of each other that served as a desk, and there were also a chair and a couple of wood benches. Across from the guard room was a jail used for imprisoning soldiers for various offenses.

As he allowed us to walk beyond the drawbridge into the fort through a brick tunnel, my eyes fell on the torches flickering on the parade grounds. Stationed about the garrison in the fog, the soldiers seemed to have an ethereal quality about them. With each step on the wet ground, we could feel the years roll away—until we were there, finding ourselves in 1861.

Within the walls of this self-contained site, we had somehow stepped back in time. We felt as if we were in a vacuum or a time warp. In the isolation of the site, we were transported back 129 years.

Somehow the drawbridge had been a connecting link from the twentieth to the nineteenth century.

We were directed to the adjutant's office around the corner and up the stone steps. He was quite a well-educated fellow who could read and write and remember lots of facts and figures. The Confederates' blockade of the Potomac had given him problems getting fresh vegetables for the troops. Apparently, the men had also complained about the infrequency of the mail. Getting straw from the local farmers was another issue to handle. Most of the local population were Southern sympathizers and couldn't be trusted.

The adjutant made a disparaging comment about the lack of bravery of the Southern soldiers. Barry bristled. He'd been born and reared in Georgia. His great-grandfather had fought in most of the major battles of the war, had been wounded, imprisoned, and then walked home to eventually father nine kids. He died many years later with a bullet—a minie ball—still in his leg. Barry immediately jumped to the defense of the bravery of the Confederates. He'd clearly been drawn into the drama.

As his senior officer entered the office, the adjutant snapped to attention. The officer discussed their recent trip up in Washington City to sign for ordinance stores. After he left, the adjutant complained about all the record-keeping and form-signing such a trip entailed.

Leaving his office, we moved past the parade grounds. It was eerie to be the only civilians present and there was something strange about the stillness. The air hung heavy. The moon was just a hazy glow. We walked past the flickering torches.

Officers' quarters loomed in the background. On the other side of the flagpole and to the back were the soldiers' barracks. Breaking the silence, some of the soldiers marched up to the flagpole, repeated their instructions, and relieved the guards on duty.

The little bit of moonlight that streamed through the clouds fell on the artillerymen who explained how the cannons worked. They used various forms of ammunition—from spherical case shells to shrapnel and canisters. While they expounded on the pros and cons of the various fragmentation and bursts that would result from each, I looked out over the Potomac. On this murky evening, the lights of Alexandria and Washington City were indistinct, almost obscure.

The soldiers illustrated that it took seven of them to load and fire a cannon. It seemed almost like a ballet in the sense that everyone had their roles and they were all reliant on each other's movements.

The men said that on a clear night, downriver, you could see the large trees of Mount Vernon, and upriver, the lights of Alexandria. In the daytime, you could see the red roof of President Washington's home to the south and Washington City to the north. The Federals exuded a strong sense of pride at defending the nation's capital via the Potomac. If the Confederates shelled Washington City from ships, they believed it would do more political than physical damage. Another reason for their presence in Maryland was to hold the state in the Union, even under force of arms.

As the light shown on their faces, their eyes lit up with passion. They told us how Robert E. Lee himself had approved the construction design for the sinks when he was still an army chief engineer.

Soon, it wasn't so much what they were saying that intrigued me. It was as if I were tapping into some inner sanctum of their souls. These ghostly figures had become visibly more animated, their enthusiasm radiating. They spoke with an intense conviction that went far beyond the facts. Could this conviction have come from beyond the grave? It was uncanny how very comfortable they were in their surroundings. Had I stumbled on a secret so private that it was locked within the subconscious minds of these living historians? Was their passion so intimate that its true source was hidden from their own conscious minds?

It seemed as if time had stood still for Barry and me. We were surprised to find that it was already past the soldiers' bedtime. Through the mist, we quietly walked back across the parade ground. The torches flickered and danced, while the breeze appeared to carry a hint of echoes from the past.

As we walked through the now very dark passage and across the drawbridge, we left behind the enclosure that had triggered our time travel. We felt uncomfortable, as if we had to consciously adjust to the time frame of our twentieth-century lives.

The ride back to Alexandria was filled with reflection for both of us. Normally skeptical of such things, Barry, an engineer, was touched by the other-worldly quality of the experience. Meanwhile, being a hypnotherapist with a specialty in past-life regression therapy, I was haunted by the possibility that these weekend soldiers may actually have been replaying former lives. The men's fervor for the era had deeply stirred me.

Fourteen months later, I again came face to face with this nagging thought about reincarnation when Barry and I attended our first reenactment—the Battle of First Manassas or Bull Run. As we arrived at what is now a county park near the original battlefield in Manassas, Virginia, I began, once again, to feel the twentieth century slip away.

This time, as we stepped out of the car, the parking lot became the barrier that divided the centuries. With the sedans and convertibles clearly out of view, our senses again transported us back in time. Impressions bombarded our senses—horses neighing, bugles blowing, children laughing, men marching, flags flying.

This was different from our fort experience. Although Fort Washington was vitally important in defending the nation's capital, it saw no actual fighting during the Civil War. Here, things were gearing up for an actual battle reenactment. The area was teeming with excitement and activity. Everywhere we looked, we saw a new slice of the re-creation these one thousand people collectively and individually were producing. Their commitment to re-creating the authenticity of the battle and the 1860s lifestyle was evident.

Wandering around the Union and Confederate military encampments, we peered into tents and saw muskets stacked neatly. Some soldiers were eating hardtack and salt pork. Others were stirring a tantalizing, hearty stew with corn and other savories over a campfire. Drummers and fifers merrily played favorite camp tunes. Elsewhere, happy soldiers cavorted while lilting tunes from squeezeboxes, banjos, and harmonicas accompanied their antics. While some men socialized, others were practicing their drill.

Hospital surgeons demonstrated the treatment of wounds and illnesses. Their field kits included fine scalpels and a hack saw which they used to cut through the bones of injured limbs. Smells of men's sweat and "hacked-off limbs" came our way, causing me to leave the medical tent. Even though we knew the surgeons used cuts of meat instead of body limbs, its lifelike quality caused many a queasy stomach.

On the lighter side, ornately dressed wives showed off their fashions—hoop skirts, bonnets, the latest hair style worn in a bun. Women explained how they managed to keep their families going during the trying wartime conditions. They had to cope with problems and financial concerns while their husbands were off fighting the war.

Again, I was compelled to meet the men and women who were portraying these characters from America's past. I had to ask them why they did this.

One Confederate reenactor began a long explanation of Jeffersonian and Hamiltonian democracy. He said he was fighting for state's rights and that the Supreme Court had never ruled on the right to secede from the Union. I was impressed by the level of his historical knowledge and background. Beyond his words, however, his fervor swept over me like a wave. He was clearly impassioned about what he was doing. He began to get tears in his eyes. Slowly composing himself, he rejoined the rest of his unit in their final preparations for battle.

After a while, a long, impressive array of Confederate and Union troops lined up. Officers on horseback led foot soldiers and artillery men onto the battlefield. At first, I was caught up in the impressiveness of the blue and gray uniforms—frock coats, sack coats, kepis, and Hardee hats. The authenticity went beyond the uniforms and accoutrements. There was something about their demeanor, their gait, and body language that was unique. Something was different and yet uniform about the way the men carried themselves, the way they walked, and their posture. Their facial features, hair, moustaches, and beards looked reminiscent of another era. Their faces expressed mixed emotions. Fear, camaraderie, courage, adventure, righteousness. Why were they doing this?

We watched in awe as both armies surged back and forth across the million-square-foot battlefield. Volleys of musketry and cannon fire now began to roar and smoke from a thousand black powder guns billowed across the fields. The smell of gunpowder permeated the air. Horses reared. Soldiers fell to the ground. It was particularly strange being one of the thousands sitting on picnic blankets in the hot sun watching a 130-year-old battle take place before our eyes. The truth is, that hot July day in 1861 also had the appearance of a holiday picnic. Once word got out, amazingly, Congressmen and their ladies in carriages, adventurers on horseback, ordinary folk on foot, newspapermen, and sutlers with wares to peddle had all arrived to watch this battle as if it were a sporting event. The exception was that, then, men were going to die!

What transpired was no picnic, but instead a shattering defeat for the Union. Demoralized Union soldiers fled. Panic-stricken spectators created a stampede in their hurry to return to the safety of Washington.

At the reenactment, spectators were leisurely sipping fragrant sarsaparillas and enjoying musical entertainment by a regimental string band. Meanwhile, in a wooden shed decorated with bunting a distance away, a civilian band played camp songs and other popular nineteenth-century tunes.

Several soldiers spontaneously rose to their feet and danced a jig. Their unbuttoned field jackets showed checkered shirts. Some were still wearing their kepis and brogan shoes. It was as if these young men with the scruffy beards were on liberty or had come home for a visit from the battlefront.

Civilians and soldiers strolled around the sutlers' camp browsing through the merchandise—much of it being authentic reproductions targeted at the reenactor. Most everything in the sutlers' tents appeared to be handmade. Youngsters tried on kepis and played with guns. Women modeled hoop skirts and bonnets for their husbands. Even the candies were hand dipped and hand wrapped. The smells in the tents were reminiscent of the old Woolworth "five-and-dimes" with the wooden floors and the glass cabinets. Barry found a book that listed his great-grandfather and his regiment's history (the 21st Georgia Infantry).

Meanwhile, I was captivated with the story of a sutler who took pains to explain in great historical detail the authenticity of his wares. Then, there were those tears again. There was that reverence. This was more than coincidence. It was a consistent thread connecting everyone I met.

The sutler reminded me that these reenactors pay nearly a thousand dollars for one period uniform and accessories. They sometimes spend a weekend a month doing these activities. Some came from as far away as Florida, Kansas, and Germany, and many research their roles by studying old documents, letters, and photographs.

Around the same time as my attendance at the reenactment, I was furthering my education in metaphysics, which required that I write a dissertation. While I was talking to the sutler, this compelling question once again occurred to me as to whether any of these men had actually lived, fought, or even died during the Civil War. I could not ignore the overriding passion that these reenactors exhibited in re-creating battles, studying military tactics, and creating encampments as a hobby. Although they had come from all walks of life and appeared very individualistic, this serious enthusiasm seemed to be a common thread uniting them. Why would they spend their spare time sleeping on the ground without sleeping bags and eating hardtack? I wondered if this could be a suitable topic for my dissertation.

Having a background in both traditional and alternative forms of counseling, I was generally fascinated with digging to the bottom of what motivates people to do what they do. There was some strong motivation among these people, but it was only after seeing another reenactment and the movie *Gettysburg* that I began to mull over the idea of actually regressing these men and women through hypnosis to see if my hunch was right.

There was something about the movie *Gettysburg* that moved me deeply. As Barry and I left the theater, I turned to him and said, "I'm going to research these Civil War reenactors to see if they can recall a Civil War lifetime." Barry scoffed. He said that I'd never get the people for my study. They'd think I was a nut. After years of working in the holistic healing arts, I was used to that response, but being a former reporter, it was my turn to bristle. "Watch me," I said. "Even if I have to go to Alaska, I am going to get the people I need for my study."

I immediately contacted the woman who organized the reenactments at Manassas. She wasn't sure of the response I'd get, but gave me a list of reenactors from the greater Washington area. I began the enlistment process by contacting individuals by phone.

Because of their reverence for the Civil War, the men were initially apprehensive about participating in the research. They were determined to keep Civil War reenacting as close to traditional history as possible. Some had been in the forefront of making their living history events as accurate and realistic as possible. They were very protective of their reenacting hobby. But once they began telling me about their involvement with the Civil War, it was as if they couldn't stop. During the initial recruitment phone interviews, some of them even shared déjà vu experiences and admitted that they questioned the reason for their own obsessiveness. Even after the phone interview they were still skeptical. The first reenactor to agree to a regression, David Purschwitz, a museum technician from Manassas, decided to hold off on recommending the regression process to others until after he had tried it. We did Dave's regression session at his home, which was itself like walking into a museum. The Civil War filled every one of his rooms—period furniture and flags, old coins, photographs, and books were everywhere.

After giving me the "tour" and a pre-regression interview, we were prepared to start. We were both nervous—neither of us knowing what to expect. I sat down on a period couch that Dave had made, while he stretched out in a recliner. I slowly and carefully led him into a hypnotic state using various techniques that included visualization. Once Dave was in a state of hypnosis, I held my breath. Would he recall a lifetime in the Civil War? I now suggested that he go back to a time that would correlate with his current interest in reenacting.

For the next several hours, I was amazed and mesmerized by his narratives (recounted in chapter 5). As he spoke, Dave went through a myriad of emotions and what seemed to be a lot of pain. His apparent "memories" had been heart wrenching. I felt like a reporter experiencing the Civil War right beside him. Through his narratives, I was there at each major event of his life as a soldier.

What an assignment! In my capacity as radio anchor and TV reporter in California, I had interviewed Sally Ride and Chuck Yeager, Muhammad Ali and Sandy Koufax, and covered the Mondale-Ferraro Presidential Democratic Convention. I had been on oil rigs, at toxic waste dumps, and nuclear power plants, and I'd covered missile launches. Even so, the chill that went through me as I was transported back to the time of the Civil War with Dave couldn't be matched.

Dave and I were both shaken by the dramatic trance narrative. By the time it was over, we had clearly shared an incredible experience together. We both were convinced of the veracity of the information that had come through under hypnosis. As I was leaving his home, Dave handed me a list of names of some of the other reenactors in his unit. Dave's past-life regression experience confirmed my decision to continue pursuing this as the subject of my dissertation.

Within the next few weeks, I had similar success with several other volunteers in Dave's unit and other units during past-life regressions conducted at my home, and it convinced me that I was on the right track. Fortunately, word-of-mouth was beginning to replace my need to recruit subjects for my study.

Not long after the series of regressions had begun, Dave went to his Confederate unit's Christmas party where the main topic of conversation was past lives. The reenactors who had already had their regressions were sharing their experiences with the others. As they compared their past-life stories, they also began to divulge their feelings about what was revealed. They were amazed with one fellow who wasn't particularly history minded, but who had, under hypnosis, delivered a past-life narrative that was historically accurate. The next day, another member from their unit eagerly volunteered to have his own encounter.

This is the way it went in other units. After a regression, the subject would be on the hot line with the others, sharing feelings and validating historical information. One historian, Brian Pohanka, held back until he was so intrigued by the others' escapades and so amazed at their historical accuracy that he also took the plunge (see chapter 14). Along the way, he historically substantiated for me many of the other regressions, even when what they had experienced conflicted with what they thought to be correct. For the most part, these fellows were incredibly well read when it came to the Civil War. Some interests were very specialized—like military tactics or historical costuming. In Brian's case, he was amazed that, unlike in reenacting, in over six hours under hypnosis done in two sessions, there was not one unauthentic detail. He was so moved by his regression experience he suggested that I regress a woman reenactor he knew, and she agreed.

So, there I had it. Eleven men and one woman who, as a hobby, re-create the Civil War and the life of the period. Their ages ranged from twenty-seven to fifty-one. Of these, three were single, eight were married, and one divorced; seven had families. All but one had some college; one-third had degrees in history, and one-third were making careers out of their passion for the Civil War.

Much to my delight, all twelve subjects were able to recall a lifetime in the Civil War era. Each had a fascinating tale. Some had been maimed; others imprisoned. Some had been killed in battle, while some had homes or businesses that were partially destroyed during the war.

Although I had no intention of trying to prove the validity of reincarnation, I thought the results were interesting, particularly when compared with another study. When psychologist Helen Wambach hypnotically regressed 213 subjects in California to a lifetime in 1850, only three recalled being Civil War soldiers. This sharply contrasted with my findings of 100 percent past-life recall of these reenactors to involvement in the Civil War. Using Wambach's study as a control group, I realized that the contrast of my findings could be an indication that the interests and hobbies we choose to pursue could conceivably be rooted in past lives. The fact that all twelve reenactors who participated in my study did have recall of a lifetime in the Civil War, and the regressions are consistent with regression studies and related literature by others, strongly suggests cause for intelligent speculation and further research on the subject.

In the course of my research, I felt somehow bonded to each participant and was quickly swept into the fascination of the Civil War. I had originally been trained to be a history teacher, because I knew there must be a way to make history come alive. Finally, for me, history was not only alive, but vivid, in the words and re-created experiences of the subjects under hypnosis.

For me, the phrase "history repeats itself" was taking on a new, much more personal meaning. I was beginning to appreciate a fresh perspective as to why we choose the hobbies or even class curriculum, careers, and friends that we do.

The regressions turned out to be the easy part because I also wanted to try to document the names, units, and stories that would be revealed during hypnosis. Drawing the names out of the hypnotized subjects wasn't always easy. I knew that it would be challenging even before I started. Having conducted lots of past-life research and many regressions, I knew that it's much easier to remember an emotional incident from a previous life than a name or number. Even in one's present life, it's harder to remember what you had to eat on a nondescript day a month ago, than it is to remember what you ate on your wedding night ten years ago.

I also believe that under hypnosis we tap into the creative side of our brain. During the process, we are directing the practical side of the brain to pop in and fill in the information we want.

It wouldn't be a stretch for me to believe that once we finish a lifetime, it's not very important what our names were. It's more important what we did or didn't do and how those things affect us now. At death, that part of us may still be retained, while the ego simply slips away.

If I hadn't been so results oriented during my research, I would have found the reenactors' resistance to bringing forth the Civil War names humorous. I asked, and sometimes cajoled. I even guided them under hypnosis to ask their buddies in the memory. Sometimes they couldn't. Sometimes they didn't want to appear stupid. At other times, however, they asked and got answers. I asked them to look around at their uniforms, corps badges, flags—anything that could provide identifying details. Some got irritated that I was interrupting the flow of the scene. Others felt anxious or befuddled because they couldn't draw on those answers as easily as the rest of their recalled experiences. Perhaps with more hypnosis sessions, they could have refined the names and facts. In spite of all this, eleven of the twelve people recalled names and other data.

Another difficulty I encountered was in the interpretation of the life stories. When someone died in a field, we would probably assume they had been wounded. And yet, soldiers in field hospitals were sometimes treated outside, in the fields. It's possible that someone who remembered dying in a field but didn't recall a battle could have died of infection. Soldiers on the move rarely knew the destination of their march or the name of the area in which they were fighting. Only with detective work and help from historians, particularly Brian Pohanka, would the puzzles be pieced together.

Verifying historical data had its own difficulties. For example, it was not uncommon for people, particularly Southerners, to go by their middle names. As I worked, my concern was that those were the names the reenactors had most likely recalled. I feared that somewhere in the reels of microfilm the perfect match would be found under the first name and not the middle.

If the reenactors were slightly off on the recall of their state or last name, it would be nearly impossible to exhume the correct soldier's records from the correct dusty file folder. I simply wouldn't have the proper access code.

As I first began the regressions, I felt that the recalled Civil War personages were so real that they would be relatively easy to document. I almost felt that it was my duty to locate them and dust off their stories. When I couldn't find them immediately, however, I worried about missing records, soldiers changing units, and unknown soldiers buried at battlesites. In the seventy-nine national Civil War cemeteries, fifty-four percent of the graves are those of unknown soldiers.[1] One historian told me they didn't much care who died in prison back then. Of the more than 12,000 Union prisoners buried at Salisbury Prison, North Carolina, ninety-nine percent are unknown.[2] One of my reenactor subjects said he spent four years tracking down a single Civil War ancestor. Even Barry Wood's great-grandfather had been listed in the wrong unit at the surrender at Appomattox.

During my research, however, providence was with me on more than one occasion. I had managed to stumble across reenactors whose regression narratives were so legitimate that they valued their regression sessions almost like a religious experience. I appreciated their earnest approach to both the study and their Civil War hobby, knowing that they took the authenticity of both seriously. Secondly, historian Brain Pohanka was helping me with the facts.

Another serendipitous event occurred one day at the National Archives when, slightly discouraged, I decided to ask an archivist for help. I had already spent many hours sorting through military and pension records. The matches weren't as forthcoming as I had hoped. After telling the archivist about my attempts to track down soldiers from past-life regressions, he stifled a smirk and haphazardly tossed a book on Salisbury Prison my way. Like a hungry dog just given a bone, I opened it. As I glanced down at the first page that fell open, I was amazed to discover the name for which I was looking. After many hours of painstaking research, I had found a missing soldier! (See additional documentation on Edward White in photo insert on page 8.)

In the final countdown, I was encouraged by discovering that eleven possible matches of twelve had some conformity to names, units, and life stories recollected by the reenactors. All my efforts checking grave sites and battlegrounds, talking with historians, and researching had paid off enough to convince me that the narratives were indeed past-life memories.

I felt I could finally put these soldiers to rest as I completed my research project. Turning to other endeavors, I traveled to Natural Bridge, Virginia, to give a lecture on hypnosis to junior college Wellness Program coordinators. While there, I discovered that Appomattox was only about an hour away. The next day, I ventured to the site where the war ended.

When I pulled into Appomattox and stopped where Grant had set up his headquarters, it was about 1:30 p.m. Another tourist informed me that it happened to be the 130th anniversary of the surrender at Appomattox. I hurried to the center of the little town. Reenactors—soldiers in uniform and their wives in their colorful hoop skirts—were strolling among the buildings and along the tree-lined walkways. I had begun to get a headache—something unusual. The informational film mentioned the time Grant had ridden into town. It was 1:30 p.m.! It also mentioned that he had a headache until he received word from Lee about the truce.

Touring the McLean House, I recalled how the reenactment of First Manassas had motivated me to launch my research. The Civil War's first battle literally began just outside this house, when the McLeans lived in Manassas. The family then moved away, to Appomattox, to avoid the war. Four years later, the parlor in the McLean House in Appomattox was the setting for the restoration of peace to a war-torn nation. I thought it was strange that I had begun my research at Manassas and, upon its completion, had found myself at Appomattox. Maybe I had come full circle. When I think of the Civil War lives that have been relived in my living room, I hope that some measure of healing can result for the twelve reenactors. Perhaps their accounts are breathing new life into a spirit that people believed to be dead—a spirit echoed in the souls of those who have reincarnated in this time. Perhaps these reenactors have unwittingly opened an eyewitness window into deeper insights into the Civil War and into the immortality of the soul as well.

2

Do We Live Again?

I can still recall sitting on the veranda of a posh hotel in New Delhi reading a book and sipping ice tea. Having just come back from a shopping spree, I was upset that I couldn't use the pool. It was being repaired. The laborers worked slowly and diligently. One was an Indian woman about my age. She was dressed shabbily. I watched her laboriously carry load after load of bricks on her head. If we had only one lifetime, why was I the one being pampered while she appeared to have a life of drudgery? It didn't seem fair. That's when I began paying real attention to the philosophy of reincarnation. But it wasn't until I became a past-life regression therapist and later launched my own research project that I uncovered even more about the process of recalling other lifetimes.

Past-life regression using hypnosis isn't new. Just because psychiatrists have stumbled upon it and the talk shows have covered it recently, doesn't mean it's a contemporary phenomenon. I was sur-

prised that nearly 100 years ago, psychiatrist Albert de Rochas researched his clients' past-life recall.[3] He found that people are actually recycled within decades. This startling new information
challenged previously held beliefs of a minimum cycle of 1,200
years. Following on de Rochas's heels, English psychiatrist Alexander
Cannon regressed nearly 1,400 volunteers.

Then, in 1956, hypnotist and businessman Morey Bernstein
shook up traditionalists and brought past lives to the attention of
the American public. Readers of over one million copies of his ex-
plosive book, *The Search for Bridey Murphy,* followed a young Colorado housewife's hypnotic regressions back to Cork, Ireland, where
she grew up, married, and died at age sixty-six. The *Denver Post* sent
columnist William J. Barker to Ireland to conduct the only intensive
hunt for "Bridey evidence." He found that a number of Bridey
Murphy's statements were consistent with historical fact.[4]

At about the same time, L. Ron Hubbard, founder of Scientology
and author of several books, including *Have You Lived Before This
Life?* created his Dianetics techniques. This allows "auditors" to fa-
cilitate people's accessing their past lives by using a present trauma
to go back to an original trauma found in another lifetime.[5] I have
used a similar, effective process that's been popularized among professionals by Dr. Morris Netherton in *Past Lives Therapy.*[6] He has his
clients access past lives though repeating emotionally charged
phrases like "I'm seeing red."

A true "marriage" of science and spirituality led to what has been
some of the first scientifically reported studies of past-life regressions to be published in the 1960s. The marriage and professional
union of psychiatrist Denys Kelsey and psychic Joan Grant led to
their uncovering of clients' memories of birth, the prenatal period,
and past lives. Grant, not unlike Taylor Caldwell, drew on her past-
life memories in writing her novels. Grant's were conscious recollections; Caldwell was regressed by journalist Jess Stearn to discover
that this was her source as well.

Dr. Kelsey was amazed to find evidence of prenatal memory recall before the fetus develops a nervous system to retain the memories. In *Many Lifetimes,* he concluded, "In a human being there must
be an element which exists and is capable of function even in the
absence of a physical body."[7]

I remember when hypnotherapist Dick Sutphen used television

to interest people in his past-life regression work. In 1976, the hypnotherapist, researcher, and author appeared on Tom Snyder's NBC *Tomorrow Show* and conducted the first nationally televised past-life hypnotic regression. Sutphen, author of *Past Lives, Future Loves,* is particularly well known for his research into the past lives of mates and lovers.[8] My friends and I participated in one of his research seminars in Los Angeles. Later, in the comfort of our homes, we would lie on the floor and listen to his regression tape. They would recall exotic lives; I would usually fall asleep. I still remember Dick droning, "Deeper, deeper, deeper, down, down, down." These days, I occasionally find myself using the same intonation during a hypnosis session.

Like Sutphen, I have found that, during regression hypnosis, many of my clients focus on relationship issues and that they have benefited tremendously from their past-life work. Afterward, they seem to have a whole new perspective and understanding of their relationships. Other therapists have had similar results, Dr. Edith Fiore among them.

Using hypnotic age-regression techniques in her clinical psychology practice, Fiore, like psychiatrist Brian Weiss, more recently stumbled upon the concept of past lives. Fiore and Weiss have found the results extremely effective in treating patients. Both are convinced that many current problems have their roots in former lives. Dr. Weiss described his remarkable results in *Many Lives, Many Masters* as well as in *Through Time into Healing.*[9] In *You Have Been Here Before,* Fiore revealed that most of her patients with chronic weight problems have had a lifetime of food deprivation or starvation.[10] I've had clients who began dropping weight immediately without effort after one session in which the past cause of their problem was revealed.

While Dr. Fiore focused on the clinical aspects of regression, psychologist Helen Wambach focused on scientific research. Using hypnosis techniques, Wambach regressed large groups and compiled data from various time periods. In *Reliving Past Lives: The Evidence Under Hypnosis,* Wambach tabulated what her subjects wore and ate, their race and social status, their death experience, and prenatal period.[11]

Netherton, Fiore, and Wambach were original board members of the Association for Past-Life Research and Therapies, which began in 1980 with Hazel Denning at its head. Today it is a viable international society and, since 1986, has published *The Journal of Regression Therapy.*

To date, hypnosis has been the most common method of recalling past memories. Many pioneers in past-life regression therapy—Edith Fiore, Ph.D.; Irene Hickman, D.O.; Ernest Pecci, M.D.; Chet Snow, Ph.D.; Hazel Denning, Ph.D.; Barbara Findeisen, M.F.C.C.; Bruce Goldberg, D.D.S.; Charles Tebbets; and Thorwald Dethlefsen, Ph.D., rely on hypnosis techniques. However, like myself, they disregard the basic accusations against hypnosis: control by the therapists and the use of special suggestions.[12]

Author of *Mind-Probe Hypnosis,* Irene Hickman, D.O., one of the strongest proponents of hypnotherapy, regards hypnosis as probably the finest tool available for probing the mind.[13] Psychiatrist Brian Weiss believes hypnosis accesses the wisdom of the subconscious in a focused way in order to achieve a healing. In *Through Time into Healing,* he described the hypnotic state: "We are in hypnosis whenever the subconscious plays a more dominant role. The client is always in control and the mind can comment, criticize, and censor."[14]

That's what I tell my clients right up front. Hypnosis is a deceptively simple tool that can plumb the depths of our subconscious and make major repairs. That's all hypnosis is: quieting the conscious chatter so that we can hear the subconscious. There's no mystique to it. I remind my clients that they are in the driver's seat. I'm just helping them read the map.

As a result, my clients have experienced healings in areas ranging from relationships to fears, phobias, and depression, sexual dysfunction, body image, self-esteem, and physical health. It has been rewarding for me to see the dynamic, quick, effective changes that can result. This contrasts sharply with my experiences in social work. As a hot-line listener and, later, case manager for a men's homeless shelter, I found my work sometimes discouraging. Just a few months after I had assisted the men to get jobs, housing, and clothing, many would be homeless again.

Because thousands of clients have been helped in healing a wide range of physical, psychological, and emotional issues through past-life regression therapy, it is becoming increasingly popular. The therapeutic results and education have led to an increasing acceptance of past-life regression therapy by the medical community and the public.

Another therapeutic use of past-life regressions that I've wanted to explore in more depth, both as a therapist and a client, is understanding the antecedents of how we develop talents and interests. I had primarily done group regression work in this area and received immediate positive feedback, but did not do any follow-up. One of my colleagues once gave a suggestion to a woman under hypnosis to bring forward artistic abilities. After the session, she bought paints, took a sculpting class, and was amazed at her creations.

It made sense to me that these Civil War reenactors could have carried forward their interest and knowledge of the war from a former lifetime. I had often wondered why I felt more comfortable in one country than another and why some people excelled at a particular skill or talent.

Psychic diagnostician Edgar Cayce often touched on this theme, as described by Gina Cerminara in *Many Mansions*. Giving readings while in trance, he identified these pre-birth memories existing below what might be called a trap door—and at deeper levels of the unconscious than those commonly tapped by traditional psychotherapists.[15]

In trance, as reported by Noel Langley in *Edgar Cayce on Reincarnation*, Edgar Cayce said, "We don't have to remember past lives because we are the sum total of all our memories. We manifest them in our habits, idiosyncrasies, likes and dislikes, talents, blind spots, physical and emotional strengths and vulnerabilities."[16]

Throughout nearly 2,000 of his over 14,000 readings, Cayce counseled youngsters and adults to develop certain career paths, which would enhance skills acquired in other lives. Langley cites a Cayce reading on a six-month-old boy, which tells the parents that their son should be given the opportunity to be in the field of medicine because of his prior relationship to disease in France. The parents later reported that the child showed a particular interest in the physical body as a tiny child and had a phobia about germs. At ten, he had a paper route to save money for medical school.[17]

In his landmark study of children described in *Children Who Remember Previous Lives: A Question of Reincarnation*, past-life researcher Dr. Ian Stevenson found the same thing. Many children expressed in their play the vocation of the previous personality: a child who opened a pretend biscuit shop (formerly a shopkeeper), one who would lie under the family's sofa pretending to repair a car (former auto mechanic), a child who created her own broom to sweep (former sweepstress).[18] When I was three years old, I used to chant and dance around the house in a heel-toe fashion, with my little fingers up. Everybody used to kid me. Years later, we attended my brother's Boy Scout jamboree. We were amazed to see American Indians doing my dance!

The Cayce readings place talent and interest firmly in the heredity of the soul rather than the heredity of one's grandparents.[19] He said it took thirty-five lifetimes to develop a talent to the degree of a child genius. Composer George Frederick Handel's father was a barber-surgeon and opposed the interest in music that his son showed in early childhood. The family had no known ancestors with an interest in music.[20] Since I've received this information, I have a healthy respect for my friends who are fabulous musicians. One plays for the Kennedy Center Opera in Washington, D.C. I tell her she must have spent thirty-something lifetimes practicing!

The Cayce readings reveal that sometimes former talents that have lain forgotten needed reawakening. In *You Have Lived Here Before*, Dr. Fiore described helping patients reawaken abilities by going to previous lifetimes to find the source of talents, skills, interests.[21] Researcher Hans TenDam, in *Exploring Reincarnation*, even goes as far as to say that the practice of such skills in one life may lead to abilities in the next, while neglect can lead to atrophy.[22]

Hobbies or any impelling interest very probably stream from activity in a previous lifetime: i.e., an interest in things Spanish argues a Spanish incarnation, according to Cayce.[23] It may serve to reawaken facilities acquired in that lifetime and even lead to people with whom we had previous connections in the same lifetime. When my friend Barry and I visited the Prado museum in Madrid, I was astounded to find a painting of a woman who resembled a woman I had just met in Virginia. In the next hall, Barry found a painting resembling a man he currently knew in Virginia. Interestingly enough, the people depicted in the paintings were related.

Hobbies and interests, historical periods, costumes, furniture, art, and music that have a special attraction can help jog memories of another lifetime. Michael Talbot has found this to be the case and describes specific techniques in *Your Past Lives: A Reincarnation*

Handbook.[24] One of my reenactors became interested in "the hobby" after acquiring a Civil War coin, another through historical costuming.

Reincarnation, the philosophy that people are reborn, is how several reenactors explain their regression experience. They are not alone. Roughly two-thirds of the world's modern population believe in some form of rebirth. The belief has long been accepted by Hindus and Buddhists and is becoming increasingly adopted by Westerners. In 1969, a Gallup poll showed that twenty percent of Americans (two percent more than Europeans) and twenty-six percent of Canadians believed in reincarnation.

Many more Westerners would believe in the philosophy today if it hadn't been for politics in the early Roman Catholic Church, according to Noel Langley's *Edgar Cayce on Reincarnation.* Some historians look to the Council of Nicaea in 325 A.D. as the point at which the Emperor Constantine negotiated the condemnation of the doctrine. Others credit the Byzantine Emperor Justinian and his wife with obliterating most of the references to reincarnation from the Bible in the sixth century.[25]

Belief in reincarnation is also present in Judaism. Kabbala, which is Jewish mysticism, mentions reincarnation in numerous texts. Rabbi Yonassan Gershom, who explored incidents of reincarnation from the Holocaust in his book *Beyond the Ashes,* says that the Hebrew term for reincarnation is *gilgul.* Like the subjects in Gershom's book, I encountered two students in a Reiki healing class who believed they may have lived during the Holocaust. Interestingly, one had been Jewish, the other a Nazi soldier. Religious historians say that belief in the afterlife was in place from biblical times throughout the Middle Ages. Gershom writes that several Jewish sects, particularly the Hasidim, include reincarnation as part of their beliefs.[26]

Dr. Stevenson further states that the belief is currently held by Islamic sects of western Asia and tribes in East and West Africa, North America, the South Pacific, central Australia, and northern Japan.[27]

Some define reincarnation as the state of being "embodied anew." The soul of a deceased person, after an interim period in the other world, is reborn according to the merits acquired during his or her previous life. Some believe the human soul is a fragment of the Divine and will ultimately return to its divine source. The soul must evolve or mature through experiencing a wide range of knowledge and suffering in more than one lifetime.

This evolution is not haphazard, but follows the law of karma or cause and effect. All actions have consequences, some of which are delayed to future lives. We punish ourselves by our actions, and the very defects and difficulties under which we suffer offer scope for perfection.[28]

On reincarnation and karma, Theosophist Annie Besant wrote: " ... in the memory of Nature every act of each of her children is self-engraved and from this self-written record, the changing destiny of men and nations flows ... nowhere any injustice, caprice or favoritism."[29]

In my lectures on past-life regression therapy, I tell my audiences that people who believe in reincarnation are in good company. The thread of belief in reincarnation has found its way to modern times from ancient Roman writers and the Greek schools of Pythagoras to the Essenes. Head and Cranston, in *Reincarnation in World Thought*, listed some of the world's greatest thinkers as having espoused the philosophy: philosophers Plato and Aristotle; statesmen Cicero and Julius Caesar; poets William Butler Yeats and Robert Frost; scientists Ben Franklin and Thomas Edison. Pythagoras claimed that he had been Euphorbus in a previous existence.[30] General George Patton "knew" where Caesar had pitched his tent and where the old Roman temples were when he arrived in Langres, France, to assume his first command.[31]

However, that "good company" doesn't include most research scientists. Even regression investigator Ian Stevenson himself found only one case of hypnotic regression credible. In that case, reported in the *Journal of the American Society for Psychical Research*, over 100 facts about a woman regressed to sixteenth-century Spain were verified by therapist and researcher Linda Tarazi.[32]

In general, though, there is very little scientific data that supports the authenticity of hypnotic past-life regressions. For starters, scientists question the very mechanics of hypnosis. Hypnotherapist Dr. Masud Ansari, in his book *Modern Hypnosis: Theory and Practice*, describes hypnosis as "an altered state of selective hyper-suggestibility brought about by relaxation, fixation of attention, and suggestion."[33] Scientists also point to the concepts of the suspension of the critical faculties and suggestion as unavoidable problems.

The scientific evidence of memory enhancement under hypnosis is also mixed. Hypnosis has been found to be such a useful tool in memory recall that it has been used in some criminal investigations. Studies, such as one conducted in 1980 by Reiser and Neilsen and reported in the *American Journal of Clinical Hypnosis,* show that memory has been enhanced through hypnosis, particularly when trauma to the victim is involved.[34] Other studies, such as those empirically reviewed by David Payne in 1987 and reported in *Psychological Bulletin,* have also indicated that the ability to recall memories of films, movies, pictures, or live events are strengthened when using hypnosis.[35] Meanwhile, scientists such as Yuille and McEwan point to their 1985 study which found that no memory enhancement took place with hypnosis.[36]

The confusion of fantasy with reality in the hypnotic recall process has been the focus of both clinical and experimental studies, notably one researched by Steven Lynn and Michael Nash in 1994.[37] In "Truth in Memory: Ramifications for Psychotherapy and Hypnotherapy," one client, under hypnosis, was reported to have told her therapist that she had missed a prior therapy appointment because she had gone to a cemetery and gotten into an open grave. Her son denied this and said that his mother was at home sleeping through the missed therapy session.

I found at least one study in which researchers Wilson and Barber labeled people "fantasy-prone" when they experienced a previous life, their own birth, or went off into the future. These "fantasies" have been described as having "hallucinatory intensity."[38]

Because of such studies, some researchers believe that age regressions, returning to an earlier time in life, may be a mix of fact and fantasy. I did find several studies, one of which was conducted by Philip Spinhoven and his colleague in 1992, that have been favorable to age regression in a clinical setting.[39]

In a 1991 study conducted by Eric Van Denburg, when regressed to age seven, all the adults had more childlike handwriting and recalled many vivid details of the second grade.[40] But this doesn't seem convincing enough for scientists. Some research now suggests that the age-regressed adults score higher in cognitive tasks than children and thought the way the adults predicted children would think.[41] I tell my clients when they prepare to be age regressed that they may still be aware of their current personality.

Further research revealed that science has had particular difficulties backing reincarnation, especially in the past century. A researcher named Burnham debunked reincarnation by stressing the role "illusions of memory" plays in the creation of past-life scenarios. After reviewing the literature on memory, he concluded that these illusions were an important aspect of normal cognitive functioning and that they were particularly present among people who have vivid imaginations.[42]

Researchers, such as Stevenson, Perry, Hilgard, and Spanos, focused on the role suggestibility plays in the subjects' ability to be hypnotized.[43] In one experiment referred to in Nicholas Spanos's essay, "Past-Life Hypnotic Regression: A Critical View," an experimental group was told that it was not uncommon to change sex, race, or live in exotic cultures in past lives. This group was much more likely to manifest these changes during hypnosis than a control group who was not given those suggestions.[44] This does not necessarily invalidate the possibility of past lives, but demonstrates only that the experimental subjects felt freer to select those lifetimes. In another study, Spanos found that thirty-five people who reported past lives during hypnosis scored higher on hypnotizability. They were more likely to have had déjà vu experiences. Those subjects who thought the concept of reincarnation was plausible assigned more credibility to the experiment.[45]

Investigative police and others, however, have shown that the hypnotist can unknowingly cue his subject and elicit memories that others can't duplicate.

Over ninety percent of age-regressed subjects could remember the day of their tenth birthday after being asked, "Is it Monday, Tuesday, etc.?" When other researchers tried to duplicate Orne's study using the same procedure but without asking specific days, they didn't get nearly as good results. They had not prompted their subjects by reviewing the days of the week and speculated that the researcher in the prior study had unknowingly suggested the answer through his specificity.[46] Taking my cue from these studies, I was careful not to direct the reenactors to go "back to the Civil War" during their regressions so that scientists could not claim that I had suggested Civil War lifetimes to my subjects.

So, how did I achieve credibility in my study? I was already aware of the possibility of confabulation, improvising, or filling in the gaps, during hypnotic recall sessions. As early as 1932, scientists J. Stalnaker and E. Riddle hypnotically age-regressed college students and asked them to recite poems committed to memory earlier in life. These poems were typically a part of a school assignment. Students under hypnosis appeared to show a dramatic increase in remembering the poems, when compared with their performance while awake. After some scrutiny, the improvements in the poem recall were attributed to confabulation. The researchers concluded, in "The Effect of Hypnosis on Long Delayed Recall," that the students, under hypnosis, had improvised and filled in the gaps somewhat imperfectly.[47]

I was even more intimately aware of the phenomenon of cryptomnesia during my research. This involves the tendency of people to incorporate, as their own experience, what they have forgotten that they read or saw.[48] The much-publicized case of Bridey Murphy has been criticized as being fraught with cryptomnesia. The *Chicago American* published an article that maintained that Virginia Tighe had an aunt who was Irish and had "regaled the girl with childhood stories of old Ireland." Another discovery, as reported by Ian Wilson in *All in the Mind*, was that, as a girl, she had lived across the street from a Mrs. Bridie Murphy Corkell from County Mayo, Ireland. She had been in the home often, but had never remembered knowing the woman's maiden name.[49]

The most amazing case in Dr. Reima Kampman's research on cryptomnesia, entitled "Past-Life Regression: The Grand Illusion," was of a young girl.[50] In one of eight recalled past lives, she remembered dying in an air raid in 1939. She knew the address of the home and the name of her former parents. The address was correct as was the exact date of the air raid. When the girl was age-regressed, however, she remembered herself as a little girl turning over the pages of a book with photographs. She recalled seeing the exact date of the air raid and a picture of a mother and daughter killed that day. Another possibility, however, is that the book could have served as a trigger for her recall.

As a hypnotherapist, I had been so acutely aware of cryptomnesia that I debated whether to even conduct my study. I knew before I started that the very nature of my study—selecting a population that is more aware of an historical period than most, one that even participates in re-creating life during that period—was fraught with scientific pitfalls.

From a scientific viewpoint, these academic barriers could deter the bravest past-life therapist from a study such as this. Not only the subjects' knowledge, but the very nature of reenacting—re-creating the Civil War experience, the reenactors' ability to do first-person dialogue, and even participation in a lifelike movie—makes the apparent cracks in Bridey Murphy's story seem small by comparison. My regression of Civil War reenactors would definitely provide grist for the critical scientific mill, well beyond the risk of cryptomnesia.

But to ignore this great thirst for knowledge is to ignore the passion behind it. If psychologists, sociologists, and history teachers observed the reenactors' passion for the Civil War and its influence on their relationships, marriage ceremonies, careers, diets, and home decor, they might find it inspiring. One reenactor feels so strongly about events that happened over 130 years ago that he would give his life to preserve its history. The reenactors' overriding passion for "the hobby," one that is not mainstream and attracts individualists, has caused many reenactors to ask themselves what drives them to focus so intensely on a war that occurred more than 130 years ago. Even if some philosophers and scientists were open to the possibility of reincarnation or genetic memory, the question of which came first—the former lifetime, sensitivity to genetic memory which created the passion, or the passion which created the memories—may never be successfully determined.

Armed with all the explanations scientists could give about my study and the reasons why these reenactors recalled Civil War lifetimes, I carefully analyzed the reenactors' themselves and how they may have influenced the narratives.

Psychodynamic factors could certainly have played an important role. This suggests that some unconscious need could have been the motivation for creating a lifetime. Although most of the reenactors were voluntarily recruited for the study, they have strong ties—some even seemingly spiritual—to the Civil War. Although practically all were skeptical of reincarnation, some may have had a subconscious desire to have lived in the Civil War.

Most of the reenactors were very selective in sharing their regression experience with others. Several felt it had almost a spiritual quality. Some couldn't explain it or how they got the information. The only thing they received from participating in the study was the opportunity for the regression experience, so there would be no apparent motivation for fraud.

Because the reenactors were generally knowledgeable about many aspects of the Civil War, it would have been possible for some to have filled in the gaps and improvise, relying unconsciously on confabulation. But, while under hypnosis, several distinctly expressed being uncomfortable about not knowing what would happen next. Others were not able to make adjustments in the scenes they experienced. Another feared an outcome that he expected from his prior knowledge and was relieved when it didn't turn out as he feared. Still others experienced events that they thought contradicted what they believed to be accurate, and the unexpected information turned out to be historically accurate. This indicates convincing evidence that at least some were not able to "write the script," but rather waited to see what information or experiences would come up next. This inability to control the script may or may not go beyond the confines of confabulation.

Cryptomnesia, the previous exposure of the subject to relevant information through books, movies, or conversations that are subsequently forgotten and later recalled as a past life, is another possible influence. One of my subjects, Paul Jones, said that on a conscious level he didn't know that Lincoln's funeral car was built in Alexandria, Virginia, but worried that he may have read the material and forgotten that he had. My lone female subject, MaryLynne Bauer, says that one of the names that came to her she later remembered she had typed a month before. David Morse's first regression as a bearskin-capped guide for Red Coats marching to the fort in Albany reminded his wife of a Revolutionary War movie he had watched. But Dave says that his past-life recall was prior to that period, possibly around the French-Indian War, with log buildings. Even so, no movie could have accounted for his sore legs, aching calves, rumbling stomach, feeling cold, and seeing a flame and a blackened face with a shocked expression. No movie could have prepared him for the vivid death he experienced while a Civil War soldier.

In his regression, Brian, the Civil War historian, was amazed that he saw distinct faces and personalities who interacted with each other. With his current or even prior knowledge, he had no sense of how they could have been created. Brian, like the other reenactors who had read diarists and Civil War writers, found that their regression material could be documented as being quite different and unique from what they had previously read. It could even be possible that certain movies and books have a particular impact because they resonate with certain actual memories of a previous life.

I took care during the hypnotic sessions not to mention the Civil War or allude to uniforms or anything of that nature until the reenactors had made it clear on their own that they were in the Civil War era. I did, however, suggest that they recall memories "that related to their interest in reenactment."

Although researchers point to the influence of suggestion while in hypnosis, the reenactors were not always able to follow my suggestions. Some had difficulty recalling names, units, and concrete details. One displayed irritation at being asked his name, as if his activities or thoughts had been disturbed. Four of the subjects were not able, even through will power, to make the slightest alterations to what was occurring in their regressions.

Imagination is often used effectively in hypnosis, but it can also create paramnesia or pseudo-memories (false memories). Most reenactors, however, appeared not to have any preconceived ideas about their past lifetimes. Only one may have fought at the battle of Chickamauga in his past life, a battle that he had found particularly moving in reenacting. Another always had the sense that he had died early in the war. This may have happened in his past life.

Fantasy may or may not appear to be an element in the regressions of the reenactors. If they could have created what they wished, there probably would have been more officers, even famous men. Two of the men resemble famous Civil War generals in this life. But they were not even officers in their regressions. One may have become a sergeant later in the war.

Six subjects were killed, five wounded, three prisoners of war. Nine out of ten soldiers experienced hunger and not knowing where they were going at times. One said, "You're not supposed to die in a dream." They couldn't stop from getting a limb cut off, going into a battle that could be fatal, or getting captured.

Unlike in a dream, reenactors were able to remember vivid details of their regression months later. One drew several maps of the Richmond area and the layout of his office building months after the regression.

It would also be unlikely that imagination and fantasy could produce the historical verification of most of the details and chronology in each regression. After about six hours of continuous regression material, there was not one small detail that was not 100 percent authentic in the historian's regression, including some personalities and information he had not previously known.

Possession is another method of gaining past-life information. It is the possession of the living person by a dead entity. None of the reenactors appeared to show any of the common signs of possession as described in Dr. Fiore's *The Unquiet Dead.*[51] The death experiences described by the subjects were not indicative of an attached entity: uncoached, they went to the light and followed Moody's near-death description in *Life After Life.*[52]

I feel that it is possible that some reenactors may have attached entities. For one thing, they spend weekends at a time at Civil War battlefields. Dr. Fiore says that people who work in hospitals and cemeteries are targets for possession because of the number of people who died there and remain earthbound.[53] Because of the traumatic deaths, some Civil War soldiers most likely remained earthbound. Because reenactors are so simpatico to their cause, they would be the perfect hosts for the entities. The entities would even be able to replay the Civil War through the reenactments. This could perhaps enhance a reenactor's obsession with the Civil War.

A research proposal by the psychology department of Colorado State University in 1987 hypothesized that post-traumatic stress disorder found in Vietnam veterans is the result of attachment by the souls of soldiers killed in battle to comrades still alive.[54] Unfortunately, the study did not receive funding.

It is possible that reenactors who are highly sensitive could tap into the actual memories or "souls" of those who lived in the past, telepathically reading their thought patterns. I could conceive of this, particularly at Civil War battlesites where emotions ran high and still run high during reenactments. Years before I embarked on this study, I was at the site of the Battle of Chancellorsville where my friend Barry's great-grandfather had been shot. As we stood on the site, I got impressions of war that I knew weren't mine. I got the sense of adventure, camaraderie, fear, being where the action was, and being a part of something much bigger than myself. I had never looked at war that way before. To me, it had always been a "male" perspective.

The genetic memory theory presupposes that the memories of

the past life arise from the experiences of the subject's ancestors. Ian Stevenson says this can account for a small number of cases in which the personality returns directly to the same family.[55] In one reenactor in twelve, this was the case. Dave recalled being his own great-grandfather.

Nine other reenactors had ancestors in the Civil War era, six had ancestors who fought in the war. There were some similarities between two of the past lives. One reenactor recalled a past life as a prisoner—perhaps at Point Lookout, Maryland—which happened to an ancestor. Another owned a business in Richmond in his past life; so did an ancestor. After becoming reenactors, most researched those ancestors who had been soldiers. Only one did research prior to joining reenacting.

Genetic memory, therefore, could account for some of the knowledge of the reenactors. But this does not account for descriptions of specific life events, personalities, details, and feelings that each individual experienced during his or her regression.

The concept of racial memory explains that knowledge, attitudes, and feelings about historical events are imprinted on entire cultures. The Civil War was an American phenomenon. If the Civil War was imprinted on the cellular memories of Americans, why is it that there are Civil War reenactors in England, Germany, and Australia? One reenactor grew up in Panama. Why would he be drawn to the American Civil War and reenacting?

Swiss psychologist Carl Jung's concept of the collective unconscious plumbs even greater depths than the concept of racial memory. He saw a rich vein of universal patterns or archetypes, not individual but collective, into which the mind can tap. This collective unconscious is the part of the psyche that retains and transmits the common psychological inheritance of humankind.[56]

Meanwhile, scientist Rupert Sheldrake's morphogenetic energy field theory—which seems to encompass racial memory and the collective unconscious—builds on pooled memory of similar species. Sheldrake postulates that we attract what we most resonate to. That may be our own past states, Sheldrake says in his essay "Can Our Memories Survive the Death of Our Brains?" Through this energy field, Sheldrake theorizes that the conscious self could retain the ability to tune in to its own past states, even after the death of the brain. This is similar to endocrinologist Deepak Chopra's concept of a "network of intelligence" grounded in quantum physics. In *Quantum Healing* he says, "A cell's memory is able to outlive itself . . . Your body is just a place your memory calls home."[57] This could explain how each reenactor's regressions could be so specific about details of a particular individual's life, feelings, and thoughts.

For various reasons, I have come to believe that reincarnation could be one possible explanation for the reenactors' recalled lives. I was impressed with the distinctly different personalities, events, emotions, and details that were evidence of completely individual cases. The real emotions, physical feelings, and vivid descriptions were hard to ignore. The fact that adult men and one woman expressed their fears to a female hypnotherapist they had just met was telling. Also of importance is the intense interest in the Civil War that most of the reenactors exhibited as youngsters. Characteristics and findings of these narratives, taken individually and as a group, were consistent with much past-life literature, such as the fact that no one was famous. In addition, the documentation of historical events, the historical authenticity, and facts that were either not known or contradictory to what was believed lead me to consider reincarnation as a viable explanation.

From my perspective, the most plausible explanations for the Civil War past life of all twelve reenactors in the study appear to be: the morphogenetic resonance theory, genetic memory, cryptomnesia, confabulation, and reincarnation. Other plausible explanations are obsession, soul tapping, and a psychological desire for a lifetime in the Civil War.

Nevertheless, given the fact that all twelve reenactors did have recall of a lifetime in the Civil War and that the regressions are consistent with studies and literature by others, these narratives serve to stimulate professional speculation and should inspire readers with the possibilities they present.

3

A Short Course in Reenacting
and Civil War Buzz Words

After attending my first Civil War reenactments, I wondered how long they had been going on. Was this a relatively new phenomenon? I was surprised to find that there is not much literature on Civil War reenacting and its history. Most of the periodical literature merely entices tourists and history lovers to attend one of the living-history reenactments.[58] Journals and newspapers for reenactors, such as *The Civil War News*, the *Camp Chase Gazette*, and *Reenactor's Journal*, feature articles on historical perspectives and list upcoming events and reenactments.[59] Reenactors can also find where to purchase Civil War uniforms and other items. The *Camp Chase Gazette* has been keeping reenactors informed for more than twenty years. To compensate for the lack of the written word on reenacting, I drew on my media background and went to a live source for my information: Civil War historian and reenactor Brian Pohanka.

According to Pohanka, troops performed a few mock battles and training sessions for civilian entertainment even during the Civil War. After the war, large veterans organizations would don old uniforms for parades and functions.

Between 1880 and 1940, eight to ten of the Civil War battlefields were historically preserved and fell under the auspices of the War Department. Battlefield parks like Chickamauga and Gettysburg were used as campgrounds and training areas for U.S. soldiers during the Spanish-American War of 1898 and during World War I. As late as the 1930s, they were also used as the location for war games by modern soldiers armed with machine guns and supported by tanks and airplanes. Some battles purported to re-create the tactical situations of the original Civil War battles.

Since the late 1950s, interest in the hobby of reenacting has grown. Prior to the anticipation of the Centennial, there were only a few groups of reenactors, and the first large-scale reenactment was held on the Manassas battlefield in July 1961. About 3,000 participants attended. At the time, current standards of authenticity were virtually nonexistent.

At this point, the Park Service controlled the battlefields and had been disturbed by safety violations that had occurred at Manassas. After the reenactment of the Battle of Antietam in September 1962, the Park Service discouraged reenactments on battlefield sites. In July 1963, the Centennial of Gettysburg was reenacted at the battlesite, but no shots were fired. Since then, most reenactments take place on private land or state parks.

After the Centennial, "the hobby," as it is referred to by reenactors, grew in numbers and authenticity. Several thousand men were reenacting on a regular basis up until the late '60s and early '70s, when there was a slight decline in interest. This was due to a question of appropriateness while the Vietnam War was in progress.

By the mid '70s, interest in reenacting and authenticity flourished. With the celebration of the Bicentennial of the American Revolution, Revolutionary War reenactments became popular. It did not, however, continue to attract the numbers that the Civil War ones did.

On July 4, 1976, the Battle of Gettysburg reenactment brought out 4-5,000 reenactors, thousands of spectators, and television newscaster Dan Rather. It was the largest reenactment up to that time. Authenticity was improving. Some groups were making the transition to upgrading their uniforms. From that point on, interest mushroomed. "The hobby" spread to groups in Germany, England, Australia, and former Soviet-bloc countries. The 125th anniversary of the Civil War, from 1986 to 1990, ushered in the largest reenactments yet. Between 6,000 and 7,000 reenactors participated in the 125th anniversary of First Manassas. Nearly 10,000 reenacted the Battle of Gettysburg in 1988 for 40,000 spectators.

There are now between 12,000 and 25,000 reenactors, about 12,000 to 15,000 of whom are regulars. The largest concentration is in Virginia, Maryland, Pennsylvania, Kentucky, Tennessee, and Georgia. There's a sizable contingent in the Midwest—Ohio, Indiana, Michigan. There are also significant numbers of troops in Florida and California. Interest in Civil War reenacting is sluggish in New England states since reenacting the Revolutionary War seems to take precedence there.

Today, many organizations strive to master the same tactical manuals that the original soldiers used. Reenactor officers spend much time poring over the diagrams and complex instructions in Hardee's [60] and Casey's *Infantry Tactics*.[61] Some larger umbrella organizations, like the National Regiment, hold a yearly two-day classroom instruction to perfect training, knowledge of drill, parade, and army regulations of the 1860s. The tactics and drills are far more sophisticated than three decades ago when battlefield reenactments were much less structured. At the first reenactment thirty-three years ago, clothing and equipment were also inaccurate. Confederates wore khaki pants and J.C. Penney shirts, while Union soldiers wore blue jackets, blazers, jeans, and blue hats. Any weapon would do. Thirty-three years later, 150 to 200 vendors or sutlers make their living supplying reenactors with reproductions of wool uniforms, shoes, belts, cups, muskets and bayonets, tents and knapsacks. The average uniform runs about $550, musket $450 to $800, and tent and knapsack, $200. Most reenactors have at least two uniforms.

A *farb* is a slang reenactor term for unauthentic. "It's a farby unit" or a "farbfest" are descriptive derivatives. The popular term is rumored by some accounts to have originated from early reenactor George Gorman who originally began producing authentic uniforms in wool. When someone criticized the unauthentic dress of those not wearing Gorman's garb, he said, "Far be it for me to criticize." The term *farby* stuck.

In general, one-third of reenactors take authenticity seriously. They eat hardtack and wear linen suspenders and cotton underdrawers. One-third is split on authenticity and may sneak in an Igloo® cooler or eat a steak when the public's not around, but will stay in character when necessary. Another third is primarily out for fun, may have trouble with authority and discipline, and may balk at the military structure.

On the unit level, most officers are elected, although some are self-appointed. A typical unit includes a captain, lieutenant, lst sergeant, 2nd sergeant, and several corporals, along with anywhere between twenty-five and sixty privates. Most units incorporate and have a president and board of directors for administrative purposes. A board includes a secretary and treasurer. Unhappy with internal politics, sometimes splinter groups break off or individuals find another unit that suits them. Now, a bigger organizational structure is beginning to emerge. The larger umbrella groups include smaller organizations, and some, such as the Confederate "Army of Northern Virginia," fields up to two thousand troops, divided into several battalions. Their purpose is to re-create larger battles with a substantial military structure as its base, which will result in more historical reenactments.

Fitting into this military structure are the reenactors who come to "the hobby" from all walks of life. There are a large blue-collar group and a cross section of teachers, government workers, doctors, and lawyers. Some reenactors are as old as seventy or more years, but most are in their thirties and forties. They are generally older and heavier than the average Civil War soldier, who was thin and in his twenties. This has become a cause for some concern among "authentics."

These reenactors devote many hours to their military activities. Summer activities can average two to three events a month, dwindling down from late November to April. Reenactors think nothing of driving hundreds of miles to converge on reenactments, living history demonstrations, and parades for the public. Tacticals and war games are strictly for reenactors. Some events are fund-raisers to preserve the battlefields.

Reenacting meets many needs. Reenactors' reasons for continued involvement range from enjoying the camp, camaraderie, relaxation, respect, and escapism, to being able to live history,
preserve it, and educate others. Some speak of romanticism, hon-
oring the dead, portraying the warrior, or a deep spiritual connection. One sees it as experimental archaeology.

Manassas Battle reenactment organizer, Prince William County
Park Ranger Tracy Hormuth, observes reasons ranging from getting
back to simpler times in the nineteenth century to getting away
from family pressures, from feeling more comfortable with clearly
defined gender roles to having no outlet in their personal lives, and
from obtaining positions of power and rank on the field to escaping
from a life or job over which they have no control. She says that units
bond like fraternities.

As to why this incredible absorption with the Civil War, Lew Lord
reported in an August 1988 *U.S. News and World Report* feature article that the answers lie deep in both history and the American
psyche. "It's a fascination for history as much as a lust for gunpowder that makes people play Civil War soldier." Princeton historian
James McPherson told Lord that the Civil War was by far the most
vivid, dramatic, and violent single event in our history.[62] Perhaps
the issues aren't dead. Reenactors still emotionally argue in favor of
the legality of secession and the merits of Jeffersonian democracy.

Other historians interviewed by Lord included Frank Vandiver
and Emory Thomas. Frank Vandiver said, "The Civil War keeps coming back the further we get from it. The war itself may be remote in
time but not in geography." Emory Thomas, a historian at the University of Georgia, said, "The Civil War is as close to Americans as
their grandfather's trunk in somebody's attic."[63] Clinical and research psychologists like Fiore and Wambach, as well as psychics
like Edgar Cayce, would say it may be even closer than the attic.

Meanwhile, reenactors are helping to bring the Civil War back to
life in films and making an impact on Hollywood. They have acted
in the *North and South, Part II,* and the *Lincoln Miniseries* made for
television; and in the movies *Sommersby, Glory, Gettysburg,* and
Andersonville. They are making their voices heard and Hollywood is
listening. Civil War movies, such as *Gettysburg,* are much more accurate and authentic because of the demands of the reenactors.

Because reenactors are so concerned about authenticity, they are familiar with various marching terms and Civil War uniform items. My subjects referred to many of these during their regressions. For an amateur like me, it's helpful to have a reference guide. Consider these your Civil War regression crib notes.

Marching Terms

BREASTWORK: A low, quickly constructed barrier of earth or logs to protect the soldiers.

BY THE RIGHT (or THE LEFT) FLANK, MARCH; or RIGHT, FACE (or LEFT, FACE), FORWARD, MARCH: Bringing soldiers into a column of fours; this was the typical way soldiers marched along the road or into battle before deploying into the line of battle (two ranks deep).

CASEY'S INFANTRY TACTICS: A field manual written by Brigadier General Silas Casey. Used primarily by Union officers, it included exercises, marching and military maneuvers, music, and instructions for skirmishers.

DOUBLE-QUICK: A jogging step used in a charge. This was the way soldiers marched quickly or advanced.

FIX, BAYONETS: The command given by which soldiers draw their bayonets from the scabbards and attach them to the ends of their muskets.

GILHAM'S MANUAL OF DRILL: A field manual for drilling and military tactics used primarily by the Confederates. Techniques were derived from General Scott's manual used in the Mexican-American War.[64]

HARDEE'S TACTICS: The standard textbook on drilling and military maneuvers for rifle and light infantry written by General W. J. Hardee. Used by both Confederates and Federals, it included regulations for dealing with misbehavior, making known the watchword, and the roles of chaplains and sutlers.

RIGHT SHOULDER SHIFT, ARMS: The command brings the soldiers to the right shoulder shift. The musket was brought up so that the butt of the piece was held atop the palm of the right hand. With the lockplate just below the shoulder, the muzzle was up at an angle over the right shoulder. This command was usually used when the men were moving or charging at a double-quick pace. This allowed for the weapon to be more easily managed and not in the way of the men in front.

ROUTE STEP: This command allowed soldiers to march comfortably, carrying their muskets any way they wished. A casual, go-as-you-please manner; no one had to be in step. Troops still had to keep their place in the column of fours. This was the way soldiers marched long distances.

SHOULDER ARMS: This was the standard position from which other movements of the musket were made. The weapon was held parallel to the right side of the body, while the right hand was wrapped around the trigger guard.

SKIRMISH LINE: Skirmishers were deployed forward in single rank, five to ten paces between each man. They screened the advance. Once the fighting began in earnest, they fell back into the line of battle elbow-to-elbow with everyone else.

TRAIL ARMS: This was the command by which the musket was carried in the right hand, at the right hip or thigh level. It was used to go through brush so that the weapon was not tangled in tree limbs.

Civil War Uniform Fashions, Accoutrements, and Supplies

(As told to me by Robert Hodge, who has had a lifelong interest in Civil War period military fashion. See his regression story in chapter 7. Note: It originally cost the Federal government $727 million to clothe and feed the army and $339 million for supplies and transportation.)

BROGANS: Made of leather, these ankle-high boots were among the first mass-produced footwear that distinguished between right and left feet. These shoes became the standard military footwear.

CHEVRONS: Noncommissioned officers' insignia. Usually V-shaped, they were worn on the sleeves to show rank, years of service, and enlistments.

ENFIELD MUSKET: This weapon was one of the most widely used by Confederates. Standard issue in the British army; the Confederacy imported 400,000 of them. It fired a .577 caliber conical ball. The rifled musket was the most accurate by Civil War standards. Firing a musket required eleven separate motions. Soldiers were required to fire three aimed shots per minute. At the time, a musket cost about $13.[65]

FORAGE CAP: Cap of wool with a leather bill and chinstrap. Worn by both the Northern and Southern enlisted troops, this was a take-off on the kepi. Looser and taller than the kepi, it had more material hanging down in front, which would slope toward the bill. It was also called the "bummer's cap."

FROCK COAT: A single-breasted dress coat with a full skirt reaching to the knees. It had more buttons, was better made, and was tighter fitting than a sack coat.

GALLOON KNOTS: A braid of cotton, silk, worsted, or metal thread used for trim. Found mostly on Confederate officers' sleeves, it indicated rank and was nicknamed "chicken guts."

GAUNTLETS: High leather gloves worn by mounted officers and cavalrymen.

HARDEE HAT: A big-brimmed, Federal military hat. The hat had a tall, seven-inch-high tapered crown that was stiff when new. After use, it broke down, became soft, and took on the character of a slouch hat. Some of the hats were worn pinned up on the sides. This was also called a "Jeff Davis" hat.

HARDTACK: A staple food for the Federal soldier, the crackers were made of flour and water. They were often so hard that they earned the nickname of "toothduller." Some Confederates were also provisioned hardtack.

HAVERSACK: A bag, often made of canvas and painted black with waterproof paint. Worn almost like a purse, it was slung over the right shoulder and hung at the hip. Soldiers carried their rations such as hardtack, salt pork, and coffee in their haversacks.

CONFEDERATE JEAN JACKET: A Confederate jacket made out of jean cloth; 85 percent wool and 15 percent cotton, it was a tight, coarse, burlap-like fabric.

KEPI: A French-style military cap of blue or gray wool with a band around the base and a bill in front. A circular disc is sunken into the crown so that the sides of the fabric can curl inward.

KNAPSACK: Usually made of cotton cloth painted black with leather straps. The knapsack often contained half a shelter tent, a rubber blanket, toilet articles, and spare clothing.

LANYARD: When pulled, it sets off a spark from friction primer in the vent hole of the cannon, firing the cannon.

MINIE BALL: A conical bullet for a .58 caliber rifle musket named after the French army captain who designed it.

SACK COAT: A simple four-button garment of blue flannel. This fatigue blouse was widely issued throughout the war to soldiers in the Union army. This loose-fitting coat came to the middle of the thigh and was mass produced.

SCABBARD: A sheath for the bayonet made of black bridle leather with copper rivets and a brass tip. The blade of the bayonet was generally eighteen inches long. The most common style was a triangular blade.

SHELL JACKET: A waist-length (just below the belt line) jacket. Generally, Confederates wore shell jackets. One variety, the CO-LUMBUS DEPOT JACKET, was medium blue jean cloth and had solid blue cuffs. There were several styles of RICHMOND DEPOT JACKETS, with or without epaulets and belt loops. Another term used for Richmond depot jackets was EASTERN JACKET.

SHOULDER STRAPS: Rectangular boards which displayed an officer's insignia. Worn on both shoulders, they were more commonly seen in the Federal army.

SLOUCH HAT: A big-brimmed, wool felt hat with a beehive-like crown. The brim could be worn flat or turned up and worn with a plume. Soft-brimmed slouch hats were popular throughout the Confederate ranks.

SOFT PACK: A type of knapsack, different from a haversack.

ZOUAVES: Patterned after the French Zouave units during the Crimean War, Zouave uniforms and drill were popularized in 1859 by a company of cadets from Chicago. Some Civil War Zouave units were recruited from fire companies, known for teamwork and bravery. Uniforms vary. One of the most distinctive is the 5th New York: short blue jackets with red trim, baggy red trousers, and fez. Zouave uniforms were also found in the South, particularly in Louisiana.

Military Structure

COMPANY: In theory, a company consisted of 100 men and was commanded by a captain. Because of losses, many companies had only twenty-five to fifty men.

REGIMENT: A colonel commanded a regiment which incorporated ten companies. Early in the war, a regiment consisted of 1,000 men, but gradually many dwindled to 250 to 500 men.

BRIGADE: Usually three to six regiments comprised a brigade, which was supposed to be led by a brigadier general.

DIVISION: Three to four brigades comprised a division. It was supposed to be commanded by a major general.

CORPS: Three to four divisions comprised a corps, also usually commanded by a major general.

ARMY: Several corps comprised an army. In the Union army, starting in 1863, each corps had its own symbol, worn as a cloth badge on the cap or uniform.

Interpreting Codes

When you see something like this: Company K, 17th New York Infantry, it will mean an infantryman in the 17th Regiment of New York in Company K. You may hear or see some clues as to the various branches of service: blue trim on the uniforms stands for infantry, yellow for cavalry, and red for artillery.

Other Terms

DISTRIBUTION CAMP: Recruits or men who had recovered from illness were returned to distribution camps before being sent on to their units in the field.

PROVOST MARSHALL: The commander of a force who functioned as military police.

RETINUE: A group of persons in attendance on a person of rank; an escort.

SKEDADDLER: A soldier who had deserted or fled the battle. *Skedaddle* means "to scurry away."

A Key to Major Battles

Although more than 10,000 military actions took place in the Civil War, only a small proportion were big battles like Gettysburg. There were two main arenas in which the major military operations took place. They were divided by the Appalachian Mountains. Everything to the east was the Eastern theater. This area encompassed both the Union and Confederate capitals. The Western theater went to the Mississippi River.

This guide includes battles mentioned by the reenactors. It can help put the battles in perspective. It appeared that most of the battles were fought in the Eastern theater.

Eastern Theater

Surrender of Fort Sumter, S.C.—April 12-13, 1861
First Manassas (Bull Run), Va.—July 21, 1861
Jackson's Shenandoah Campaign, Va.—March 23-June 9, 1862;
   Winchester—May 25, 1862
Seven Pines, Va.—May 31, 1862
Seven Days Battles, Va.—June 26-July 1, 1862
   Battle of Mechanicsville—June 26, 1862
   Battle of Gaines's Mill—June 27, 1862
   Battle of Malvern Hill—July 1, 1862
Second Manassas, Va.—August 28-30, 1862
South Mountain and Antietam, Md.—September 14-17, 1862
First Fredericksburg, Va.—Dec. 11-13, 1862
Second Fredericksburg , Va.—May 4, 1863
Gettysburg, Pa.—July 1-3, 1863
Wilderness,Va.—May 5-6, 1864
Spotsylvania, Va.—May 10-12, 1864
Cold Harbor, Va.—June 1-2, 1864
Siege of Petersburg, Va.—June 18, 1864-April 2, 1865
Battle of Monocacy, Md.—July 9, 1864
Winchester,Va.—September 19, 1864
Cedar Creek, Va.—October 19, 1864
Battle of Sayler's Creek, Va.—April 6, 1865
Surrender at Appomattox, Va.—April 9, 1865

Western Theater

Battle of Shiloh, Tenn.—April 6-7, 1862
Vicksburg Campaigns, Miss.—Oct.-Dec. 1862; March-July 1863
Battle of Chickamauga, Ga.—September 19-20, 1863
Chattanooga Campaign, Tenn.—October-November 1863
Battle of Bentonville, N.C.—March 19-21, 1865

Now you are armed with everything you need to know to begin this Civil War past-life adventure. You already know far more than the average young recruit who had never been away from home before. If you are not yet eighteen, just print "18" on a piece of paper, slip it into your shoe, and you can honestly state that you are "over eighteen." Although the typical Union soldier was twenty-five and most were between eighteen and forty-six, nearly 200,000 were only fifteen or sixteen.[66]

We can dispense with tying the hay to the left foot and straw to the right to tell them apart. As recruits, you would be far too smart to be called "strawfoots" like that last unit. In fact, you also already know more about the Civil War than some of the Civil War soldiers we are about to visit.

If you've just enlisted, you've first passed through the distribution camp to find out whom to report to. You would identify your NCO by looking at his chevrons. You'd be issued kepis and uniforms, although if your pants are too short and your knapsack feels heavy, you'll get used to it. Eventually, you'll slim down your load. You'll also learn to soak your hardtack in your coffee, so you'll be able to eat it.

4

Steve:
The Soldier Returns

As a pacifist, Stephen Melko had spent most of the 1960s avoiding going to Vietnam. During the pre-hypnosis interview, he laughed at himself as he noted the irony, "Now I play Civil War." For the past eleven years, he had spent at least one weekend a month at reenactments and battlesites. For the first few years, it was nearly every weekend. Because reenacting was consuming much of his free time, Steve compromised with his wife and cut back on some activities. At the time of the interview, he was spending more time with his eight-year-old daughter and two teenage stepchildren.

The forty-four-year-old commercial property manager freely admitted that reenacting was a wonderful change from the stress of everyday life. For him, it was "R and R" within the confines of a military structure. Steve, who had earned a degree in business from Pennsylvania State University, took "the hobby" seriously. He enjoyed the recreation and camaraderie associated with reenacting.

Still, he handled his military duties responsibly, liked the physical demands, and spent as much time as possible reading about the Civil War.

Through Steve's involvement in Civil War reenacting, he said his thinking on the subject of war had matured. He realized that sometimes war is an unavoidable evil. His philosophy on war was now consistent with the old adage: the best defense is a good offense.

During our interview, his blue eyes became pensive. Steve expressed his inability to choose either the Yankee or the Confederate philosophy because the 1850s was a completely different way of life. He compared the current pro-life vs. pro-choice abortion debate with the abolition vs. state's rights issue. In Steve's opinion, abortion was the closest issue in modern times to elicit similar emotions and questions of what is morally and legally right. It even resulted in bloodshed.

Turning to other matters, Steve said that his wife urged him to participate in the regression research. She had always felt that Steve had lived before. His eyes crinkled around the edges as he smiled. With a feeling of anticipation, Steve settled back on the couch for his regression session. He closed his eyes, quickly slipped into hypnosis, and, as I tape-recorded his words and took notes, he immediately became aware of body sensations.

"My feet and legs are cold," he said. "They feel chilled as if they were in cold water." He jerked. A shiver ran through him. "I feel a chill, like being cold inside my tent. It's starting to become light and warm up a little. There's a fireplace. I'm trying to warm by the fire or trying to warm something in the fire. I'm feeling hungry; maybe I'm making coffee. The coffee is still cooking and I keep wanting it to be ready. I feel like I'm going to be called away from it."

It was clear to me that Steve was processing information kinesthetically, through sensations. He was feeling rather than seeing pictures or hearing things. He repeatedly used words like "feel" and "sense."

"I'm needed for something," he began. "I'm being called away. I've got to report to somebody. I feel that I've got to prepare the morning report. I have to assemble the men. I have to call the roll and report to the sergeant major. But I'm not getting my coffee. I'm going to miss it again. I'm getting dressed and putting my brogans on. I need to put my coat on. Now I feel warmer.

"It's time for roll and time to have the troops fall in," he continued. "The troops are in line. All you hear in the mornings is men coughing. They all seem to be present—all eighteen men.

"I guess I'm an NCO—maybe acting in the sergeant's place. It's unusual for me to call the roll. The men seem to be jocular. They want to kid me, but couldn't do that with the sergeant. They are being a little smart about it. They want to be back in their beds. Me, too. I'd love to have my coffee. I never get to finish it.

"Roll call's over," he said. "I have to take it to the sergeant major. As is customary, he has some orders. He wants a detail. I hope it's something I can delegate. After the men have eaten, we're to go to the woods to relieve the guard. One squad has to go and I have to go to formally place the guard. There goes my coffee."

During his narrative, I noted that Steve is a corporal in reenacting and, while he had similar duties during the regression, he never took roll as a reenactor. In reenacting Steve also never seemed to get a chance to finish his coffee. In this memory, he missed his morning cup for guard duty. I was aware the skeptics might suggest confabulation to explain these similarities.

"The guard has given me the new sign—'daisies' is the password." I saw Steve smile at the password. "He's asked permission to be relieved of his post. The detail is posted. We're in the woods. It's hurry and wait—nothing going on. I wish I could go back to my coffee.

"There's a messenger. He's saying we'll be relieved at three o'clock. It's only 6:30. I don't like this duty. It's boring. I don't think the men have eaten unless they did while I was seeing the sergeant major. I haven't eaten. We can't have a fire where we're at. Don't want to alert the enemy of our position. I sense they may be close. I don't want to take any unnecessary chances.

"There's something strange. I sense there's somebody beyond our line." He laughed with relief. "Oh, it's just a deer. Better a deer than the enemy. We call the enemy Johnny Reb. I haven't seen any Rebs close up."

Steve's sense of humor and his easy but professional way of dealing with the troops impressed me.

"My head hurts. When I haven't eaten, I get headaches sometimes. A good cup of black coffee wouldn't hurt."

Steve was on a roll. I thought it was time to try to elicit some details like his name, rank, and unit. Through suggestion, I moved him in that direction.

"I've been doing this for too long," he answered. "Two years. William Snyder. They call me 'Corp.' I must be a corporal. I'm from North Carolina. The men don't talk like I do. I'm not from where they're from. They're from Michigan. It just seemed like the right thing to do to join them—4th Michigan Company B 'Black Hats' (I think). Sometimes they kid me about the way I talk. They're good men. Things have been quiet."

Steve had just identified himself as a Federal, although he was originally from North Carolina. In his twentieth-century life, he has always reenacted as a Union soldier. His sympathies lie clearly with the North. Because of his antislavery views, he has no bond with the South. In reenacting, he wore a Confederate uniform only once. While acting as a Union soldier for the movie *Gettysburg*, he spent a lot of time waiting. He decided to borrow a Southern uniform and get into the action, rather than sit idly.

At the time of my research, Steve was living in Virginia, however he grew up in the North. As a youngster, he would only take the role of Yankee. He grew up playing with his great-grandfather's musket and bayonet, and he still remembered the vivid stories his mother made up about blood dripping from the blade.

Steve was one of just a few reenactors in my study to do research on his ancestors before getting into reenacting. It took him nearly four years to track down his great-grandfather's unit, military and pension records. His great-grandfather, a Connecticut soldier, had died at Gettysburg.

Another relative had received a pension for having contracted "bloody piles" during the war. Steve laughingly reported that he was called "old bloody ass Murphy." Murphy had stood picket duty at Hartwood Church, Virginia. Coincidentally, Steve's current reenactment unit was also at Hartwood in the winter of 1862. And interestingly enough, Steve's employer owned the Hartwood Plantation on the same site.

As Steve's Civil War life memory continued, I guided him to the next significant event, in which he found himself on a campaign.

"It's daytime. There are leaves on the trees. It's hot. We're marching on the roads. I feel tired and dusty. We have our coats on. The roads are very busy with lots of men and movement. I feel uneasy because there's something happening.

"There's a sense of urgency," he said, "like we're needed somewhere soon. The pace is quick, but there's lots of stuff on the side of the roads. The mounted men—the cavalry is passing by. Something's up there. I can feel it. I hear the shuffling of the feet and cups rattling on the canteens as men march. (He laughed.) A scared jack rabbit ran across the road.

"Someone's crying. He's sitting down on the side of the road. I think he's a drummer. Oh, God, is he young! Maybe ten or twelve. I'm twenty-two. Most of the guys are the same age as I; then there's a couple of old geezers. I think the drummer's crying because he can't keep up. His drum must be awful heavy.

"My musket barrel feels hot. It must be the sun shining on it. Damn, it's hot out. We were in Culpeper, Virginia, a few days ago. We've been going for several days now. I think we camped there for a day or two. We're going away from there. They got the slip on us. We're chasing Johnny. He must be up there. They're moving us awful quick. I'm not sure how I feel about this. I suppose we have to catch up with them sometime."

Steve's regression flowed like any other regression I had facilitated, evolving sequentially. The inherent nature of the regression experience is that the participant doesn't know what will happen from moment to moment. This element of the unknown is the reason Steve preferred military maneuvers to re-creating battles where the outcome has long since been predetermined. Tactical maneuvers require skill and cleverness, and Steve found them more realistic—not knowing where he was, where he was going, or what would happen next. The element of confusion, of not knowing whether you'll meet friend or foe or whether you can turn the tide, was a challenge to Steve.

Next, he recalled an Allentown, Pennsylvania, reenacting event where he camped at a church and drilled at dawn amid fog so thick he couldn't see. When the fog lifted, his unit found that the Confederates had sneaked into the fort with Union uniforms on. Basically, the South had captured the fort using their wits. This unpredictable element triggered Steve's most emotional reenacting experiences. He believed that all reenactors were trying to get as close as possible to the essence of what it was really like. Unpredictability is exactly what Steve was finding in his past-life adventure.

"They're getting us off the road," he continued. "Something's going to happen. They want us to load our muskets. I load it. We're in line. There's another regiment beside us. We're stopping. We're way off the road now and straightening the lines. 'Fix bayonets.' I can hear 'em coming—like screaming banshees. I don't like that sound. I've never heard it like this. They're sounding louder and closer. There seems to be lots of 'em. I can't see 'em.

"My stomach feels funny. I have a knot in my stomach." His body visibly jerked on the couch. "The hair on the back of my neck is standing up. It's strange. I can see some smoke, but I didn't hear the noise for a while. Maybe they're a couple hundred yards off. It's getting louder."

Steve now called out commands that would be audible to his troops.

"Keep the alignment! Keep the alignment! Forward!

"We can't lose contact with the other regiment. We have to keep aligned with them. I can't see the colors. I'll know where I'm at when I see the colors. They're over a hill. I can't see the whole regiment. We are higher than they are, but there is a slope.

"We're stopping. We're getting ready to fire. I've got to load again. We're moving off. We're going forward again. It's harder to load while you're trying to move. I'm nervous. God, I'm nervous. I can't tell whether I'm excited or scared. We're stopping again. I can see 'em now. They're very close. They can't just stand here."

Now, the commands flowed more swiftly.

"Come on! Come on! OK, here we go. All right. We're firing by files. OK, reload. Easy.

"God, I can't see a thing. There's lots of smoke. I don't know what the heck I'm shooting at. Damn, I dropped my cartridge. I have more."

Steve repeated the commands as he heard them.

"Come on, boys! Cease fire!

"We're moving again. There's still a lot of smoke. It's starting to clear, but we're not getting fired on now. We're moving forward. There they are. Do you see 'em? They're protected behind a fence or logs. They got some breastworks."

While in hypnosis, I saw the expression on Steve's face change to one of apprehension and then fear.

"Oh, no, they want us to charge the breastworks. I'm scared to death. What? No. This is crazy. They have us uncap our weapons. They don't want us to fire when we charge. They want to use us up. I don't want to go. Don't make me go."

In his waking life, Steve expresses disdain for reenactors who don't make the extra effort to stay in character. While reenacting, he doesn't take a lot of baggage along and survives without creature comforts. He had described his passionate "hobby" as an avocation, but under hypnosis what was an avocation was quickly transcended into a matter of life and death. This was more real than any reenactment Steve had ever experienced. In spite of his fear, however, he followed orders and charged the Confederates.

"It's over," he suddenly said bleakly. "I don't know what happened. We charged. I'm not with the rest. I didn't make it. Some of the others made it. I'm down. I feel numb all over. I feel weak. I'm rolled over on my back. I'm thirsty. I feel like I'm falling asleep. I feel tired. Someone is shaking me. I'm slowly waking up."

Steve was talking slower and softer now.

"Someone's helping me up," he said. "I feel dizzy. My head is sore. My head feels like it's ready to fall off. Jim, my friend, is helping me. He's taking me back. There are some trees. I can hear shooting, but it's not nearby. There are men under the tree. Some are hurt. Others are just winded and exhausted."

Steve laughed with relief.

"Jim says I got a lump on my head. No big wounds. Yeah—I made it! He's giving me some water. I think I'll be all right. I have red hair, haven't shaved for a while, and have a little bit of a beard. I've looked better." He laughed again. "I lost my hat. Jim made sure I still got my gun. My cup's all bent up—I think I fell on it."

Unlike in his past life, Steve had medium brown hair and a moustache. He stood about five feet, eleven inches, and exhibited a hint of shyness. Fellow reenactors said he resembled British Major General Prettyman, who served as military governor in South Africa around 1880.

Steve's regression continued. Now, he was more concerned about how he was feeling and what would happen to him next.

"They want to take us somewhere else, those who can walk. I can walk OK now. If they're going to feed us, you're darned right, I'm going. I think it's an officer who's leading us. I don't think he's with our regiment. I don't know where the rest of my regiment is. There's a couple of my men here. Jim's here. They want to take us to the rear to feed us and sort us out."

I observed that Steve had weathered his first injury well and was in good spirits.

"I'm walking OK now, but my head still hurts. It's getting dark. There are still things happening about a mile away. Just as long as it's over there and not here. They found our regiment. Jim and I are to report to our new positions. I'm happy to be alive." He sighed with relief. "The men seem to be none the worse for the wear. There are some people missing, but it doesn't look like we got it too bad."

The elusive element of authenticity Steve had sought was right here—the pathos, the fear, the companionship, the pain. What he had been trying to re-create in reenacting—the experiences of the common soldier—was unfolding in the regression. These memories nurtured an even greater level of appreciation for the Civil War soldiers by Steve.

Now, Steve found himself on the march.

"We're moving again. I feel OK. I'd rather be doing something else—most anything. My God, I can see our column. It's very, very long—maybe the entire corps. I don't know who's in charge. We've been moving. It's like we're snaking through a mountain road. I can look back and see the column. I think we're in Maryland—we just crossed the Potomac. The last battle was several days before we crossed the river.

"I have a new black hat—it's still stiff. I'll have to break it in. I can hear the artillery, far away, echoing in the mountains. I sure need a bath. The last one was when we crossed the river—two days ago. As far as I can see in front and behind me is a column of men. The hats are all different. There are some different uniforms." He laughed heartily. "A guy's got his leggings on backwards. Must be a fresh fish. Where do they find these people?"

In this lifetime, Steve treasured his Civil War uniforms. He purchased most of the equipment for his first uniform before he became a reenactor. His first uniform was the more traditional Union uniform. At the time of this research, Steve was reenacting as a Zouave, wearing a blue jacket with red trim, red pantaloons, white gaiters, and a white turban with a gold tassel (see page 5 of the photo section). He liked the exotic impression. Steve said he just couldn't discard a piece of his uniform, even when it was all tattered, because he was too attached to it.

Steve's focus now shifted off uniforms and onto a rest break.

"We're stopping. I think they're camping us here. It feels good to sit down. My feet always hurt. I don't think we're going to stop long enough to cook. They're just giving us a rest. I'm hungry, though. Maybe I can have some crackers. Better than nothing. Yuck. My water's warm."

Steve was right. Soon, he was back on his feet.

"OK, all right. We're back on the road. God, I feel so stiff when I get back up. I see stars. They're marching us at night. I see campfires in the distance. They look like fireflies. Maybe the rest of the army's up there. We should be there soon. They're gonna rest us here. We get to spend the night. We don't get a lot of sleep—two hours here and there."

Steve's night sped away in just moments.

"It's morning," he said shortly. "There's corn in the fields. It's high. We're marching through it. It's been three or four days or longer since we crossed the Potomac. The corn's about ripe. I put some in my haversack. I'm going to roast those ears tonight. It sounds real good—the first fresh food for a long time. The guys are having a great time taking the corn. The marching is slowed up. We're not marching now. We're in battleline. We're going through the corn in battleline."

Periodically, the men talked about food or the lack of it. Steve was delighted to have stumbled on what he planned would be a feast. Quickly, his attention shifted to his surroundings.

"You can't see a damn thing—you can only get a glimpse of the guy beside you. It's very confusing, very strange. I don't want to go any farther. They want us to keep moving. This is crazy. I can't see a thing. Ow! I twisted my ankle. It's rough. There are stones in the field. I kicked one up.

"I hear noises. Someone else is in the corn. I don't know who. I hear people walking. I can hear the corn leaves. They're coming toward us. I think the whole regiment's in here. I can't tell. I can't see but a few people from where I'm at. I can hear 'em, but I can't see 'em."

Suddenly, what had seemed like a romp through the fields had become frightening. Steve stiffened.

"They're shooting up the line. What are they shooting at? I can't see anything."

Steve began to speak in a whisper to the others around him. "I think he's out there. I know he's out there. Yeah, Johnny's there. He's coming toward me, but I don't think he sees me."

He now began to hear and relay commands in a stage whisper. "What was that? I think I see him.

"What's the command? Kneel. Down. Down. Everybody down. Front rank. Ready. Rise. Fire. Load. Kneel. Rear rank—rise. Fire. Kneel. Front rank—are you loaded? Ready? Rise up. Fire. Kneel."

Steve tried to remain calm, but I now detected panic in his voice. "I don't know what's happening. They're not moving.

"Hold your position.

"Damn—what a mess! What a shame—destroying all this corn. It's getting beat up—shot up and trampled on.

"We're gonna move again. Bayonets. Fix bayonets. Right shoulder shift. Forward."

I was amazed. For probably ten minutes now, Steve had been relaying commands. He had never gotten out of character or departed from his role as corporal. Steve, who found the wheat fields at Gettysburg particularly stirring, was now grappling with the difficulties in the corn field. Then, the commands stopped.

"I'm sinking. I think I'm hit. Strange—it's like I'm there, but I'm not there. I can't get up. I'm trying. I think it's real this time. I think I'm really hit. I'm hit in the chest. It feels like someone is sitting on my chest. It burns real bad. It really burns."

Steve's breath became labored at this point. I paid careful attention.

"I feel weak, really tired. I wanna sleep. I can't let myself sleep—I won't get up. Don't let me go to sleep."

Steve was now taking big breaths, gasping for air. "I feel tired and can't see anything. I'm trying to catch my breath. I know I'm not going to make it. I feel the life drain out of me."

Steve now began to sound peaceful and speak softly as if he were moving away.

"I wanna sleep. I'm not afraid any more. I don't know why. I feel very light—just white—like a light coming to me. If I can reach it—I can almost touch it—everything will be all right if I can get to the light. There's no pain. I just feel better."

What he described next seemed confusing at first.

"I'm happy, 'cause I'm home. Mamma's there. Mamma's made me an apple pie. I love apple pie. Everything's OK now. I'm back, Mamma. I see the floor of our house. I'm moving. I'm rocking in Mamma's rocker by the fire. I feel very good. Just sitting in the rocker by the fire. Can I stay here? I want to stay with my mamma for a while."

What did this mean? Had Steve just been wounded and then sent home on leave? Over the course of several reenactor regressions, I found that when the men got wounded, they often thought they were dying. They sometimes described the same elements as those who have reported "near-death experiences" (NDEs). Was Steve now dead and making a visit to his mother? After the passing of someone they love, people often claim that they have been visited by their departed loved ones—often before being informed of the death. Could it be that this was how he envisioned meeting his mother in the afterlife? NDE researchers have found such examples of meetings among friends and relatives.

While I was still mulling over the possibilities, Steve threw me another curve..

"I feel like I'm being drawn in," he said, "like I'm being pulled in. I don't know." He sighed. "I'm breathing. I'm waking up. It's strange."

Steve appeared puzzled as he touched his body and his hair. "It's hard to describe—it feels like I'm part here and part somewhere else. I don't know where 'here' is, but I can sense it's familiar to me. I don't know what 'there' is; it's like wherever it was, I left a part of me there. It feels like it's happy here and I don't want to leave. Like maybe where the light was."

At this point, I was perplexed. I now felt that Steve didn't think he was waking up after the battle or resting at his mother's. "Is your name still William?" I asked. I held my breath and waited for his response.

"I don't think so. It's Daniel Haynes. I'm at home." We were clearly out of the Civil War life. Although I was fascinated to know more about Daniel Haynes, who I assumed was a baby, Steve had been in hypnosis for hours. Reluctantly, I brought him back to our twentieth-century reality. When he opened his eyes, we both shook our heads in amazement.

Although he had been raised Catholic, he was open to the possibilities of rebirth. Steve believed in the immortality of the soul. He felt that, as souls, we go through many stages of evolution and development before we "retire."

While in his teens, Steve had a paranormal experience. His young friend, Ernie, who meditated and did yoga for hours at a time, had told Steve that he was developing his skills of astral projection. One day, Ernie came to visit. They watched *Lost in Space* on television and chatted. During the visit, Steve's mother came into the room and asked Steve why he was talking to himself. No one else was there.

The death scene Steve described during his regression shared commonalities with other reenactors' death scenes. Altogether, they fit the scenario of NDEs as described in the research of Raymond Moody, M.D.[67] Steve was one of six of the reenactors who described their deaths as soldiers. Like Steve, four others felt pain and then felt it leave; two others felt sleepy; three others saw either light or dark; and one other saw friends or family. Although Steve didn't voluntarily describe viewing his body, like most of the others did, I didn't ask him about it since he had already moved off the battlefield and onto his mamma's rocking chair, perhaps transitioning into his afterlife experience.

Interestingly enough, when my subjects, as soldiers, were wounded, their ordeals had some of the same characteristics as the death experiences. Of the four who were wounded and who did not die, all four felt pain; one then wondered why the pain had subsided. Two expressed a fear that they might be dying; three wanted to rest; and three saw light, darkness, or both.

Five of the six reenactors who died in battle were very interested in the Civil War as youngsters. At least three of them played as Civil War soldiers. Noted past-life researcher Ian Stevenson had cases of children who have relived in play how the previous personality died. Some played at drowning, others hanging.[68]

The death scenes of Steve and the other men could have left psychological marks on their present lives. Most past-life therapists agree that death is the great unresolved trauma.[69] The unfinished business we leave at death—whether physical, mental, or emotional—gets carried forward to the next life to be relived or resolved. Could this be one of the main reasons for the reenactors' fascination with the Civil War? Deep in their souls are they really seeking to resolve unfinished business from their lives in the 1860s?

As regards the soul experience, war deaths are particularly traumatic. Past-life researchers tell of soldiers who continue fighting after they have died.[70] Some, particularly those with violent deaths, may remain in the vicinity of the death.[71] With all the carnage on Civil War battlesites, some nineteenth-century soldiers could still be manning their posts.

Edgar Cayce[72] and others[73] were concerned about war children who, bewildered by their violent deaths, wandered the lower astral planes and returned to earth too quickly. In his past-life regression experience, Steve appeared to return almost immediately. He does, however, recall experiencing the light, which might suggest that he moved on to more celestial arenas in between. Steve did spend a little time visiting his mother before moving on.

Aside from the apparent credibility of Steve's death scene, his experiences also checked out historically. Steve described his unit being attacked by surprise. The Iron Brigade was attacked by surprise at the Battle of Second Manassas, August 28-30, 1862.

The 24th Michigan Volunteer Infantry joined the Iron Brigade a month after Antietam, although the 4th Michigan Volunteer Infantry was not. However, the 24th Michigan was engaged at the Battle of Brawner's Farm, August 28, 1862. The 4th Michigan was engaged at Manassas, although not at Brawner's Farm. The Iron Brigade then crossed the river and moved on to the Maryland campaign.[74]

As Corporal Snyder, Steve had said that he had been from North Carolina. Although it may have seemed strange for a Southerner to be in a Michigan unit, General Gibbon, commander of the Iron Brigade, was also from North Carolina.

Although Steve had dreaded it and was shocked by it, his company was ordered to advance on the breastworks (protective barrier of the enemy) with guns that were not capped. Percussion caps were needed to be placed on the muskets' nipples in order for the weapons to fire. Historian Brian Pohanka confirms that this was common practice, when officers didn't want their men to stop and shoot, but to quickly keep advancing, thus cutting down on casualties and using their bayonets.

Steve saw a rookie putting on his leggings backward, and early in the war it was common for the Iron Brigade to wear leggings, although many other units didn't wear them.

Events in Steve's regression follow historical chronology. The Battle of Second Manassas was August 28-30, 1862. The march on the mountain (the long column snaking through Maryland after having crossed the Potomac several days earlier) was probably the march through South Mountain, Maryland. That could have been just enough time to have put Corporal Snyder in Miller's cornfield at the

Battle of Antietam, September 17, 1862. The corn would have been ripe at the time. This was also the bloodiest battle of the war to date. Not only did the details in Steve's regression appear historically correct, but also the person he recalled under hypnosis. In an Antietam Civil War cemetery, I found two Union soldiers' tombstones whose names, units, and life stories may be close matches. Edwin R. Snyder, Company D, 3rd Wisconsin Volunteer Infantry, was mortally wounded in action at Antietam. According to his military records, he was a twenty-one-year-old sergeant. William Snyder, Company D, 97th New York Volunteer Infantry, was also a casualty of Antietam. He died shortly after the battle at Smoketown Hospital near the battlefield. The 97th New York was in the First Corps, the same corps as the Iron Brigade.

National Archives military and pension records yielded some correlation to two other soldiers. Twenty-one-year-old Pvt. William H. Snyder, Company G, 2nd Michigan Volunteer Infantry, was killed in action near Petersburg, Virginia, on June 18, 1864. Although the name and unit were a very good match, we had earmarked Snyder's last battle as Antietam. It is possible, however, that Snyder died in a cornfield other than Antietam. It was rare when a soldier knew his location. Another good unit match was Harrison Sneider, Company F, 3rd Michigan Volunteer Infantry. Although he did picket duty, the similarity ends there. Harrison was sick in the hospital, had been a prisoner of war, and then dropped from the rolls, possibly for desertion.

I was grateful that there weren't too many spellings for Snyder as I ordered Union pension records at the National Archives. Researchers have to wait two hours after ordering the records and are only allowed to view three files an hour. I was encouraged about the possible matches.

Besides that, I was haunted with the visions of Steve enthusiastically picking corn for an evening meal he would never have, sinking to the ground as he whispered battle commands, and watching his shocked reaction at finding himself in another body after leaving the battlefield behind.

5

Alan:
Beginner's Luck

There was something that made Alan McBride stand out from all the other reenactors who participated in my study. I couldn't quite understand the reason. For one thing, he gave short concise answers in the pre-regression interview, as compared with most of the other reenactors, who seemed to get on a roll and then talk nonstop about the Civil War.

Alan was one of the younger reenactors in my study. He was twenty-nine at the time of the regression. The others ranged in age from twenty-seven to fifty-one, with the average age being forty. By far, Alan was the rookie reenactor. At this point, he had been reenacting for about two-and-a-half years. The next most junior reenactors had between six and seven years' experience, and the remainder of the group had from twenty-two to thirty-two years' experience. This adds up to a life investment of more than 167 years among twelve people or an average of fourteen years per person.

Alan was married and, at the time of the regression, the couple was expecting their first baby in about four months. Three of the reenactors were married, one was divorced, and the rest were single. Alan told me that his wife was very supportive of his reenacting. Although some reenactors get so consumed with reenacting that it can create tension in their relationships, she didn't mind the time Alan devoted to "the hobby." Although she never cared to "dress out in period costume" and camp with the unit like some other wives and girlfriends, she did watch Alan's unit in local parades and reenactments and helped as needed.

Unlike most of the other subjects, Alan didn't believe that he had any Civil War ancestors and had never done any research. Besides that, he freely admitted during his pre-hypnosis interview that he didn't even know much about Civil War history. He hadn't done much reading on the subject. Alan's focus had been on his unit's background and his particular speciality was bayonet drill. He excelled at this, the *Manual of Arms,* and all the nuances of nineteenth-century military drill.

Unlike some of the others, Alan didn't feel particularly comfortable doing first-person dialogue historical interpretation. He said that it required an incredible amount of knowledge to do it right. Another difference between Alan and most of the others was that he did not participate in the movie *Gettysburg.*

Another distinction was that Alan, a computer specialist, was one of only a few reenactors in my study who had ever been hypnotized before. Working on a degree in accounting when his regression was done, Alan remembered being hypnotized one time in a psychology class. He told me that he didn't think he had been hypnotized because he hadn't been in a trance. He said that he hadn't been able to feel, hear, or see anything unusual. In fact, he was still able to hear what was happening in the room. His soul didn't leave his body, and he couldn't see himself in his chair. He described a wave of relaxation moving through his body. Then, he sank deeper into relaxation and stayed that way until the end of the evening.

What Alan had reported was just how hypnosis is actually supposed to feel. Almost everybody feels the same way Alan did. Before each session with a new client, I explain the realities and misconceptions about hypnosis, and what the client should and should not expect. Inevitably, clients will still say that they were not hypnotized, even if they have been "under" for hours.

When I give lectures on hypnosis, I sometimes bring along a T-shirt and show it to the group. It illustrates a client elevated about a foot off the couch. The caption reads something like, "But I wasn't hypnotized. I heard everything you said."

To set the record straight, clients are in control during hypnosis and are often aware of their surroundings. In fact, their senses are usually heightened in the hypnosis process. It's really just a shift in consciousness, much like a meditative state. The only difference is that the subconscious is guided in a therapeutic direction.

Anxious to get on with Alan's hypnotic regression, I began a visualization and countdown process. Alan moved quickly into a relaxed hypnotic state. His eyes began fluttering, which is the sign of entering into an altered state, and his eyes continued to flutter throughout the regression. Responding quickly to my questions, he found himself outside with others. He was wearing black shoes.

"A man's leaning against a wall or tree," he said. "He's wearing gray pants, jacket, and hat with yellow trim. He's wearing black shoes. He has short blond or red hair and a darker moustache. He's young, in his thirties. He's tall, slender, clean. His uniform looks new, but the shoes don't. I don't know him.

"He's in a grassy inclined area. Others are lying in a flat, small area without trees. The grass is short. The sun's shining, but not straight up. It's afternoon. It's warm, dry.

"Everyone else is lying on dirt not moving. They're wearing dirty pants and open white shirts, and aren't wearing hats, coats, or carrying anything. They look alike. They're hot. There are no tents.

"The first man's the only one with a uniform. A few others, standing next to him, are also dressed in gray with yellow piping. One new person has dark brown or black hair, a beard, and the same gray hat. The first man is watching the men on the ground. He has a musket."

Ironically Alan, currently a stickler for uniform grooming, found himself in the midst of a disheveled band of men. Even on a hot day, when he imagined that Civil War soldiers would have taken off their jackets, he preferred to keep his coat completely buttoned. He kept his brass polished and his shoes blackened. Alan liked to look neat in military fashion because people notice, and it showed discipline. He wore his hair short, had good posture, and wanted his presentation and his marching to be correct. As a reenactor, he felt that his goal was to be the best soldier in his regiment. In his regression, Alan found the standards and morale not up to his current expectations.

"Men are marching in long narrow columns without weapons," he continued. "They're not carrying anything. They're like the guys lying down—unkempt, no uniforms, nothing distinguishing or organized. They're not the gray and yellow uniforms.

"They're walking from my left to my right, as if they're walking past me. They're not stopping in front of me, and I can't see the front of the column to the right. They're walking through an open gate. The walls of the compound are high and dark brown creosote. Dusty posts look like telephone poles. The place is open and wide.

"The ground is dusty. The dust is thick and it's making a dust cloud. I'm several feet away, so I'm not in the dust cloud. No grass. Very dry. Nothing there. It's open. There's wire. Before I had the impression there were poles and spaces several feet between the poles. But not here. This is a wall."

From Alan's description, it seemed to me that this probably was a prisoner-of-war camp and he was a guard. It would take Alan several more minutes to arrive at the same conclusions.

"The men are still lying down. I'm near a pole. The first man I saw was by a pole. When the men were marching in, I saw them from my perspective. Several men are looking right at me. They're hostile. They're several feet away and standing still. I don't think they like me, but they're not coming toward me. I haven't done anything to them. They don't seem to have any rank. They really aren't in uniform.

"I feel like I'm wearing gray. I think I'm a guard and this is a prisoner-of-war camp. I feel more comfortable than they look. I'm always near the wall or post and they're lying or standing around in the dirt several feet away."

Alan shifted uncomfortably on the couch. He said he was sensing the hostility. At other times, he'd get flashes, impressions, or snapshots that weren't always connected. It wasn't a running film like most of the others had experienced.

"No one stands out—it's just a group. I see more faces, now that they stand up. When they're lying down, they lie on their sides and I can't see their faces. One man is bald on top, clean shaven, not tall.

He's in the center of the group. This guy's jacket is so dark it looks black. They wear coats darker than their pants, dark or white shirts. They're all unkempt, dull, dingy. This could be in Virginia or North Carolina."

So it seems that Alan was in a prison camp and hadn't found himself in a battle. Interestingly, he, like Steve, said he preferred military exercises to reenacting battles because the outcome was not determined. In exercises, troops are given scenarios and have freedom to decide what tactics to use to win. Judges decide which side has the advantage.

It also occurred to me that in contrast to some of the other reenactors, Alan has never had a déjà vu experience. He also said that he felt differently about reenacting than the others in his unit. He never had the emotional charge many reenactors express. It had never brought tears to his eyes. He thought that maybe someday he would have a spiritual experience like theirs—perhaps he just hadn't been in "the hobby" long enough. He felt as though he were missing out. At Civil War events and ceremonies, Alan simply felt a quiet respect. Always conscious of the present, he never found himself pulled totally back into the past. Is it possible that his emotions were stifled or somehow different in prison camp than they would have been on the battlefield?

"It's dark," he was saying. "I'm breathing heavy. (Alan was now breathing hard.) It hurts when I breathe. My stomach hurts—in between my chest and stomach. Two people are with me. I'm by a pole. The dark-haired guy is on my right side. I'm lying down. It's just the three of us. They're talking to me, but I don't know what they're saying. (It sounded as if Alan were snoring.) I see them from the chest up. They're beside me." (His breathing now calmed down.)

"It's not dark any more. My friend is still with me. He seemed concerned about me. It's light—not bright. I'm breathing better. I'm not out of breath now. There's just a tightness, an aching. I feel OK."

Something had happened to Alan. It sounded somewhat similar to a near-death experience. By now, I was carefully monitoring him. When he began having trouble breathing and felt a pain between his chest and his stomach, I remembered that, in this life, Alan has asthma. In my regression therapy, I have often found that a physical malady in this life corresponds to an injury or trauma in another lifetime.

"I'm inside now," he continued. "I was stabbed with a stick." He winced. "My friend is asking me who did it. I think the bald-headed guy did it. I haven't done anything to him, but he's still hostile. He's lying down with the others who are lying in rows. I just see white shirts—no legs, arms, head, or feet. I can just see a wall. I'm lying flat."

In the regression, Alan had mentioned his friend. In reenacting, camaraderie is one reason why Alan likes "the hobby." He feels particularly bonded to about five men in his unit and feels a brotherhood with the rest. He was introduced to reenacting by a co-worker, who had piqued his interest with Civil War adventures. Moving back to the regression, the next thing Alan recalled was that his friend was no longer by his side.

"My friend's not there now. An older man with a white shirt and no hat is standing to my right. He's doing something to my stomach. He doesn't seem to be in a hurry, just busy. It feels like pulling and tugging—my skin feels tight. The doctor finishes and turns and walks away. He looked me right in the face and never said a word."

Up to this point in his regression, there was no conversation between Alan and the people he was experiencing. Although he felt vivid sensations, like discomfort and pain, he said there was always a silence.

"There's just a small window, up high. It's daylight, but cloudy. It's light in the room. I feel like I had a dark jacket on after the doctor turned and walked away. I feel my friend has gray and yellow."

This was a startling new piece of information for both of us. Wearing a dark jacket meant that Alan was probably a Yankee prisoner, not a guard after all.

"The crowd's not angry with me, they're just angry," he continued. "They're hungry. They wanna go home. They're a long way from home. I'm from a rural town that's green with lots of trees.

"I'm in the hospital—not really a hospital, just one big room. Three men in faded blue uniforms with light blue pants and dark blue jackets are standing in the doorway. The one in the center who's bigger than the others has a forage cap. He wears it pulled to the front."

From his bed, Alan could see some sky.

"The door leads to the outdoors. It's daylight. It's bright, but the sky is overcast. It's white, though, not stormy. I'm propped up, not lying flat. It's warm."

Still mulling over this latest information about Alan having remembered wearing a Yankee uniform in his regression, I recalled that, although Alan had spent his formative years in Kentucky, his reenactor activity was clearly aligned with the North for ideological reasons. In contrast, most of the other reenactors' current allegiance to the North or South was in line with their geographical upbringing or family influence. Several reenactors have reenacted on both sides and have even changed units. But Alan had no intention of changing his unit.

Still, with the war over, he admitted during his pre-regression interview that he didn't know which side he would have chosen in 1861, whether he had lived in the North or South. He acknowledged that, at the time of the regression, he was a different person with different life experiences than people had in the nineteenth century and that he was not prepared to make any judgments. Alan now saw the Confederate reenactors taking everything more personally—including winning at tacticals—and said that there were about two Confederate reenactors for every Union reenactor. While I was still integrating Alan's reenacting with the regression he was experiencing, Alan's next words brought me back to the life he was experiencing under regression.

"Now I'm standing," Alan said. "I'm walking out of the building. I feel like I'm wearing blue. The other three men in blue are in the doorway: one just outside, the big man in the doorway, and one inside. They seem friendly.

"I'm with a crowd of people. I feel happy, comfortable. They're milling around in a group—not just because I'm there. The gathering doesn't seem to have a purpose. It's daylight. We're outside. The ground is dirt. I don't feel familiar to anyone. They're not talking to me or paying attention."

I wondered if Alan had volunteered to assist the Confederate prison guards. Could this have been why he got stabbed? In reenacting, he volunteered for time-consuming duties and didn't hide during battles, trying instead to be on the front lines. Meanwhile, back in the prison camp, it seemed that Alan and the others were being freed. Surmising that the war must be coming to an end, I asked Alan for his name and unit. "Stephen Wright or White, Company D, Pennsylvania 42," he responded. Then he recalled his parole.

"A woman is hugging me. I'm almost a head taller, although I'm just medium height with brown hair. She's a motherly figure; she's stocky. We're embracing outside on the porch. The two-story white house has a porch that runs the length of the house. There are lots of trees. There's a small brown dog and a small girl in white on the porch.

"The woman and I are now in the kitchen. She's crying and very sad. She's telling me my father is dead."

Alan had been through his own war experience only to come home to find his father dead. Assuming his father had died in the war, his family had paid a high price. In the twentieth century, Alan believed that war was ugly and he hoped that we wouldn't have any more wars. He said he reenacts to remind people how ugly war can be. In reenacting battles, those who predetermine themselves casualties or run out of ammunition end up as bodies strewn all over the battlefield. He said that the number of casualties at even the larger events with 6,000 to 8,000 reenactors pales in comparison to the actual casualties during the Civil War.

But Alan, who had loved history since he was a school boy, was still optimistic about human nature. Although he believed in the possibility of reincarnation, he focused more on the afterlife. He said that he was not sure where the soul goes or whether it spends time in purgatory or in heaven after death. He was not sure whether the soul keeps reincarnating until it becomes perfected, but he felt confident that as long as one is honest and treats people fairly, one will get to heaven.

It was interesting to find elements in Alan's story that were easily matched to historical data. This may be meaningful, considering that he admitted to knowing little about the Civil War and was relatively new to "the hobby." Although he didn't give as many details as some of the others, his story checked out historically.[75]

Alan thought he was in a prison in North Carolina or Virginia. Salisbury Prison, unknown to him, was in North Carolina. He hadn't heard or read about it, but had visited Fort Schuyler in New York. Nevertheless, his account of the prison camp in the regression sounded like Salisbury, North Carolina, or Andersonville Stockade, Georgia. He described the construction of the stockade with telephone poles and an open pen with men lying on the dirt with no tents. He also portrayed prisoners without belts, swords, hats, or any accoutrements—picked clean and ragged—and doesn't remember seeing any officers.

It was common for prisoners to help the Confederates.[76] Prisoners were detailed to work around the buildings about the post at Andersonville Prison. It would be understandable that doing the work of a Confederate and associating with them could lead to some confusion about whether Alan had been a Confederate or a Union prisoner. It is also possible that he identified with his captors and tried to please them, much like hostages who become attached to their captors. Resentment could have built up because some of the prisoners who assisted Confederates received privileges.[77] They were viewed as traitors. In some prisons, such as Andersonville, raider gangs robbed, terrorized, and even murdered their fellow prisoners. At Andersonville, prisoners were eventually allowed to hold their own trials and punish such offenders. After one reign of terror, six of the raiding leaders were hung, while others were beaten with clubs.[78]

With regard to Alan's being stabbed, possibly by a raider, he was not alone. Many others were wounded while in prison. Between March and August of 1864, there were nearly 43,000 reported cases of wounds and disease at Andersonville alone. Because there were only thirteen surgeons for the 26,000 prisoners at Andersonville, many men died without ever having been seen by a physician.[79]

Aside from a lack of knowledge about Civil War prisons, Alan had no idea of the 42nd Pennsylvania Volunteer Infantry, which he recalled in his regression, and had no affiliation with them. Called the "Bucktail Regiment" because the troops wore deertails dangling from their caps, the 42nd fought at the battle of Dranesville, Virginia, where some were killed and others were captured.[80] Alan had never heard of Dranesville or Sycamore Church, Virginia. A Union Zouave reenactor, he had never worn a blue uniform—always Zouave.

In his regression, Alan saw one Confederate whose body and body language resembled a reenactor whom Alan recognized as the captain of the 1st Pennsylvania Reserves. Alan had never seen him wear a gray uniform in this life. Historian Brian Pohanka said that the captain of the 1st Pennsylvania carried himself well and had nineteenth-century mannerisms similar to those many nineteenth-century Civil War soldiers would have exhibited.

In reenacting, Alan aspired to be the "spit and polish" soldier. As a prisoner, Alan could not maintain those standards and admired the Confederate officers who had flair.

Besides the real possibility of his story, the name and unit Alan recalled as his own in the regression was more easily authenticated in Civil War files than some of the others. Alan had given me the name of Stephen White or Wright of Company H or D of the 42nd Pennsylvania—also known as the 13th Pennsylvania Reserves. After I had sifted through volumes of prisoner lists, a National Archives historian handed me a book on Salisbury Prison authored by Louis Brown.[81] The book fell open to the "W's," and my eyes immediately fell upon two names.

There was a Sergeant Edward White of Company D, 13th Pennsylvania Cavalry (also known as the 84th Pennsylvania Reserves). He had been a prisoner of war at Salisbury Prison and was released. A laborer, he died in 1915. There is no record of Edward White being in the prison hospital.[82] Perhaps in his regression, Alan was in some type of recovery room rather than a hospital.

Another prisoner of war at Salisbury was a Jasper R. White of Company G, 45th Pennsylvania Volunteer Infantry. He is recorded as having been in the Salisbury Prison hospital for pneumonia. He also was paroled.[83]

A less probable match with some conformity is Sylvanus White, Company D or A, 54th Pennsylvania Volunteer Infantry. National Archives military and pension records indicate that he was a prisoner of war in Richmond Hospital after being wounded at New Market, Virginia. The soldier was later paroled. A perfect name and unit match was an S. White, Company B, 14th Pennsylvania Cavalry. This Andersonville prisoner of war died there in August 1864.[84]

After my research was complete, I wondered if perhaps Alan wasn't the Civil War beginner that he thought he was. Perhaps Alan knew more about the Civil War than he ever thought possible.

6

Dave:
Strange Coincidences

Normally, the first thing one hears on David Purschwitz's answering machine is the tune *Dixie*, the battle hymn adopted by the Confederates, but, because it was nearing Christmas when I called to set up Dave's regression appointment, I was met with a cheery message from the "South" Pole.

Weeks later, as I entered his home, I felt as if I were walking into a Civil War museum. Dave's place, just miles from the Manassas battlefield, was filled with Civil War photos, books, memorabilia, and antiques. Dave showed me the minie balls he purchased for a quarter each nearly three decades ago. Those inexpensive minies were the beginning of an expensive interest in the Civil War that has permeated nearly every area of his life. Dave's next purchase was a cuff button from a NewYork uniform. His wife thought he was crazy to pay six dollars for a button.

Less than one year after buying the Civil War bullets, Dave became a reenactor. Because of a heart problem as a child, he had been prevented from participating in sports, but, as an adult, he found that he could handle the physical rigors of reenacting. In fact, his love for reenacting spilled over into his career. Formerly an art director, at the time of the regression Dave was working at the Manassas museum, which is devoted in large measure to the Civil War.

At first, we browsed through the library of 800 Civil War books which he had accumulated and read over the years. I fingered some of the antiques, such as Dave's canteen from the 20th Maine. In the living room, surrounded by Confederate flags, Dave gave me their history and pointed out a priceless handcrafted Civil War "command post" travel desk, complete with pigeon holes and secret compartments for messages.

My eyes next fell on a photo of Dave and his family in Civil War attire. The fifty-two-year-old Confederate reenactor told me his family had become involved in "the hobby" over twenty-six years before when his youngest child was just a baby. The family of five had spent many a weekend at Civil War encampments. His wife had made his uniforms, as well as period clothing for the rest of the family. Years later, after a separation from his wife, he thought about selling everything and getting out of "the hobby." Having contacted an interested buyer, he found his efforts unsuccessful and, after much soul-searching, he decided to keep his Civil War collection.

Holding a position of particular prominence on his living room wall was a photo of his great-grandfather who had fought in the Civil War. His grandmother had taken the picture with her to a nursing home and later gave it to Dave. The first time he heard about his relative, James McNally, was after Dave had been in Company F, 8th Virginia Infantry reenactor's group for six years. It was another four years before he knew of McNally's units. While a seasoned reenactor, he researched McNally's military records and visited the site where great-grandfather McNally had been wounded. He shivered as he relayed his strong gut feeling that the battlefield looked familiar. That same déjà vu feeling would sweep over him every time he looked at pictures he had taken of the battlesite. Episodes of emotional waves that flooded Dave at various battlesites had opened him up to the possibility of reincarnation.

Ready now to begin the regression experience, Dave moved off his handcrafted couch and settled into a lounge chair. After the hypnotic relaxation phase, Dave began answering my questions. Of all the reenactors, Dave's had a surprising twist, but like many of the others, it involved painstaking effort to move it forward. *(Note: The following discourse serves as a fine example of the questions and answers that assist the recall process during a regression. My questions are in italics.)*

"It's daytime," he said. "I'm outside. No one else's around. I'm wearing brogans, my military boots, and light blue pants. My jacket is wool; it's darker blue. My belt is over the top coat of the jacket. The metal buttons have an 'I' for Infantry. My hat is a black wide brim hat.

"There's an open field in front of me and some woods in the distance. On my left, that's our camp."

"What's the name of your unit?"

"I can't remember."

"Are you by yourself?"

"U'hum."

"What season is it?"

"Trees are blooming. It's gotta be spring."

"How old are you?"

"Twenty. I'm scared. I don't have my family around."

"Where are they?"

"I don't know. Home, I guess."

"Where's home?"

"I can't remember."

"How long have you been gone?"

"Six months."

"Why are you scared?"

"It doesn't seem right. I'm in camp. I don't see anybody.

"I got a gun. It's a rifled musket. I've been practicing with it. I'm a pretty good shot."

"Hit anybody with it?"

"No. Just targets. I'm still scared."

"Why don't you go into the camp and see if anybody's there."

"They're there, asleep in their tents. I feel better."

"Miss your family a lot?"

"U'hum. I haven't got mail for three weeks. My mother told me not to worry. Dad has fallen ill, but it's not necessary to rush home."

At this point, Dave's hands were twisting nervously. "They won't let us go. There's a rumor that the Secessionists are near."

"Who's the enemy?"

"Secessionist rebels. Going to have to shoot 'em." Tears began to fall. "I'm scared."

"Where are you?"

"I think they call it the Shenandoah Valley. We're down in the valley. Mt. Jackson is nearby."

"The others are getting up?"

"Not right now. I see several guys still in their tents. The sun is just coming up over the mountains. It's almost time to eat, but the food's not so good."

"What do you eat?"

"We got salt pork and eggs. We got 'em at a little farm right over here." He chuckled, "I haven't had eggs for weeks.

"Sometimes I get hungry. We're issued a certain amount, not what I'm used to eating. Some's pretty grubby, impossible to eat."

"What do you do at home?"

"Work the farm, tend the animals, cows. I'm wishing I was back there. I'm scared."

"Where are you from?"

"New York."

"How did you get to the Shenandoah Valley?"

"We came part of the way on the railcars, the rest of the way on our feet. That hurt. My brogans are tight. They're the only ones I could get. When they gave 'em to me, they were too small. Some of my comrades told me I'd better not complain, because I may not get any shoes to replace 'em. So, hopefully they'll stretch a little bit."

"Why did you enlist?"

"Mr. Lincoln put out a call that he needed men—and I'm a man. The country needed help."

"What do you think about the cause?"

"Ours is good. To preserve the Union. We gotta get the country back together again."

"What about their cause?"

"It's all wrong. They shouldn't break away. We were a strong country before seceding. That would make us two weak countries. There's trouble in other parts of the world—we were growing stronger. We'd be too weak to defend ourselves."

"What do you think about the enemy?"

"Even though what they're doing is wrong, I don't hate 'em. I have no desire to look down my gun barrel at 'em. I might have to and that's what I hate. I'm scared."

"Look around the camp for any identifying company flags."

"The U.S. flag with thirty-two stars. Even though they want to drop out of the Union, that flag over there still holds their stars on it. It's at headquarters' tent. There's also a blue flag."

"Anything on your uniform to tell what company?"

"There's a New York State seal on my belt plate."

"Ask one of the guys what company you're in."

"Harry's over there. 'Harry, what regiment are we?' Oh, now I know who I am." He laughed. "We're 5th New York Heavy Artillery, Harry said, 'F.'"

"What does Harry call you?"

"Sometimes he calls me 'the Irishman,' sometimes 'Mack.' Jim Mc . . . McNally's my real name. We weren't neighbors, but we enlisted together up in Monroe, New York."

"Is Harry about your age?"

"He's a couple years older. Harry's a good buddy. He keeps encouraging me. It keeps me here. I could find it easy to skedaddle, but I'd be in big trouble. The provost marshall has people who go around looking for skedaddlers. A few weeks ago they killed a man that they brought back. The first time I ever saw anybody killed, I felt terrible. I'm scared.

"The bugle's sounding. It's calling us to form up—fall in. I have to go."

"OK, are you falling in with the others?"

"Yeah. We're standing at attention. The officer of the day is reading something. I can't hear him. I'm not close enough.

"The commander's not here. David 'H'—like 'Hunt.' Guys like him. He seems fair, although I don't think he should have had the man shot. He treats us well. We could use more food, but he's doing the best he can. He's thirty-five. He's a general. Normally we don't address him."

"What is the officer saying?"

"He's telling us we're going to march. We are being marched back into the camp to our tents. We're told to pack our knapsacks, cook up three days' rations, and get on the march."

"*Where to?*"

"They never tell us. In case we're captured, they don't want us to know. We haven't been in battle, but some straggling behind were either captured or skedaddled home. We think they might have been captured."

"*How's the march going?*"

"We've been four hours on the march. My feet are killing me. They never tell us how far, but word is coming through the ranks it's not much farther. They never tell us anything except 'pack up, cook your meals, and march.'"

"*How are you doing?*"

"Gonna get off my feet for a few minutes. My feet are swollen. I got my shoe off. Ow, that hurts. Some of the others are taking theirs off, too, and so is Harry. Harry's only got one shoe that's bothering him. I have a twenty-minute break. The sun's mid-sky. It's got to be mid-afternoon. My pocket watch was stolen.

"I'm hungry. Goin' to eat some rations—salt bacon and hard-tack—if I can break it. I'll soak this hardtack in coffee. It's time to go. I'm putting my shoes on."

"*Painful?*"

"Yeah. I'm tying 'em loose."

"*Marching again?*"

"Yeah."

"*When do they let you rest?*"

"I don't know."

"*Have you seen any well-known generals?*

"No, I don't think so."

"*How do you feel about the other guys? Do you get along?*"

"Yeah. Some call me 'Young Irish' and other nicknames," he chuckled. "I don't think I'd better tell you. Some guys are about my age, a couple a little older. Harry's my best buddy."

At this point, Dave didn't need my guidance very much as more complete thoughts began to flow.

"It's getting late. The sun's on the horizon. We got the order to make camp. I'm glad. My feet are killing me. Even my legs hurt.

"I saw a dead rebel lying beside the road. Made me sick to my stomach. He'd been hit with a minie. Ugly. Ghastly. He'd already started to rot. The air reeked. But we're away from that now. The air's fresher.

"There are beautiful mountains on two sides. It's quiet and peaceful. The guys are settled in. My legs are hurting. I don't think I can sleep. I'm tired, weary, and scared as hell.

"They're all scared. Word is circulating that we might meet the enemy soon. I'm not sure I'm ready. My legs have eased up. I'm going to turn in."

After Dave rested for a moment, I directed him to the next significant event, where he found himself in the midst of battle.

"We're down in the valley," he said. "I had to raise my weapon in anger and fire on the rebels. I emptied several cartridge boxes in a heavy fight. We were over on the flank, not taking the heaviest of the fighting, and unloading on them. I must have thrown 150 minies at 'em. Don't know if I hit anything. In one way, I hope not.

"We're on the march. Oh, no. Our brigade's being sent onto the field. We're going to fight. I'm scared, trembling. Their artillery's firing. The explosions were close.

"We're moving out onto the field. A cannon fired and then another. That one's close. One shot went over our heads. It fell behind us. Didn't do us any harm. More cannons firing.

"Oh, Harry's down," he suddenly said urgently. "Oh, Harry's been hit. I can't help him. They won't allow me to fall out of ranks. 'Harry, I'll come back for you.'" He was noticeably distraught. "I have to go on.

"I'm scared. Our cannons open up now. It hit close. We're out in the middle of this field. About 300 boys are way behind.

"Ouch! I've been hit. I got smacked in the chest with a spent minie ball. It hit another guy, bounced off him, and smacked me. It hurt. I'm OK. I probably have a bruise. I don't think he's going to make it.

"We're going across the field. We're trying to hold our formation. Minies are kicking up dirt all around us. John is down. Lord, spare me. We're taking a lot of hits. I'm scared. I'm throwing as many minies out there as I can.

"I just got hit again. Oh, oh, I'm hurt. Oh, I'm really hurt. Blood. I got hit in the arm. I lost my weapon. Lord, bring me through." He was now greatly distraught. "I got to get down behind these other guys. The field is covered with bodies. I'm lying behind them."

The next thing Dave remembered was being taken prisoner.

"'No, no, no. Don't take me. No, don't take me.' A rebel got hold of me. 'No. I'm hurt. Let my surgeons take care of me. No, I don't want to go.' I'm being dragged off.

"'Please, let go. Have mercy. Take it easy on that arm. Can't you see I'm hurt?'" He sniffed. "'You're taking me to a surgeon? Thank you.' My whole sleeve is covered with blood. 'Lord, please spare me.' Men are all around—some dead, some dying, some with no arms." He sniffed again.

"'Lord, why are you taking me into the church?' Oh, it's a hospital. Oh—a pile of arms and legs. Some of the legs still have shoes on. The surgeon's looking at my arm. 'You've got to save it.' " Now, Dave was sobbing. "'No, Doc. You can't take it off.'"

Now I told him if it's too painful to just observe.

"It's gone," he sighed. Against his protest, his arm had been cut off. "There's agonizing pain. Oh, my whole body just wracks with pain. I need some rest."

I was amazed that his previously active arm was now not moving. Dave never moved his left arm again for the next ninety minutes. Wondering if Dave survived the amputation, I was anxious to find out where he was headed now.

"They're putting us on cars—some on wide-open flatbeds. A lot of our guys were captured and not hurt. Some I know—Zeb over there. Some guys got lucky and got boxcars. Rain is falling." He shivered, "I'm chilled, I'm scared, I'm hurt—not a good combination.

"'Please, Lord, see fit to help me survive. I have a wife waiting. What is she going to think now—me being a cripple?' We're heading south. The sky is clearing. I need sleep.

"The train's stopped. Men are getting off. There's lots of noise. Now, they're gettin' us off the train. They roughly grab me. It hurts. I see a stockade. They're leading the guys in that direction." He jerked. "Several of us are being sent in another direction—the walking wounded. They've got our men carrying some. We're completely surrounded by armed rebels.

"There's another hospital. The sign says, 'Hospital Camp Sumter.' I'm being directed to a cot and a surgeon is looking at my arm. I'm running a fever. I'm very hot. They're wrapping me with heavy wool blankets.

"My arm hurts like hell. Don't know if I'll get away from here. My body's hurtin'. I'm scared. I think I'm dying. I don't think I'm gonna see my woman again.

"'Ellen, Ellen! Can you hear me, Ellen? Ellen, my love for you is the deepest I've felt for anyone.' Haven't got anybody here to write a letter for me.

"Now I got chills. The surgeon's looking at my arm again and says it's healing. It hurts. I've got to sleep."

Dave now appeared to be sleeping. Though he was still in hypnosis, the rest seemed to have assisted his recovery. He gradually "awakened" into the next regression experience.

"My body's feeling better," he said. "I've been asleep three days. I'm soakin' wet. It's like a creek came inside my blanket cocoon. I'm thirsty. Does my arm hurt! I thought nothing would ever hurt as much as my feet had. I was wrong."

During his recovery, someone offered to write a letter for him.

"Yes, I want you to write a letter. Please."

"'To My Dearest Ellen.' I don't know what to say. I can't say, 'I take pen in hand' to write this letter because it's not in my hand. That's the way I always used to start my letters.

"'My Dearest Ellen, I have been through a very traumatic (and I hope you can spell it, 'cause I can't) time. We were in the heaviest fighting I have as yet seen and I was seriously hit. I'm told now it was a minie ball. At the time I wasn't sure whether it was a minie or a shell fragment. Oh, my darling (Dave was now overwhelmed with emotion), it shattered my arm. I'm telling you now in this letter so it doesn't come as a total surprise to you when we do meet. I have faith we will.

" 'But the bones in my arm were shattered—not a clean break. And they had to cut off my arm. It was my left arm (he sniffed) and, when I get back and we start attending church together again, I can still bless myself with my proper hand. My surgeon is telling me I should recover and be OK.

" 'Someone is writing this for me so you will not recognize the hand. For that reason I'd better keep it short. Your devoted husband, James McNally.'

"'You'll see that gets off to her? Thank you.' I'm tired."

Once again, Dave fell into what appeared to be a deep sleep and then "awakened" to some good news.

"It's a beautiful morning. I feel pretty good. My arm still hurts though. (He was holding his arm below the elbow.) I don't know how I'm going to be able to work. It's kinda difficult handling farm tools with just one hand."

While contemplating his future livelihood, Dave received good news.

"'Oh, thank you. Thank you.' I'm being paroled. I've been here three or four months. I can't do any more fighting, so I'm no danger to the Rebs. The longer I stay here, they have to feed me and have a space for me."

"How are you leaving?" I asked, beginning another series of inquiries.

"Yeah, they're loading us onto cars. Thank God. We're going away from this hellhole. They're burying guys—laying 'em in one long trench—not even a decent burial. What a shame! All those lives lost."

"What do you think of war now?"

"I hate it," he said. "All my friends lost. I haven't heard if Harry's dead or alive. He could be in that trench. Why did I ever come in? It looked like the right thing. Maybe it was. So many lost souls.

"The train's stopping. We've been bounced around for hours. My arm is throbbing. They're taking us off the cars and loading us on a boat." Dave began to visibly relax as he waited for the boat to pull away from the dock. "Hallelujah! Thanks, Lord. What a gorgeous sight! They dropped the canvas. A full sail. Nice wind. I'm heading home!

"I hope my Ellen's there waiting. No way to let her know I'm coming—except 'Ellen, if you can hear my prayers. Ellen, I'm coming to you. Please be there.' I'm sick—it's this rocking back and forth. But I'll make it."

"Your destination?"

"We're going up the Chesapeake Bay around Annapolis. We're docked. The ship's stopped rocking. They're helping us off and putting us in wagons. Before we pull away, the surgeon looks at my arm. He says it doesn't look good, but might be OK. It's full of sores. Can't stand looking at it."

Dave had now arrived at his next destination.

"I see a bunch of tents and several hospital tents. It's a distribution camp that redistributes men. They'll take care of us. If we're healthy enough, they'll send us back to the line.

"I don't think I'm going to make it. I hope they'll send me home. I don't see how I could handle a musket with one hand.

"The surgeon just looked at it again. He said I'm unfit for duty. I'm going home."

Finally given the go-ahead to be released from active duty, Dave had one final journey ahead of him.

"I'm having a wagon ride. Now, they're putting me back on the cars. We're heading north. This time, it's a passenger car, not a box-car—an actual car people ride in. Instead of being treated like cattle, I can rest now. It'll take a couple days.

"The train's stopping. It says 'Monroe.' It seems like a lifetime ago I lived here. Where is she? I'm on the platform. Please be here. I guess she doesn't know I'm coming. I had hoped that somehow my message had gotten through. I can make my way home. It's not far.

"I'm gaining strength with every step. There's our beautiful brownstone house! There are stairs up to the porch with a little covered area. What a beautiful door!

"She greets me at the door with two kids. She's holding one in her arms. I don't know who the other one is crying in the background." He laughed. "They're *ours!*

"I feel good being home. My arm still hurts. She got rid [sic] of the babies. She's got me wrapped in her arms. It's been a long time. I love her so. She says the arm doesn't matter. It makes me feel good.

"I'm tired. My room is still waiting. She's warmed the bed and told me to get some sleep. I still want to know about Harry. I need to get some sleep."

An intensely loyal Confederate in twentieth-century reenacting, Dave found himself, in his regression experience, having to shoot Rebels. Dave, whose father was a Northerner, grew up in Maryland and had always had leanings to the South. At the time of the regression, his ideologies were transformed from supporting the Confederates to judging the Rebels harshly for "being all wrong and breaking away."

What was even more surprising, he had just relived his great-grandfather's life. As a researcher, I was impressed with the long process of memory that eventually yielded the startling information that Dave had lived his great-grandfather's life.

Dave's love for reenacting began twenty-two years before when he was instrumental in starting Company F, 8th Virginia Infantry. He claimed to have just picked the unit and company "out of thin air." Oddly enough, the first unit of his great-grandfather, Jim McNally, was Company F, 8th U.S. Infantry. Dave didn't know this information until conducting research on his great-grandfather years after becoming a reenactor.

General George Pickett initially served in the 8th U.S. and later switched sides and commanded Dave's 8th Virginia. The 8th Virginia had a ninety-two percent casualty rate during Pickett's famous charge at Gettysburg. Interestingly, Dave acted in the movie *Gettysburg*. Although he did not portray a member of his own unit, he followed directly in the historical footsteps of the 8th Virginia and carried the unit flag in his haversack. He made sure that each time he approached "the wall," he "took a hit" or fell to his knees in prayer at a spot approximating where the 8th Virginia flag was felled at the real battle of Gettysburg.

About eleven months after his regression, Dave also acted in the television movie *Andersonville: The Diary of Josiah Day*. Amazingly, after more than a quarter century as a reenactor, this was Dave's first time in Yankee blue. Dave admitted to feeling uncomfortable in the Federal apparel, but felt he was healing wounds between his great-grandfather, who had been a Federal prisoner, and himself, who had always worn the Confederate uniform. At the site of the prison hospital, Dave walked the same ground where McNally would have spent time recuperating from his amputation.

An eerie feeling overcame Dave when, during the shooting of the movie, he was jammed into cattle cars with other "prisoners," chest-to-chest and back-to-back. They would remain like this for twenty-five minutes at a time in the dark. This scenario was much like Dave described in his regression. He was choked with emotion as he experienced the inhumane treatment the prisoners had received. Once again, he was overwhelmed with emotion when the rail cars pulled up to the prison and he and the other prisoners walked down the planks.

One year after the regression, Dave met a researcher of the troop movements at the Battle of Piedmont, who had done some new research. Dave's prior research had suggested that his great-grandfather was shot on what is now private land. This new research, however, indicated that the troops had advanced farther than what Dave had previously believed. The site where McNally had been shot was probably on the public ground that correlated to what Dave experienced in his regression. In his visit to Piedmont, Dave had also retraced the actual footsteps of his ancestor without knowing it. While visiting the battlefield, he had the sensation that it looked familiar.

But the similarities don't stop there. According to Dave's calculations, he was born the same month exactly 100 years after his great-grandfather's birth (January 1943). Dave spent four years in the air force—from July 1961 to July 1965. These were the same years, 100 years later, as the Civil War, most of which his great-grandfather had spent in the army.

As a reenactor, Dave was a regimental commander for twelve years as well as brigade commander. But he prefers being a private. Jim McNally enlisted as a private and remained a private throughout his military career.

Although Dave had been familiar with his great-grandfather's involvement in the Civil War prior to the regression, he was unprepared for the heart-wrenching, physical, and emotional pain he experienced as his Civil War regression memories gradually unfolded.

After getting shot in the regression, Dave never moved his left arm for the remainder of the session, which lasted more than an hour. He said the pain was so real it was excruciating. During the war, most amputees went through surgery fully conscious. Lucky ones received a little morphine to deaden the pain.[85] He prayed for his life and begged that his arm would be saved. His arm was later amputated. He even protected it with body language. When his captors were rough with him, he would reach for the spot where it had been amputated. Prior to that time, he had been using both hands while talking and would wring them when agitated or fearful.

After the regression, we observed a photo of Dave in his Civil War uniform, taken about eight years before. He had never noticed that it could appear as if his left arm looked limp, almost lifeless.

Another point of interest is that Dave's former wife and their son both have cerebral palsy which resulted in problems with an arm. This is not hereditary, and doctors said it was rare that his son would also develop the condition.

It was coincidental that Jim McNally got shot in Virginia. The New Yorker later moved to Virginia where his first wife, Ellen, whom he had written to from the prison hospital, died. He then remarried and six months later moved to Maryland. Dave, who was aware of Ellen McNally prior to his regression, moved from Maryland to Virginia. Years after Dave's divorce, he, too, has enjoyed having a lady friend in his life.

At the time of the regression, Dave had made his own Civil War-era furniture, flags, and some clothing. His great-grandfather also did some carpentry and made furniture. Apparently, besides farming, he did harness work after the war with one hand. After the regression, Dave found that a relative had a wooden toolbox that Jim McNally made after the war.

Dave was the only reenactor out of twelve whose memories appear to have been those of a present ancestor. This fact correlates closely to the research of Karl Muller,[86] who found only nine percent of reincarnation cases reported to be their own ancestors.

As stated in chapter 2, researcher Ian Stevenson also found that ancestors returned to the same family in five to ten percent of the spontaneously recalled reincarnation cases that he reviewed. Although ancestral return was rare elsewhere, Stevenson uncovered cases among the Tlingits of southeastern Alaska.[87] In about seventy percent of the revealed cases, the subject and previous personality were related on the side of the mother. Interestingly, Dave's great-grandfather was on his mother's side.

Whether Dave's regression experience was generated because of genetic memory or prior knowledge, nothing could have prepared him for the vivid experience of excruciating pain and humiliation of losing his arm, or the concern for his buddy, and the heartfelt letter he composed to his wife from a prison bed.

Only one reenactor in my study had actually learned of research, sketchy as it was, that had already been done on his Civil War ancestor prior to becoming a reenactor, while six others had conducted research on their ancestors after becoming reenactors. Like Dave, they all indicated that reenacting had been the catalyst for the research.

My study revealed a few additional possible links between ancestral knowledge and reenactors' past-life memories. One reenactor, Edward Embrey, felt that he had been a prisoner at Point Lookout as one of his relatives had been. Another subject, Dale Clarke, owned a business in Richmond and so had a relative during the war. In a third Civil War-era regression, Thomas Galleher had been stationed in New Orleans and had the name Cates. An ancestor, Thomas Kane, had moved there from Ireland. A fourth reenactor, Brian Pohanka, who is an officer in reenacting, was revealed to have been an officer in the regression. A distant relative of his had also been an officer. Only Dave had relived the experience of his own great-grandfather.

According to historical records,[88] Dave's ancestor James McNally had emigrated with his brother from Northern Ireland to the U.S. at about the age of fifteen. He settled in New York state while his brother went on to the west coast.

That same year, claiming that he was nineteen, McNally enlisted in Company F, 8th U.S. Infantry—possibly to gain citizenship. His unit was sent to Texas, and upon the outbreak of the Civil War his company was imprisoned. James's company was paroled in early 1863, and, after an honorable discharge, he came back to New York City and married Ellen.

Within six months of his discharge, he reenlisted, this time into Company D, 5th New York Heavy Artillery. Three months later, he was wounded near the village of Piedmont, Virginia. A minie ball shattered his left arm around his wrist, and his arm was amputated a few inches below the elbow. Once again a prisoner of war, he was sent to Camp Sumter Hospital at Andersonville, Georgia. His arm was extremely tender and festering. A family story indicates that James McNally believed the Andersonville maggots, who ate the dead flesh and dried blood of his stump, actually saved him from dying of infection.

Five weeks later, he was transferred from the hospital to prison quarters. After spending nearly four months at Andersonville Prison, he was paroled. After being discharged, James worked as a watchman for the Quartermaster Department for two-and-a-half years. He then reapplied for his pension because the stump of his arm was very tender and he was unable to wear an artificial arm. While he was married to Ellen, it is thought that the pair had fourteen children, one of whom was a nun.

In 1882, the couple moved to Washington, D.C., and five years later to Hampton, Virginia, where Ellen died. Six months after her death, James married Sarah Daisy Clear. There were at least four offspring from this union. James, who was thought to have lost his Hampton estate on a presidential wager, then moved to Hollywood, in Prince George's County, Maryland. Just months before his seventieth birthday, on October 14, 1912, James died peacefully at home. He was laid to rest in Arlington Cemetery. Sarah remarried and her next husband was killed in France during World War I. Although she later remarried, once again, at her request, she was buried with James in Arlington National Cemetery.

In January 1943, Dave was born in Riverdale, Maryland—just four miles from where his great-grandfather James McNally died.

7

Rob:
Out of the Mouths of Babes

It would be easy to pick Robert "Rob" Lee Hodge out from the others in his first-grade class picture—he was the one wearing a Confederate kepi. Since the age of four, he had already become infatuated with the Civil War while playing with his older brothers' Blue and Gray soldiers set from Sears.

In the fourth grade, he presented a diorama of Pickett's charge at Gettysburg. Every day for half the school year, Rob worked on the project which drew teachers from throughout the school. Also during that year, Rob saw the film *The Horse Soldiers,* starring John Wayne, and decided that he wanted to make a Civil War movie.

In high school, the Civil War was almost all Rob thought about. In study hall, he would look at sutlers' catalogues and figure out how many lawns he'd have to cut to get his next shell jacket. Rob was already grooming himself to be the "G.Q. Civil War fashion snob," as the twenty-six year old described himself just prior to his hypnosis regression.

At the age of nine, he saw his first reenactment at Gettysburg. He recalled how he walked out onto the field where Pickett's division attacked and his hair stood up on the back of his neck. Upon his return, he started a letter-writing campaign to contact Confederate reenactment units in Ohio, where he was living at the time. No one ever wrote back. In Ohio, interest in the Civil War did not match that of other areas of the country, and reenacting was relatively nonexistent. Nevertheless, he was "hooked."

Rob always had a strong preference for the South, influenced, in part, by his father's Southern roots. Rob was born on Stonewall Jackson's birthday, just two days after Lee's. After he was born, his older brother suggested that he be named after Robert E. Lee.

Rob was also partial to the Confederate cavalry. Interest in the cavalry may have been heightened due to his father's involvement with the last great U.S. Cavalry unit of World War II. His father, who had once slept on his saddle all the way across the Pacific Ocean to Australia, told Rob that the saddest day of his life was when General MacArthur mechanized their unit.

Rob thought the Confederate cavalry uniforms were gorgeous. When he was eleven, he ordered his first authentic reproduction of a Confederate cavalry uniform with lawn-mowing money that had been matched by his parents. At twelve, he traveled 100 miles to purchase a musket.

A year later he showed up at a reenactment at Gettysburg with his uniform. For Rob, it was a mystical experience. A reenactor who took Rob under his wing suggested that he read *The Killer Angels* by Michael Shaara, a book about the Battle of Gettysburg. It was at Gettysburg that Rob decided that reenacting would be his lifelong passion.

So moved was Rob by the Battle of Gettysburg that he had a burning ambition to be involved in the movie. In 1988, he wrote to *Gettysburg* movie director Ron Maxwell hoping to fulfill this dream. Years later, the tall lanky reenactor not only worked on the film, but acted as a soldier and lived near the battlefield for months. For some thirty days during the filming, Rob said that the fog hovered over the battlefield evoking a surrealistic feeling.

At the time of the regression, Rob described himself as a "round-the-clock fanatic." Calling it a "Civil War-gasm," he once visited twenty-six battlesites in various states in nine days. He wore his uniform, slept near the battlesites, and read soldiers' accounts. For some unidentified reason, he claimed that he always felt "weird" just before going to sleep or waking up near a battleground. In one year he attended more than thirty Civil War events. Rob admitted that he had relationship problems in the past over this, but his current girlfriend was becoming interested in sewing period uniforms and had begun to understand Rob's passion. She even said he looked better in his Civil War uniform than in modern clothes. Rob felt more comfortable and confident in Civil War clothes than in contemporary attire and wore his uniform whenever possible.

The Civil War consumed every area of Rob's life. Although he was close to completing a degree in history and art, he worked odd jobs that gave him the finances necessary to support his "unpaid profession." This flexibility allowed him to pursue additional work in movies and television documentaries and accumulate experience which he planned to draw on as an aspiring writer of screenplays.

For the Arts and Entertainment network's (A & E) *Civil War Journal*, Rob has done his "bloat" impression—with puffed cheeks and swollen belly—to achieve a more authentic dead soldier look.

But in another recent A & E documentary, he had a genuine brush with death while acting as General Nathan Bedford Forest, whom he physically resembled. During the taping, Rob fell off his horse and was dragged fifty feet when his left boot stuck in the stirrup. The horse's hooves trampled him, breaking three ribs and a left toe, and seriously bruising his leg. At one point, Rob was convinced that he was going to die. Since then, he has taken some ribbing since Nathan Bedford Forest, claimed to have been the "Wizard of the Saddle," is said to have killed thirty-eight men in hand-to-hand combat and had thirty-nine horses shot out from under him. Ironically, Forest is also identified as having been the first Grand Wizard of the Ku Klux Klan.

Rob's near-death experience, however, has not dampened his passion for the Civil War which was so intense that he lost thirty-five pounds to look more authentic. He picked the units in which he participated by how "hard core" they were. He and his colleagues were so detail oriented they even discussed the thread counts and stitching on their jackets. Some soaked their uniform buttons in urine to dull the brass, making for a more authentic look.

His obsession motivated him to do an internship with the National Park Service and has made him aware that the Park Service owns only two percent of all Civil War battlesites. Saying he'd lay down his life to preserve "the hallowed ground these men died on," he's even contacted congressmen and raised money.

Besides preservation, Rob's mission was to pay homage to those who died in the Civil War and to educate people about their suffering, hoping that it will never be repeated. In uniform, he went into classrooms and made the Civil War come alive for students.

Because of his deep spiritual and emotional connection, Rob wished to have his ashes scattered over Antietam's Bloody Lane or Richmond's Hollywood Cemetery on the bluffs overlooking the James River. At the eventual time of his death, he hoped to be able to go back in time and be an invisible observer to the Civil War in progress.

With Rob's background established, we thought we'd see where this regression would take him. I hypnotically relaxed him in the usual manner and his regression soon proceeded.

"I'm in the woods," he began slowly. "I thought I was in the Wilderness in the East, but I don't think so because they're wearing Confederate western jackets made from jean cloth with blue trim, cuffs, and collars. Otherwise, I'd think it was in the East. They're wearing tannish slouch hats a similar color to their jackets. One guy has a knapsack on. There's leaves on oak trees. It's late summer."

Rob said he was viewing his regression like a dream and was comparing everything he saw with his current knowledge. Meanwhile, I was getting a complete fashion description. Suddenly, Rob was diverted from the uniforms.

"There's a panic—a surprise!" he said. "There's Federal soldiers on the other side not far away. They don't know if they should shoot. There's about twenty Federals and maybe ten Confederates. If an officer was with them they might shoot.

"Gunshots. We started first. The wind's blowing. Maybe there's a storm coming. The sun's out. I can't see if anybody's going down. One guy shook his head and looked around, not knowing what to do. Different voices; different opinions. Confusion. If we don't shoot, they'll kill us.

"More troops—over to my right, several hundred yards away. I don't think they're ours. Through the woods, there's a clearing and you can see the Federal brigade. Maybe the guys we were shooting at were a skirmish line."

Once again, Rob said things didn't jive. He said that things didn't make sense because the Federals were so close together. "We're exposed—out too far. We could have been out in front as a buffer to the main line. We might be in trouble. Maybe that's why the panic. We're being flanked, but we're not important. We're just the outpost. We have to be taken out. The main attack is to my right. Lots of soldiers in a big field are coming at a double-quick, right shoulder shift, moving fast. Shells are tearing into them."

Rob expressed his surprise that everything was in slow motion. Nothing he observed at this point was at regular speed. "The Confederate line opens up," he continued. "The main Confederates are to my right, behind us. There's some to my left."

Now, Rob chided himself for thinking too much. I suggested that he just report what he saw and try not to critique it. He agreed and tried again.

"A small body of Federals are on top of us. We're in a skirmish line. One guy gets shot in the belly. I couldn't stand to watch it. I'm afraid I'm going to get caught. I'm trying to go backwards. We're staggering. We should be running quicker, but we're hesitating, afraid to leave our friends who are down.

"The Blue guys are mean. I'm petrified they're going to kill me. I just saw someone get killed. It's savage; it's brutal. I feel I'm gonna die. I've never been that scared.

"One Federal, a big guy with a blondish-brown beard and light blue eyes noticed me. He looks mean. He was purposely after me. I was going to be his next victim. He killed a friend of mine. He has his bayonet on, but that doesn't make sense. He probably stabbed somebody, even after he was shot.

"I'm really scared. I don't know if I've been in battle before. I might have been, but not something so up-close. They're wearing Columbus Depot jackets with blue trim. I didn't drop my gun. I'm moving back and can't see anything—as if the action disappears. They might be gone. Guys have run past me. Somebody tells me to hurry up and come with them; otherwise, I'm done for. But I'm just awed by the brutality. A real animal!" It was apparent that Rob was nervous and becoming emotional, but he continued with the regression experience.

"There are tears in my eyes like I'm on an emotional roller coaster. I want to kill the guy who killed my friend and wants to kill me. If I don't, he'll kill me."

Rob composed himself and began analyzing again. He was surprised the scene wasn't as brutal as he had imagined it to be. Compelled to notice everything, he laughingly admitted that even in the midst of battle, he had wanted to interrupt a soldier and ask him about whether his jacket was made in London!

"I see artillery. The Confederate line is pulling out. I see red kepis. One fellow has a saber on. He's helping to hook the gun up. Shells and fire are raining down through the trees. Horses are being shot. It's real confusing, real noisy. It sounds like a thunderstorm. There's chaos—a mix-up in orders." Once again, Rob questioned whether the artilleryman should have been wearing a sword. Then he continued.

"Generals are arguing. One has a black slouch hat and galloons, the sleeve insignias, and stars on the collar. He's got a bushy moustache and reminds me of Isaac Trimble. Artillery's pulling out. The horses that went down were replaced. Infantry's staying until they get all the guns out.

"Infantry's falling back. I'm in a battle line, but I don't know if they're shooting. They're standing fast, until they get the order to fall back. It's organized. It seems more stable now. I think the concern was the artillery. I lost my hat."

Rob said that at times he was so interested in soaking it all in that he felt more like an observer than a participant. And then he was back in the scene.

"The fighting is farther away now. When we were the picket post, we saw the brutality. When we got back to our line, the people chasing us stopped. They were an advance of the main line. The Federals on my right are a separate brigade.

"The order is to fall back. There's power and a steady momentum behind the Federal movement. Our morale's not good. We've been defeated before. Guys feel lack of hope. I feel safer around my friends in the line. There's thousands of us.

"We have the same jackets on—light gray jackets with blue trim. The stuff looks pretty new and we're well equipped. We 'about face' and march back. We don't turn our backs on the enemy, but we leave people there for a delaying action. The main line's going to retire. Then we move back. We are all at right shoulder shift. It looks pretty impressive."

With the lull in the battle, I was amused that Rob was once again noticing the fashions and the marching techniques. "The battle has died down and the Federals have taken some ground. Maybe they felt that's an accomplishment and they're not going any farther. It makes more sense to go farther and push. "It's strange. It's not hurried. It's almost like routine. Not to necessarily retire. There's not much panic. I first thought that the brutality was so wicked, this might be my first battle. Maybe the up-close brutality is something new."

While the shooting had been going on, Rob heard soldiers talking in the ranks. He found it peculiar, but realized that they might be talking to calm their fears. Meanwhile, his sense of hearing during his regression was improving.

"There's music—the fife and drum. It's *Hell on the Wabash*—my favorite. The fife's just hit a real high note."

The contrast between the shooting, which had died down, and the fife and drum, which sounded so pretty, haunted Rob.

"The fifers and drummers are playing like there's no fear. They're behind the lines. I think they're Federals. There's battle smoke all around them. They're playing right through it, just like statues. I would think they would be stretcher-bearers by now or pulled out for hospital duty."

Rob was confused because these Federals were wearing plain black hats, while the one he was initially scared of had worn a forage cap. He also didn't understand how he could see them if they were behind the Federal lines.

"There's lots of volleys. We've turned around and fired. Our rear guard wasn't much of a rear guard—more like a skirmish line to stall. They're back up with us now, so we don't have to worry about shooting them. We all have enfield muskets.

"I can hear the whiz of the bullets. It sounds like a bee—'buzz.' It's weird. You never know when you're going to get hit. Lead's in the air and it's hot. I'm always scared to get shot in the head. I can almost feel it—this hot, spinning lead coming right into my skull. I want to hide, but there's no place to hide. We're all standing there shooting. The men aren't going down as much as I thought. Maybe I'm so worried about loading as quickly as I can, I never noticed. I'm supposed to be focused on the Federals anyway.

"I see Federals going down a lot farther away. The smoke is real thick. When the Federals went into the woods, they pushed through the brigade to my right. They first started advancing in a clearing on my right. Now they're into the woods. They're still going straight ahead. I guess there's Federals in front of them that met up with them. Maybe we're facing two brigades. We have a lot of guys, too. This is big."

With all the explosions, Rob found it strange that soldiers weren't being hit and began to wonder if people were invincible.

"One of our officers got shot in the neck. He was in the rear of the company and the bullet passed through two ranks of men and hit him. His sword's drawn, he's wearing a kepi, and he was walking up and down the line. He's in bad shape, he's bleeding, and his expression is bad. I don't know why I was glancing behind me. I'm supposed to be looking forward. I might have been reaching over for a cartridge. Now I'm really shaken.

"I'm still loading and having a problem biting that thick paper. I get the cartridge down too deep and get gunpowder in my mouth. It tastes like sulphur. I'm having a hard time ramming these damn bullets down because the barrel is swollen from all the heat and velocity. I'm bending my ramrod."

Since shorter men were usually in the front rank, Rob found it strange and dangerous that he was tall and out in front. "I fired, but I got shot in the right shoulder around the collar bone. My left hand touched it automatically. I'm on my knees. I don't feel the pain or burn. Maybe I'm too scared. I'm petrified. I'm on needles and pins. So much's happening."

Now, Rob was telling me how anyone who was not there could ever imagine the full impact of what was transpiring.

"It's hard to imagine so many people doing this. I'm left behind. The others 'about faced' and marched away. I'm with some other guys. I don't know how I'm feeling or how seriously wounded I am. If I got shot in the shoulder, I'd think it would be bad. I'm not going anywhere. I'm looking down the line both ways, at the effects of what happened. The Federals have moved right through the wounded and left us alone. They didn't give us a hard time. I thought there would be more guys down. I see some guys now. I'm trying to make out faces.

"Now the sting starts to set in. It hurts and still burns. It's hot. You could stick something right through the hole. The bullet ripped out the back. I feel like I might die. I haven't seen a lot of gore or mutilated bodies—more clean wounds. The officer did have a gory wound, though. I felt sorry for him. He was a nice person—a teacher. "The Yanks call us 'John.' There are some wounded Yanks farther over. It's funny. You're standing there, killing each other, and when it's all over, you're friends. There's not many people helping anyone yet. I feel like the bullet went through me. Why doesn't it hurt that much? It stung for a while.

"It's getting blurry. Sweat is in my eyes. There's still smoke in the air. I'm really afraid of what's going to happen to me. If I live, which I think I will because I don't feel that bad, I'm afraid of prison camp. I'd rather die. I don't know what lies ahead of me if I die, so—I'd rather go home. I don't know where that is. People I know are farmers. I see guys lying around that have Alabama symbols, but I don't know if I'm from Alabama."

In his regression, Rob thought a shot in the shoulder or prison camp might kill him. I didn't want him to die without giving me his name, so I asked him to look around.

"I see a name on a haversack—J. W. Taylor in script—pretty writing. He's got a white haversack and his name is written in black ink. He has a smooth-side canteen that has a gray cover and a belt buckle that has A.V.C. (Alabama Volunteer Corps). The guy's dead. Taylor's haversack is the last thing I see. I feel tired. Maybe I'm unconscious. I see black."

Rob said things were becoming jumbled, dreamy, not cohesive, and faded. I wondered if he were dying. After a few moments, he answered the question that was in my mind.

"There's a hospital," he said. "I don't want to be there. It's a building. A barn would be darker; this is lit by sunlight. Maybe it's the next day. Maybe I'm alive. There's madness going around. The place is disgusting—deep, soaked blood on the floors. I feel sorry for the guys who are wounded, but I feel 'sorrier' for the people working here.

"An old guy with a white beard and glasses looks distinguished, like a town doctor. I'll be surprised if he doesn't lose his mind. He's real stern, like a rock. But it's nuts here. It's where people die. It's uncivilized—because people do this killing. They do it all the time, but we haven't seen it. We thought this would be different; now we're getting a sobering look at war. We always have to be reminded not to have it any more. We're stupid, we're ignorant, we're dumb."

As he sat in the hospital waiting, he continued to philosophize about war and human nature.

"It's funny. The Federals don't have nearly as much hatred for the people on my side. I bet some Indian guys feel the same way. The Federals that I've met are darn good people. We traded food. Some are bitter, but some are all right. I don't think there's much of a difference. You wonder whom you should be fighting."

Knowing that he was a Confederate, Rob was surprised that he didn't have a Southern accent like a twang or a drawl.

"I'm waiting for the doctor. Guess I'm not as bad as I thought. I must have been unconscious. I feel guilty he has to wait on me. He probably hasn't had any sleep. They're understaffed. It's typical.

"The doctor comes over. It didn't take long. I've got a bandage on my head. What happened to my head? But I didn't have any broken bones. The bullet was lower than I thought and just hit my muscle and made me bleed. The doctor joked that it wasn't so serious, and I felt like an idiot. I want to get out of here." Sitting outside the hospital, waiting for assistance, he anticipated his friends teasing him because so many were dead, mangled, or captured. Then, thoughts turned to family and Rob next found himself at home. Things were not as he remembered.

"Our house is deserted. My family's gone. The neighbor says they moved away after the house was taken over. It's a small, nice log cabin with flat boards on top to make it look nicer. The windows are either open or broken, and dust and wind's coming through. I'm not sure if it's Confederates or Federals that gave them a hard time. I wouldn't be surprised if it was Confederates."

Depressed, Rob returned to his unit.

"I see a flag. It could be my unit. They've got those jackets on. Men are in good spirits and making me feel better. They thought I was dead. I'm embarrassed to say it wasn't serious. They're good guys, like a family."

Now that Rob had returned to his unit, I thought I'd try to elicit his name and the name of his unit. Because Rob was having trouble recalling his name, I suggested that he ask his friends, but he said they'd laugh. I had to settle for unit details.

"I see a corps flag—blue with a solid white circle center and a white border. It's Polk's or Hardee's. It's more attractive than ours, St. Andrew's cross, which is very popular.

"The fellow with a receding hairline looks familiar. They pat me on the back, forgetting I'm sore. My arm's in a sling. I'm wearing a slouch hat."

After spending some time in camp, Rob found himself marching on a dusty road. He complained about the conditions.

"I feel tired, sick to my stomach. It's the food or lack of. We get bread, dried stuff sometimes, grits. We don't get enough. I'm used to it, but always hungry. We never know where we're marching to. They keep us in the dark. I thought I had a knapsack, but it looks like I have a bedroll. Maybe I have both. It gets heavy. When I first started, I packed too much. I threw it away, though. You learn to keep what you need.

"I hate the dust. It gets in my nose and mixes with sweat. You get filthy quick, but get used to it. I don't like the bugs. I dislike everything. I like the music. I'm afraid to like my friends for fear they'll die.

"Men complain. It's hot and bright in the middle of the day. The heat rises, distorting your vision. It looks like fall, but leaves are still green and not real orange. A guy takes his shoe off. It's all bloody. Most of the guys' feet are in bad shape. Even if the shoes are perfect, they still hurt their feet. We've been running a lot. I'm lucky my feet are OK. We have a ten-minute break every hour or so.

"We're marching again. Everybody's grumbling. There's rumors, but I learned to not listen to them. You just get your hopes up. It's boring. It's been months since the last action." All of a sudden, Rob perked up. He seemed excited as he reported that they were now marching through a big town, getting a good response. It was something that his Civil War identity wasn't used to seeing.

"People are cheering. There's nothing to cheer about. We haven't been doing very well, but maybe they just do it to keep our hopes up. They lifted my spirits."

Rob's unit must have been on campaign. He told me they had been marching routinely for a long time and he was irritated.

"We move one place and then double back and go backwards like a chess set. The generals are moving us. We do the work and they don't do anything. Some of the generals are nice, though. Everybody likes Cleburne because he seems competent."

Once again, I tried to get Rob's name and unit. I asked him to check the flags and his gear for any identification.

"The flag says 'Alabama.' I don't think I'm from there. Unit '47.' The flag doesn't even seem right. They might have changed the flags. I think my name is 'John.' You have to put your name on your stuff because you don't want people to steal it." Rob looks at his equipment. "It says 'J. J. Jackson' if this stuff's mine. I'm not a thief."

Satisfied, I relaxed, and Rob returned to the regression to find his unit bedding down for the night. It was moments like these that he became reflective about the war.

"It's so quiet. Sometimes I feel good. I'm thinking about where my family is. I'm worried. It's hard to believe everything's happening. A couple of years ago, no one could imagine this war. It's like a nightmare. Very peculiar; very unique. There's nothing like it. It's big; grand—thousands of people. The battle in the woods was a big one.

"Sometimes I think that it doesn't matter if I was a part of it or not, because I'm just one person. If more people would get involved, we'd get things done. Some people get out of fighting. If you own slaves, you are exempt to take care of them. It's not right. If the ones who own the slaves started everything, they should be the ones in the thick of things. So you get the poor people fighting for the rich's cause. We're not poor, but no one has a plantation."

After Rob finished philosophizing, I suggested he move forward to a relevant event. As he did, he heard explosions.

"We're used to the shelling. We sit around, write, play cards, or talk. Rarely does a shell go off near you. Mostly, they shoot over your heads. You hear it like a rumble. The psychological fear, more than the odds of it actually hitting, can make you old real quick."

Once again, I asked Rob to move forward. He was surprised that so many infantrymen were wearing boots and found that the troops were on the move.

"There's the drum roll. We formed up and moved ahead in formation. We look sharp, not ragged. The lines are crisp, better than lots of units. Close by, a couple of guys have taken hits. They drop like a sack of potatoes. If they don't move, you think they're dead. You're told to look straight on and dress your arms up and be disciplined. You can't help being concerned. Everybody seems distant. I'm afraid that my friends are somewhere else. I feel alone.

"I have fear but I don't know what to do. When we were sitting down, I had time to think about it and I avoided it. Now that we're up in line, I'm scared but not petrified. I'm sure everybody has fear, even the person who looks the calmest.

"We're climbing a fence. It looks funny. Fences always break up the lines. We have to re-form on the other side. A shell hits an officer on horseback behind us. He's not familiar, but he looked real sharp. "It looks very impressive—these blocks of men moving in lines, juxtaposed to each other. The chess game's about to begin."

Always the artist, Rob could see the beauty in the scenery, the uniforms, and military movements even at a time like this. "I see a wheat field or high grass. Troops moving in are using Gilham's manual of drill, which I didn't think they used in the West. We're using Hardee's. The Confederates look gorgeous. I do see some bare feet, though. Lots of slouch hats, rolls and packs; sometimes rolls and packs together. Bayonets are fixed. They shine in the sun. It's peculiar how pretty something can look before it's messed up.

"Federal artillery's shooting canister—those iron balls are tearing into ranks very well. Interesting damage is being done. We're pretty steady. We haven't gotten up into the front yet. It's a real landscape of battle. A pocket of Federal skirmishers were pushed back. I don't feel safe, but OK."

I suggested that Rob move to the end of the battle so that we could see the outcome. I wanted to see if Rob made it through another battle.

"I think we held the field. I feel relieved. Maybe there's hope. We've had a lot of bad generals."

Rob was exhausted after having been in a hypnotic state for nearly three hours. We decided to stop the regression at this point and continue with another session a week later. At that time, knowing what to expect, he trusted the hypnotic state and now found himself discouraged and disgusted with life in the trenches.

"It's real boring. We just sit in the trenches. It's filthy and smells like a garbage dump. There's sewage. I've been here too long. The trenches are filled with water. We try to bail it out with pails. When the water gets too deep, we build wooden decks to help it drain. The garbage and sewage floats on top of the water and is hard to keep clean.

"You don't see too many guys. They're spread out in different areas. We sleep in manmade, bomb-proof caves built in the trenches. I'm disgusted with the rats and want to kill them. Some guys eat them. I'd rather be hungry.

"One fellow stuck a rat on top of his bayonet and put the gun into the ground. The rat's sticking up in the air—displayed like a flag.

"It's insane. You can't go anywhere. Living in these trenches is difficult on one's mind. It's cold, it's wet, it smells. I'm sick; I have diarrhea. I have a beard now. There's a guy in an overcoat. He has a scarf around his head that goes around his ears and ties under his chin, and a hat on underneath. He might be a sergeant. His nose and cheeks are red and he has thick eyebrows. He's been around. He's so experienced.

"A guy put a mirror up so that he could shave and it got shot down. The artillery comes and goes. We're used to it. It's more miserable here than in the fields because you're confined."

In order to get a reprieve from the filth and boredom, Rob took leave to visit the nearest town. He found that the war-torn municipality and its citizenry had taken a beating.

"You can get a furlough to town but they don't like you to go. Maybe I won't come back. I've gone into town a couple of times. Maybe it's Richmond. It used to be more fun. I may have visited relatives. Time's are sadder, more melancholy, more serious. Buildings are burned out, windows are shot out. No one would think the town could look like this.

"We used to have fun playing pool. There's trouble with some bad people and we got into fights. It's desolate. Not many people around. Lots of the shops are closed. Guys in the army are not getting paid. We got French bread at a bakery—it's expensive and seems extravagant. It's sticking out of the bag. Somebody might be tempted to steal it.

"We're walking down a street filled with rubble. Suddenly, shells go off and we run for cover. Women are running, too—trying to get home. One guy is mad, frustrated, fed up. Getting up off the ground, he brushes himself off, gets the dirt off his hat, and puts it back on."

At this point, we received a glimpse into the fears and emotions of a soldier at the time, as Rob's Civil War identity seemed to contemplate desertion.

"You wonder if soldiers you don't see after a while have left or deserted. You're always watching to make sure other people don't leave. You feel jealous that they might have the opportunity to go. Quite a few have deserted. I'm envious and angry. I'd like to, too, but I don't think it would be right."

Though he found the idea of deserting momentarily tempting, Rob soon found himself once again in the foul trenches.

"Back in the trenches you sit around bored out of your mind. Guys make mud sculptures and draw."

In the midst of the sewage and stench, I found it interesting that Rob himself was doing art work. In his current lifetime, he was completing an art degree. Momentarily, however, the boredom came to a screeching halt.

"I think it's the Battle of the Crater," he said suddenly. "Federals blew up a big section of our trenches and now they're filling in the holes not far from me. It's massive with lots of Federals. I see Federal Zouave soldiers; not many blacks, though. It's near dark.

"I'm worried. I can't believe they blew a gap in our line. Men are flying up high into the air from the explosion. I see Union 5th Corps flags."

Having seen the 5th Corps flags, Rob was startled and began questioning the accuracy of what he was seeing. He saw a general and was surprised that he was on foot.

"General Mahone," said Rob, "the short guy with a long beard, is forming for the counterattack. He leads his men in somehow. He's waving his hat and he's got his sword out. I'm in the attack. I can't see the Federal soldiers yet. Now we start to see them again. There's such an impressive line of trenches that we moved back, re-formed, went back into the trenches, and took them back.

"I'm scared all the time. It's hard on your heart and your mind. It will make me an old man soon. You never know if you will die. The fighting's over. We didn't do much; maybe we were the second wave of the attack."

With the fighting over, Rob and his troops returned to some semblance of routine. By this time, Rob had seen a lot of war.

"It's night. I'm going in and out of the bomb-proof area. Shells go off and light up the sky. I'm used to it. I've got guard duty and have to keep an eye on the guys guarding the trenches. Maybe I'm a corporal or sergeant; one of the few guys who's lasted three years."

With things moving fast, Rob found himself and his unit out of the trenches.

"It's raining. It's warmer—better than being miserably cold. It's real scary. Nobody knows what's happening, but we know we're in big trouble. There's one mule pulling a wagon. The mule's sitting down like a dog and a guy is whipping him. We're on a big retreat. The artillery is chopping up the cannons' wheels. People are dumping stuff because they're in a hurry and don't want the Federals to have them. There's chaos. "It's dark. Torches light both sides of the roads. Most men just keep moving. It seems like the end of the war. I don't think we can go on. We're in trouble. We'll go anywhere they tell us. Those who haven't already deserted will listen to orders. We're out of the trenches and we had been there for months. The line must have collapsed somewhere. We're running. Guys say we're done for."

Rob's face had taken on a look of fear mixed with resignation. He seemed anxious, but then he relaxed a little.

"It's a new day. Me and a friend are talking. We have full field gear on, bed rolls, packs on. We're loaded too heavy to keep up the pace. We're taking a break, sitting in a grassy field with everybody else. There's lots of questions. There always are. They never let you know anything. It's understandable. Everybody starts talking rumors and it clouds your mind."

Even at a time like this, Rob was observant of the details.

"I don't know what I look like. The guy I'm with has bugged-out looking eyes and green teeth. He's a nice guy, but he's real messed up and dirty. His teeth aren't taken care of and they look like buck teeth. He's got chew in his mouth and he's spitting. His slouch hat is flipped up and his gun's balanced on his shoulder. His hands are stuck in his knapsack straps. We're talking about the future. It looks bleak and we don't know what to do. I don't know where I'm from, but I know that my family's not there. I want to say I'm from Alabama." Rob thought that his Civil War personality might have lived in Florence, Alabama, but questioned this because his father in this life was from Florence. Moving back to the regression, Rob sensed that the end of the war was imminent and wondered how it would affect him.

"It's real lonely," he continued. "We had lots of friends and they're not around any more. We've repeatedly had traumatic experiences. The end is right around the corner. Other guys don't think that, but we're trying to think about what we've gotta do. It's funny because we've got all our gear on and we're talking about the ending of the war. Are we going to be taken prisoners or to be taken advantage of? Will we find our families?"

Luckily, Rob and his friends were not taken prisoners, but instead found themselves being paroled by the Union at Appomattox. "Everybody has formed up to surrender. We're going through the ceremony. The formal procedures are somewhat like pageantry. We go up and stack our muskets in front of the Federal soldiers on commands and take our belts and our cartridge boxes off. We can keep the rest of our stuff. As we stack our muskets, me and my friend leave. We joke, 'We're not going to have to worry about ticks, chiggers, and lice.' We feel anger and bitterness and also lighthearted, like 'those were the cards that were dealt.' There's lots of Yanks there."

With the war over, Rob and his friend parted company. Rob would now face a long trek back to Alabama from Virginia.

"I say goodbye to my friend. I'm going home to farm. It's the season to start planting. No trains are running. I'm walking by myself. There are people walking everywhere, mostly Confederate veterans. Alabama is where I'm going. It's a long walk. I made a cane and my shoes are really beat up. I've been walking too long."

All of a sudden, Rob appeared to have fallen asleep. Slowly, he roused himself. It was then that Rob returned to his home, the house he briefly described during the first regression. This time, however, he was able to provide much more detail.

"I am getting close to home. Things look familiar. I see my home. It's been neglected and busted into. It's depressing, but I was expecting it. No one's here. I don't know where my family is, but I'm worried. It's a farm. There are no crops. I can't figure if it's been lit on fire. It has partial burns, but looks like it can be repaired. It's a log home. The logs are plain, squared, and notched. The chimney seems to be made of stone. There's a front porch. It's crude, but nice. The barn might be gone.

"The closest neighbor is far away. Maybe my mother lived with me. My wife has a couple of children. I hope they return."

After checking out his house, Rob decided to go into town to see if he could get any more information on his family.

"A guy's selling sweet potatoes by the side of the road for twenty-five cents. I'm going into the local town.

"I'm in town talking to a shopkeeper. He's a bald-headed guy with glasses; black vest, black pants, white shirt. He didn't recognize me at first. He called me 'Jim' and asked me where I've been. I'm asking him about my family. He says lots of people left, but he stayed to keep an eye on what's left of the store. People had stolen from the store. He doesn't know where my family is. I guess I'll just wait and see if they come back."

Back at the farm, Rob began repair work and crop growing. "I got a mule from a neighbor. I'm wearing boots and an interesting slouch hat, flipped up in front. It doesn't look stupid. I plow real close to the house in the garden. I'm fixing things up. I've painted the logs to seal them from the weather."

Eager to find out if Rob's family ever reunited, I asked him to move to a time when they were back together.

"All I see is plowing," he replied. "I'm sitting on the porch steps getting a drink of water. Someone I knew from years ago goes by and waves at me. When I think of the war, I realize it was very traumatic. I feel real hurt and ravaged."

A disheartened, discouraged veteran, "John Johnson" had been left without a family and with deep emotional scars from the war.

Rob Hodge's regression ended as he was struggling to pull together what remained of his life and home. After his regression, I was left to contemplate how the four-year-old Rob could have been so obsessed with Confederate uniforms. He wasn't the only reenactor to be "hooked" on the Civil War at an early age. Eight other reenactors who participated in my study were fascinated by the Civil War as children. Most of these played Rebs and Yanks as kids. This concurs with history teacher-reenactor John Robinson's observations that many in "the hobby" were "hooked" by elementary school. In fact, Robinson believes more than ninety percent acquired their interest as pre-teens.

Rob's youthful interest in the Civil War is supported by Dr. Ian Stevenson's scientific investigation of children who spontaneously recalled past lives. As noted in chapter 2, Stevenson observed that many of his subjects expressed the vocation of the previous personality while playing.[89] Two children in his study, which took place in Asia, Ma Tin Aung Myo and Bajrang B. Saxena, played at being soldiers. When they were young, they actually remembered their lives as soldiers. Stevenson ascertained that the children identified heavily with their former personalities until age seven, and then before age ten the memories began to fade.[90]

Stevenson discovered most of these cases in areas of the world where belief in reincarnation was held by the majority of the population. He speculated that cases also occurred in the West, but were suppressed by the parents or the children themselves. An explanation was given on the *Oprah Winfrey Show*, March 1, 1994, when American children talked about their past lives. The parents admitted that, in the past, they would have relegated the children's past-life recall to the category of *make believe*. An increasingly supportive philosophical climate and media exposure are now making it acceptable for some Western parents to listen to their children with a more open mind.

As a youngster, Rob had studied photos of soldiers. With the regressions, he had now just viewed his own past-life "movie." His Civil War knowledge was helpful for his in-depth descriptions of uniforms, marching, and details, but sometimes he experienced confusion when what he saw conflicted with what he thought to be correct. Rob said that he had been unaware of the troop movements of the 47th or 44th Alabama Infantry prior to the regression; however, it turned out to be true that, while both Alabama units fought with the Army of Northern Virginia, they also fought with General Longstreet in the Western theater at Chickamauga and Knoxville. They were both active in the Petersburg siege and also participated in the Appomattox campaign.[91]

Rob experienced confusion over actually having gone from the Eastern theater to the Western theater. He had seen Western (Tennessee-area) jackets, but knew that he had gone east. Historian Brian Pohanka says that this could be correct. In September 1863 the 47th Alabama went west and fought in the battle of Chickamauga.

In one battle, Rob saw blue Army of Tennessee flags alongside those of the Alabamians. This indicates that the 47th Alabama, after getting separated in the fighting, would have fought alongside some Western Confederates. Official reports say part of General Longstreet's Corps, which included the 47th Alabama, fought alongside Tennessee troops and the units were split up in confusion.[92]

Rob saw Gilham's manual of drill being used in some open wheat fields. Gilham's manual was used more in the East, so historian Brian Pohanka believes that Rob's first battle may have been Chickamauga and the next battle he described in Virginia, in 1864, after Longstreet's return to the East, thus the use of Gilham's manual.

Rob described his being in trenches for a long time. The siege of

Petersburg lasted ten months and was the longest sustained opera-
tion of the war, with thirty-five miles of trenches stretching from
Richmond to Petersburg.[93] During that time, Rob got periodic leaves
to the town he described as all burned out. Although Rob thought it
was Richmond, it was probably Petersburg, which had been badly
shelled.[94] He mentioned that bread was an extravagance. An infantry private was paid only thirteen dollars a month at the time.[95]

During the siege of Petersburg, Rob saw the Union troops tearing
through the line. This is a historical description of the Battle of the
Crater on July 30, 1864.[96] During September 1864, nearly 175 guns
fired an average of 7.8 tons of iron per day on the Confederates.[97]

Rob was surprised to see Federal Zouaves and the Union's 5th
Corps flag. He saw black soldiers in Union uniforms and General
Mahone, who looked short, thin, and wore a long beard. What Rob
experienced in regression was historically accurate. The Union 5th
Corps was present, though not heavily engaged, at the Battle of the
Crater and included a brigade of Zouave troops. Black troops were
fighting, and General Mahone, who fit Rob's description, had led
the Confederate counterattack.[98]

At the surrender of Appomattox, Rob said that the Confederates
dumped their muskets and belts with cartridges. The Confederates
did stack their arms and relieve themselves of their ammunition.[99]

Because of prior knowledge, Rob believed that artillery person-
nel he saw were not supposed to have worn swords. To the contrary,
there are photographs of artillerymen with swords.[100]

Rob observed the fife and drummer without their jackets, but just
in their shirt sleeves. Although he had not seen this in reenacting,
this was entirely possible during the war.[101]

Rob felt that he was dying after being shot. This was a common
feeling among the regressed soldiers in my study who were hurt in
battle, and one never experienced in reenacting.[102]

Other authentic scenarios that Rob had experienced during the
regression, but which are not seen in reenactments, include the two
officers arguing and lots of horses and harnesses jangling. Rob said
he hadn't seen large cavalry reenactor units. Critical of overweight
reenactors, Rob was delighted not to find even one soldier in the
regression who was overweight. He also observed that, unlike in reenacting, the dead or wounded looked totally realistic—they
crumpled when shot, fell face down, and laid like dead people. In

nearly six hours of his regression experiences, Rob, fanatical about perfection, could not find one unauthentic detail, leading him to believe this had been a past-life recall.

Aside from the details of historical chronology that matched up with what Rob had experienced, I found two possible name, unit, and story matches in subsequent research. Rob says he didn't want to say that his name was Jackson, but John Jackson just popped into his mind. Later, a local shopkeeper called him "Jim." National Archives military records showed both a John Jackson and a James Jackson in Company I, 47th Alabama Infantry. There was a John T. Jackson who moved up in rank from a private to a corporal. He had enlisted in April 1862 for three years. One year later, he was sick in the hospital. He was furloughed in November 1863, which was after the Battle of Chickamauga. Records show that he was on leave for six months. The records go through '64, and there is no indication of "a muster out date." Twenty-one-year-old James Jackson mustered in for three years one month after John did. There are no further records on James.

These name, unit, and story matches, along with the historical documentation of Rob's memories, are exciting. What's also fascinating was Rob's attention to detail, particularly to the uniforms, both in his recalled lifetime and in his current life. The art student and aspiring film maker and playwright had an eye for the artistry of the war drama, much like the young soldier whose equipment was labeled J.J. Johnson, who stopped to admire the way the soldiers appeared at the height of battle.

8

Buddy:
Heart Problems

Dallas "Buddy" Bare's wedding photographs were prominently displayed in his living room on the evening I arrived. What was so unique about them was that the entire wedding party was dressed in Civil War attire. Buddy didn't seem to think it was all that unusual. After all, he had been involved in reenacting for twenty-five years and couldn't remember a time when he wasn't interested in the Civil War.

Born in Washington, D.C., and reared in Maryland, young Buddy found it natural to play Reb and Yank instead of cowboy and Indian. Living in a "border state" (Maryland) with a father from North Carolina, he always favored the Confederates. As a kid, he made a point of never playing the Yank. Although he admitted to a brief period as a part-time Federal reenactor, he quit that unit. "It's hard for me to shoot a Confederate," Buddy laughingly said during his pre-hypnosis interview.

As an adult, Buddy carried over his youthful interest in the Civil War. While attending his first reenactment at Gettysburg a quarter century before, Buddy was invited to join in the action with the 1st Maryland Line Brigade. He made a quick trip to J. C. Penney's to outfit himself with a gray workshirt and pants, and the unit supplied him with a gun. For the next eighteen months he was a member of 1st Maryland. Later, when he met up with his friend Dave, a fellow reenactor, the pair started Company F, 8th Virginia Infantry. They were among the first reenactor units to wear 100 percent wool uniforms. Buddy is proud that he was in on the ground floor of bringing authenticity to reenacting.

In fact, because reenacting has moments of realism, Buddy believed this created a strong bond among its participants. "What else would bring people closer together than war?" Buddy mused. "Reenacting creates the illusion of depending on your partner for your life." Oddly enough, Buddy chose an occupation in this lifetime in which he often put his life in the hands of his co-workers—a firefighter. At the time of the regression, he was fifty years old and retired from firefighting due to heart problems.

After years in reenacting, Buddy has now turned his attention to researching relatives who may have fought in the Civil War. Once, while he was on a vacation in North Carolina, he spotted several Daughter of the Confederacy markers in a family cemetery. Cutting his trip short, he went immediately to the National Archives where he researched three ancestors, all of whom had enlisted the same day in Company A, 37th North Carolina Infantry. His great-grandfather, Hampton Bare, was wounded at Gettysburg in Pickett's Charge and died at Fort Delaware in a prisoner-of-war hospital. The other two relatives were captured and sent to prison at Point Lookout, Maryland, before being paroled.

Interestingly, his ancestors' unit, the 37th North Carolina, Lane's Brigade, was in Pickett's Charge,[103] and Buddy said they followed right behind the 8th Virginia, Buddy's present unit, to the wall.

Beside the 8th Virginia's connection to the Battle of Gettysburg, Buddy had his own deeply personal experience there. On the set of the movie *Gettysburg*, he experienced what it was like to be in the midst of battlefield firing from both sides. On another occasion, during a reenactment of Pickett's Charge for the National Park Service, he marched along with ten companies in formation across the field. When the Confederates arrived at the wall, the Union soldiers stood up and, instead of shooting at the moment where many lost their lives, shook hands with them. Together, the Union and Confederate reenactors tearfully marched off the field.

Another of Buddy's favorite events was the reenactment of the Battle of Sayler's Creek in Virginia. It was there that the 8th Virginia was part of the rear guard and most soldiers were consequently captured or killed. The battlefield is still relatively untouched, and reenactors march through the woods with all their equipment on their backs just like they did over 130 years ago. Buddy said that the Confederates have to "run their guts out," or they will be captured and put out of commission for the rest of the weekend. He always ended up "dying" rather than being captured. To him, the episode was not only exhausting and exhilarating, but also the closest re-creation of what the Civil War soldiers actually experienced. Even though he participated in the event—rain, shine, or snow—for at least eighteen years, he always had an overwhelming sensation that he'd been there before.

One of Buddy's re-creation specialties was being a member of the hospital staff. As assistant surgeon, he not only explained the Civil War medical equipment to spectators, but also participated in the mock amputation of a foot. The medical team would saw through a ham bone and then let "Hollywood blood" from an IV bag squirt all over. I now realized that it was Buddy's demonstration that I had witnessed at the Battle of First Manassas reenactment two years before.

Other than medical particulars, Buddy admitted that he was not too interested in the details of the Civil War. He left that to his friends. Instead, his reenacting involvement stemmed from his love of adventure and camping, which he shared with his stepson.

But Buddy realized that war was no picnic. After serving in the air force for six years, he believed war to be a necessary evil. At times, reenacting was no picnic either. The men were often half-frozen, sitting around the campfire in the rain with blistered feet.

Even at times like these, Buddy had never asked himself why he did the reenacting. He had never heard of genetic memory and hasn't thought much about reincarnation. The only time he thought about it was when his cousin used to kid him that he must be a reincarnated Civil War soldier. Fortunately, he hadn't totally ruled out the concept and agreed to allow me to regress him. So, after a hypnotic induction, Buddy's eyes fluttered and he began to move back in time.

"It's daytime," he began. "There are people around. A bunch of horses are riding by. They're pulling a cannon. I'm watching them. There are a lot of men wearing Confederate gray uniforms and black slouch hats.

"I'm going in the same direction with them. They aren't shooting at me. I'm part of them. I'm wearing a uniform coat—a little different from theirs. The markings are different. I'm infantry and have blue markings. They are artillery. Other guys are walking with me. The riders are gone now. It's a dirty road and countryside—flat land. I don't know where we're headed.

"We're going to a battle some place 'cause artillery was moving out and we're going the same direction. Some army's gathering. I'm nervous. I don't think it's my first battle.

"We're in formation. We're standing; waiting for the enemy, I guess. I see a two-story farmhouse and flat land. We're facing some woods. I'm anxious. Shooting's coming from the enemy on my left.

"They're coming out of the woods. It's getting close. I see flashes, air explosions, and guns. Our men are firing. They're getting close. Guys are being hit. I can't see too far. I see movement. We're moving forward. We're fighting harder. People are falling down. People are charging."

Suddenly, Buddy is not advancing. He's no longer with the others.

"I see lots of light. The sun's real bright. People are lying on the ground. The battle's over. I'm lying face up on the ground. That's why it's so bright. I don't know if I'm wounded; I think so. I'm real tired. My shoulder hurts. There's blood on my right shoulder. I don't know what happened.

"I feel thirsty. It's hot out. People are coming around. They haven't gotten to me yet. I'm trying to get up. I'm sitting up. I feel lightheaded. I lost my hat. Somebody came over. They're trying to help me get up. It's all right. I'm just so tired.

"They are taking me somewhere to get care. They're helping me along. I'm going to a house. I don't know where, but it's a long ways. I'm getting closer. There are lots of people down. We won. Manassas is the name of the place.

"We're at the house now. They're sitting me down. I'm waiting my turn. It must not be too serious. I don't think I'm bleeding any more. They're getting to me now. They're taking my coat off and looking at it. It just cut through the top of my shoulder. I won't lose my arm. They're wrapping it."

Relieved, he paused for a moment, and then his gripping narrative continued.

"They're putting me in a wagon and sending me to a big hospital. There are eight or ten wounded guys in the wagon—not seriously wounded. We're all sitting up. The ride is bumpy. My arm is still there. The journey just started."

Buddy then moved to the next leg of his trip.

"Now we're waiting to be put on a train. They're taking us off the wagon and putting us on a train. I'm in a passenger car with seats. Those on stretchers are put in boxcars. They're taking us to Richmond. The train is smoother than the wagon."

During his train ride, I asked for his name and unit.

"I'm Bill. From Unit 7 or 17. Company B. I think it's Virginia. The guy beside me called me 'Bill.' That's how I knew my name. My last name's Bell or Brown. This was my first big battle.

"I was fighting for my home, my state, my honor. The Yanks are the aggressor coming down to get us.

"Looking out the window, I see a bridge. I think we're coming into Richmond. It's a big town. I don't think I've ever been here before. I'm from the country. I can't read. Family is waiting at home for me. Molly must be my wife. I see a white bonnet and a brown skirt. She has a slim waist. She smiles."

Once in Richmond, Buddy and the other wounded soldiers were delivered to the Confederate hospital.

"We're at the hospital now. I'm walking in. There's a lot of white. All kinds of people are bustling around. They tell me to sit down in a chair and wait. Guess they have to take care of those who are more seriously wounded."

After a period of recuperation, Buddy was ready to go back to the front.

"I'm ready to leave the hospital now. I've spent a couple of months in Richmond. I feel all right. I have to go back. They're sending me on the train back to Northern Virginia to fight. 'If you gotta go, you gotta go.' There's a lot of people on the train. I'm not too much older than the rest, but older than the young ones. I'm thirty-three.

"We're getting off the train. I think it's Manassas Junction. They connect us up with a group. We have to walk to the camp. There's about four of us walking. It's still hot out. Richmond was hot, but exciting. I've never been in a big town. I got out into town some.

"I see the camp. I'm checking in with the provost marshall. He's putting me in the 17th Virginia—I think it was what I was in before. That's where I am now.

"I can see Captain Charles of Company B. He's a nice guy. I'm just getting into the camp. I want to know where everybody is. I haven't recognized any of the people around the campfires. It's getting dark. We're in a big camp."

It wasn't long before Buddy's unit once again got into the heat of battle.

"It's daytime. We're marching. I don't know where we're headed. I see fields and woods. I'm going to another battle. I'm excited because of the danger. Other guys are excited, too.

"We're at the edge of a woods facing the field. We're getting down low, behind a split-rail, stockade fence. We're waiting. I don't see them yet. They're coming across the hill now, way off in the distance, marching in a long line. It'll take a while to reach us.

"Our cannons are firing way off on our right. We're on the far left—kind of at an angle. They're getting closer. We're starting to shoot at 'em. We're not behind the fence no more. We're forming on the other side of the fence now.

"It's confusing because of all the shooting going on. The shots aren't too close to me, but a couple of guys have fallen and we had to move up. We're pushing them back, I can't tell how far.

"More troops are coming into the field. Our reinforcements are here. It feels good. We're still shooting at 'em. They're shooting back. The cannons have stopped. We're out in front of our cannons. Not too many down. A bunch of the other guys are down. We're pushing across the field. They told us to stop and hold the line.

"We don't want to go down in the gully because they'll have the elevation on us. We want to stay on the high ground. I hope it's the end. It's raining. We're holding our position.

"Now we're moving. I don't know where we're going. We're in town. People are waving at us and cheering. They say the name of the town is Manassas. We won the battle."

But there was no rest for the victorious, as Buddy's scene shifted once again.

"We're marching again. We're heading south. They never tell us—rumors tell us. We're going to Richmond or Petersburg or Fredericksburg—one of them that's south. My feet are tired. They're gonna be tireder. It feels like a long way."

After arriving at their destination, Buddy's unit began a new task. "We're digging in. We're in Fredericksburg digging rifle pits above the river for cover. There's lots of digging."

According to Buddy's narrative, after the fortifications had been built, his Confederate unit now began marching to the northwest, retracing some of their earlier steps.

When his unit paused for a break outside a church, Buddy suddenly saw some Yankee cavalry dash away and Yankee infantry coming out of the woods firing. Fear momentarily gripped him, since his company could be outnumbered. But his company pushed them back without incurring casualties. Relieved, Buddy relaxed somewhat. Moving to the next scene, he was again surprised to find himself back in Fredericksburg.

"We're back in the rifle pits, the one's we worked on before in Fredericksburg. It's the same area. I see the curvature of the river. They are moving back and forth, getting ready to cross the river. They know we're here. They're down river from us. That's not in the line of fire. They're going to be.

"They're crossing the river. There are cannons going off. I can't see them. They're too far away. It's getting everybody all excited and anxious. I see somebody trying to come across the river, down on the left, now. They've stopped coming. They're concentrating down river. I don't hear anything.

"We're waiting. It's a long hill. I don't recognize this place. It could be Fredericksburg. I'm part way on top of the hill in the rifle pit. Yankees are coming up the hill, in waves, like shooting ducks. We're firing down on them. They just keep coming. It's dumb. They're being slaughtered. Artillery is firing on us and hitting around us. There's some close calls." In the midst of a major Confederate victory, Buddy got shot.

"Everything went blank. I do not see or feel anything. It got light—really bright, then dark. I'm floating up—looking down. I see the rifle pit. Bodies are lying around. The battle's over. I'm lying on the ground on my stomach. "I can see blood in my ears. My hat's gone, my head's face down, my boots are on. It's sad I can't go home. I thought we were winning. "Now the body's gone. It's in line with others to be buried. I can see the front of me. My coat's tore up. I see a beard, a moustache, and blood in the ears. My eyes are closed. I'm dead."

A reincarnation skeptic prior to his regression, Buddy had just observed his own death. Besides that, after verifying historical details he experienced in his regression, he began to reevaluate his thinking. Throughout his years of reenacting, Buddy had been more interested in the adventure and camaraderie of reenacting than in the war history and details. Because of this, both Buddy and his fellow reenactors were amazed to find his story, as well as the time frame, chronologically correct.

Buddy's "change of heart" about the possibility of reincarnation following his regression experience inspired me to take a closer look at the post-regression surveys of the other participants, and I found they revealed some interesting observations. Before their regressions, the reenactors, on average, rated themselves just slightly higher than neutral on their belief in the possibility of reincarnation. The two people who had volunteered for my study rated their beliefs in past lives an average of three points higher than the ten subjects I had recruited.

Interestingly enough, Buddy was the only reenactor who felt sure that the story he recalled was a past life, even though he hadn't given the idea of reincarnation much credence before the regression. In his survey, he had rated his belief in the possibility of reincarnation the lowest of all the reenactors (three on a scale of ten). After his experience and changing his outlook, he nearly tripled his rating.

Most of the other reenactors were more cautious in attributing the results of their regressions solely to reincarnation. Even at that, eight of them changed their belief in reincarnation after their regressions.

Of the four who did not alter their views, David Morse (see chapter 13) had previously rated the reincarnation theory at ten. Dale Clarke (see chapter 10) felt the regression gave him fresh insight into his life and inspired him to think about exploring a possible life as a

Roman centurion. MaryLynne Bauer (see chapter 9) thought the fact that she recalled dying as a young soldier may be one explanation why she has felt in such a rush to have a successful career. Brian Pohanka (see chapter 15) said he now had a greater appreciation and understanding of the realism of the Civil War and the feelings of the soldiers. He claimed his regression experience had influenced his reenactment activities.

Most of the reenactors couldn't explain where their stories originated. One questioned whether the information could have percolated up from the collective unconscious. One was surprised at how effortlessly his thoughts kept flowing. Another didn't think himself capable of fabricating that well. The recalled past lives left some reenactors with unanswered questions, making them curious, unsettled, or skeptical.

Each reenactor described his or her experience differently. To one it was like a movie. Others remembered it as vivid episodes filled with emotion, fear, terror, or uncertainty. Several remembered the extreme physical sensations of pain or hunger. Several noticed that they remembered details of their regressions later, unlike a dream that fades quickly from memory. To each reenactor, the past-life regression was much more real and authentic than what they experienced during reenacting.

Taken as a group, over half reported that the regression changed their view of reenactment. They found that reenacting became more personal. They were more enthusiastic about it and had a deeper appreciation for the soldiers and felt closer to the Civil War experience as a result. Seven said that the regression experience affected them personally. One felt that it helped him to define himself spiritually; another had a new perspective on death; one felt more proud that he may have served in the Civil War and fulfilled his duty. The regression experience affected three-fourths of the subjects in at least one significant area.

In addition to the reenactors' changes of perception, I also looked at possible correlations between current health issues and wounds received then. The only apparent possible correlations were with Buddy, who now had a heart problem and recalled being shot in the chest, and Alan McBride, who now has asthma and was also wounded in the chest. MaryLynne Bauer, who has felt uncomfortable in the dark in this life, had experienced panic as a soldier when she saw blackness, and also before death. A weaker correlation could be Rob Hodge, who was shot in the arm and, in this lifetime, had trouble with his wrist.

The fact that I identified only one-third of the subjects whose health issues may have correlated with their Civil War lives appears low in comparison to the normal regression therapeutic process, since most past-life work today is done for therapeutic reasons. One possible explanation could be that the focus of my regression study was not to go back to reveal causes of current physical problems or fears, but only to see if there was identifiable evidence of memories of lifetimes in the Civil War.

Buddy's Civil War memories were a surprise to him. He was one who was never much interested in Civil War history, had not done any significant research, and was not aware of details. He was confused over the order of things. He didn't know if the Battle of Marye's Heights, Fredericksburg, was before or after First or Second Manassas. However, the time frame and chronology in his narrative between the battles, getting wounded, going to Richmond to the hospital, and returning at the end of a campaign to the Battle of Fredericksburg were correct.

In the past-life scenario, it would seem reasonable to suppose that Buddy was shot at First Manassas on July 21, 1861. He remembered taking a wagon and train to Richmond Hospital for a couple months, then was taken back to Manassas Junction where he walked back to camp. The next major battle Buddy recalled being engaged in was Second Manassas, August 30, 1862. After digging trenches at Fredericksburg and marching on campaign, he believes he returned for the Battle of Fredericksburg, December 13, 1862.

Interestingly, the line of Confederate trenches there extended seven miles, and soldiers were packed in at 11,000 per mile.[104] Historian Brian Pohanka confirms that Buddy could have gotten the rail out of Richmond to Manassas Junction and then walked to camp. The Confederate winter camp in 1861-1862 was between Manassas Junction and Centerville.

Buddy described a farmhouse on a plateau. This could have been Henry House which was located at First Manassas.[105] The 7th and 17th Virginia Infantry were both organized at Manassas Junction. Both units were at First Manassas and Second Manassas. The 7th Virginia held the line while 17th Virginia charged. Buddy's company was told to stop and hold the line. Buddy described holding the line just before a gully. This was an accurate description of Second Manassas.[106]

Both units were also at Fredericksburg.[107] Some troops were in Fredericksburg several times. Troops did retrace their steps. There were also two battles at Fredericksburg: December 1862 and May 1863. In Fredericksburg, there were rifle pits or trenches which had been dug by soldiers. After the battle, dead bodies were lined up in a row.[108]

While on march, Buddy was never told his destination. It was common for men not to know where they were going. Even officers were not told final destinations.[109]

In researching Buddy's past-life character, I found two excellent name and unit matches. However, while some of the life story matches I uncovered had some conformity, I ruled them out as conclusive evidence. W. T. Bell, 7th Virginia Infantry, enlisted in August 1862, so would have missed First Manassas. He was wounded, probably at Fredericksburg and then at Gettysburg. He was then hospitalized at Richmond. There are no further records.[110] William H. Brown, Company D, 17th Virginia Infantry, enlisted in May 1861, was captured September 1862, and paroled a month later. He transferred to the Maryland Line in May 1864.[111]

Another intriguing name and unit match I found in the National Archives military records was William Bell, 7th Battalion, who was an assistant surgeon. Interestingly, in reenacting, Buddy acted as an assistant surgeon.

There were two Browns who died at Fredericksburg. John T. Brown, Company E, 58th Virginia Infantry, enlisted in July 1861 and would have missed First Manassas. While sick in Lynchburg Hospital, he missed Second Manassas. He was killed in action at Fredericksburg and left a widow.[112] This soldier's life matched some of Buddy's remembrances: spending time in a hospital, dying at the Battle of Fredericksburg, and leaving a widow. The only way this could be a possible match is if Buddy had misidentified the first two battles. George W. Brown, 40th Virginia Infantry, enlisted in May 1861 at age twenty-five. He died at Fredericksburg, October 1861, too early for the Battle of Fredericksburg.[113] Henry J. Brown, Companies D & E, 49th Virginia Infantry, was wounded at Seven Pines and Second Fredericksburg. He was dropped from the rolls in October 1864.[114]

Of the soldiers whose records I researched, there were two possible matches. One was M. P. Bell, Company E, 33rd Virginia Infantry, who is buried in Spotsylvania Cemetery.[115] The second is Virginian R. A. Brown, who was buried at Fredericksburg Cemetery, also according to interment records.

Even before I verified the facts of Buddy's story, the former reincarnation skeptic decided that reincarnation was the only way he could explain his recalled Civil War memories. Said Buddy, "It was too real to be anything else."

9

MaryLynne: A Hoop Skirt for a Gun

An expert in historic costumes, MaryLynne Bauer had the uncanny ability to walk, run, or even climb over rocks in a nineteenth-century hoop skirt. She would get impatient when she saw other female reenactors hiking up their skirts when they walked, while she found it easy to scoop up her own skirt with her toes to keep her hemline from getting in her way. During our pre-hypnosis interview, MaryLynne told me she didn't remember where she learned this trick.

Whenever she wore her nineteenth-century attire, MaryLynne never stepped out of her tent or the house without her bonnet and gloves on, although she never felt the need for a hat or gloves in her current life.

Not only did MaryLynne feel comfortable in Civil War-era clothes, but she also believed that she looked and carried herself in a more authentic manner than some of the other women. Even though

MaryLynne looked contemporary in modern clothes, her under-graduate degree in costume design and theatre had given her the edge when it came to making her Civil War impression. The thirty year old was currently working on her master of science in historic costume and textiles.

Vain as it sounded, MaryLynne unabashedly admitted that she liked to be the best in her field and enjoyed being known as an authority in historical apparel among both female and male re-enactors.

After she graduated from college, she teamed up with a seam-stress who had planned to do costuming for a movie in Hollywood. Although the project didn't work out, it was through this seamstress that she was introduced to Civil War reenactors. She became so fas-cinated with the reenactors that she began making their uniforms.

Interestingly enough, MaryLynne didn't have any previous con-nection with the subject of the Civil War, but in fact was more inter-ested in Edwardian, colonial, and medieval history and attire. She told me that she didn't know whether this meant she never had a past life in the Civil War or whether she just didn't want to remem-ber it.

Gradually, she became more of a consultant and lecturer and less the seamstress. As a consultant to reenactors for both the infantry's uniforms and their wives' attire, she became the first honorary member and the only female of the 1st Pennsylvania Reserves.

Seven years later, MaryLynne was still involved in Civil War reen-acting and participated in all aspects of women's lives in the Civil War era. She would remind the soldier reenactors that the Civil War was only four years in duration and that they should be giving some attention to the times, their livelihoods, the politics, history, and amusements of the day. MaryLynne saw herself as a crusader for the civilian sphere of their lives.

Entirely comfortable with nineteenth-century decor, she enjoyed doing interpretations of the mechanics of home life at living history events. She said that spectators often complimented her on her abil-ity to explain how civilians spent the time we now spend watching television. Civil War knowledge and a nineteenth-century perspec-tive came easily to her.

Regarding Civil War themes, one point of view that MaryLynne was not comfortable with was the Southern cause. Although she was temporarily attached to a Southern reenactor unit, she admitted that it was mainly for fun. Recognizing that the Southern mind-set was foreign to her and aware that the war experience in the South was vastly different from that in the North, she related more to Federal reenactors, their lifestyles, and their cause. Whenever she felt uneasy with Confederate reenactors, she would remind herself that everyone was an American before, during, and after the Civil War.

MaryLynne grew up in the Midwest where she heard little talk of the Civil War. She's not aware of any ancestors who fought in the war, although she conducted some research after becoming involved with reenacting. One remote possibility was the uncle of her great-grandfather who may have fought in the 1st Delaware Volunteer Infantry.

Considering herself a pacifist, MaryLynne didn't like war. Even so, she almost joined the air force because she wanted to become a pilot. This didn't surprise her then boyfriend who once said she "thought like a man." MaryLynne acknowledged that she communicated well with men, had a good analytical mind, and was handy at plumbing. Her roommate claimed that MaryLynne could build a nuclear reactor out of a bag of scraps.

MaryLynne recognized herself as a modern woman who made her own decisions, was competitive, goal oriented, confident, and a loner. At the time of the study, she was supporting herself as a museum registrar. Although MaryLynne's present-day attitudes and lifestyle appeared to conflict with the more docile nineteenth-century females she reenacted, her own research indicated that there indeed were independent nineteenth-century women who ran businesses and broke the submissive mold.

With all this in mind, MaryLynne said she was comfortable being a woman. She took a no-nonsense approach to her "life-enhancing" interests that ranged from fashion, music, and decor to history, philosophy, and literature. Treating reenacting with the same sincerity, she claimed to be as committed to "the hobby" as the male reenactors.

Although she didn't relate to any specific Civil War battles, MaryLynne found nothing more stirring than a parade and the haunting melody of the fife and drum off in the distance. She also found it moving to sit on a porch and see the campfires glowing in the distance.

Occasionally, while sitting around a campfire with other re-enactors, MaryLynne would muse about her Civil War interest. She took the middle ground on the issue of reincarnation, being open to the possibility, but waiting for proof. She compared it to believing in UFOs. "Unless an alien lands in your backyard, you can't believe it," she said pragmatically. With a quick and creative mind, MaryLynne has had many déjà vu experiences in her life. Although none of them involved the Civil War, she often knew ahead of time how a situation would unfold and its outcome. On one occasion, it was so over-whelming, she got goose bumps and tears came to her eyes as well.

MaryLynne was a receptive participant in my study. After our successful interview, we were now ready to begin her regression experience. We were eager to see if she could explore the nineteenth-century home life so that she would gain new information and insight into the decor, dress, and activities that would enhance her studies and career. But the memories MaryLynne brought forward surprised us both.

"I feel real panicked," she began. "Something's wrong. The light is getting bright. It's all white. I can't see anything. There are swirls of black. I see lights in the bottom.

"I'm back to the panic feeling, but not as strong. The light's not as bright. I don't know what it's from. My face hurts like I was crying. I'm alone, inside something—either in a tent or under a sheet. The sunlight filters through. Maybe there's a bed. I can't see clearly. I think I'm standing up. It's dark now."

Surmising that MaryLynne had moved immediately to her death scene, I allowed her to relax and then guided her to move backward in that lifetime. Immediately she was confused. In the last scene she had felt that she had been a woman.

"It's daytime," she said. "I'm outside, alone. I'm wearing pants and a sack coat. I'm a boy. There's a town. I'm standing in a big yard with a big tree. Bob or Rob. That's what they call me. There're no houses behind this yard, just a field with a wooden fence in between.

"The house is on the other side. It's at least a two-story white wood house. There's no porch in back. I think it's where I live. It's kept up. It's summer. It's not too hot, but nice out. It's almost too quiet. I'm bored. There are other houses around.

"I'm playing with a stick in the mud. There should be a garden. I don't see it. Maybe it's not growing now. Usually there're more things

in it. There's some corn there, but it's not growing very well. It's like
somebody went in and pulled it all up."

After MaryLynne acclimated herself, I asked her to go into the
house for dinner.

"I'm in the dining room. There's a big, dark table. There are a few
chairs. My mother has on a black dress. It's plain, but neat. It looks
expensive. My sister has a brown dress on. I think I'm about six. My
chin just reaches the top of the table. I'm looking up at it. There are
some plates and a table cloth that's not big enough for the table.
There are silver things on the table and a bowl of strawberries. My
sister and I are sitting. My mother is walking in.

"I don't know where my father is. He's away. He's been gone—a
long time. I don't know when he'll be back. She's angry that he's gone.
Maybe he ran off? My sister says my name is Bobby. My sister won't
tell me my last name. She's teasing me again. B-R-O-D-? Brody?
Broderick? My father's name is Robert or Michael.

"My mother and my sister are chatting about somebody my sister knows. She's a lot older. I'm hungry. I want the strawberries and
cream. I don't care about the other stuff."

This made me laugh. We had thought MaryLynne would be fascinated with all the niceties and details of home life, but instead she
sounded like a typical boy. After the meal, I asked her to move forward in time.

"People are walking on the street. I'm walking by myself. I'm fourteen or sixteen, and tall and skinny. I have on a suit—checked pants
and a sack coat. I'm not doing anything now. I usually go to school,
but it must be summertime.

"My father never came home. I think he died a long time ago. I
don't know. I was little. They call me Robert now. I don't let them call
me Bobby. It's Brody. I'm not sure if it's 1858 or '59 or '62. I see the
name Hartford on a sign. It's rural, not a big city. But there are
wealthy people here. We're wealthy, too."

I asked MaryLynne to ask someone the name of the state.

"That's a pretty silly question to ask someone. We're out in the
West. It's not New England. Maybe it's Ohio, or Michigan, or Indiana. It's OK living here. It's awfully quiet, though. Kind of boring.

"I haven't heard any talk of the war. It's so quiet. It shouldn't be
that quiet. It's probably not quiet out East. There's probably a lot
happening out there. I wish I could go there.

"There were some horses pulling carriages. It's busy in the newspaper place. They can't stop to chat. There are newspapers all over the place in piles. They don't mind me digging around. I come in a lot. They say I'm too young to work there. It makes my eyes hurt." MaryLynne is relieved from her boredom when she moves forward to the next significant event.

"Lots of people are standing around a train depot. It's crowded. We're waiting to get on a train. We're going out East. I think we might be soldiers, but I can't tell because some don't have the right kind of hats. Everybody has big hats with wide brims. They're wearing blue uniforms.

"I'm feeling apprehensive. I don't know if I really want to go. I'd rather go to New York and be a reporter for a big newspaper there. I've been working for the newspaper here. I'm going to write things and send them back. I'm not a correspondent, just a soldier. They have correspondents for the newspapers. We are going to go down to Washington through Pennsylvania."

Leaving her hometown, MaryLynne arrived in Washington and felt anxious.

"There're always people everywhere now. It's hard to be alone. We're in the city of Washington. I'm worried. The capital's here, and we could be attacked. Washington is a nice city. I haven't done any writing yet. We just got here. I don't know anybody.

"Maybe my unit is 14th Ohio, Company D or G. It could also be 43rd or 3rd. I think they call me Harry. Maybe Robert is my middle name. I like Robert better, but they'll call me whatever they want. I still think my last name's Brody, but Mitchell also comes to mind."

After leaving the capital, MaryLynne found herself on campaign.

"It's daytime. There are small hills. It's mostly open. There are a few trees with leaves. We sleep on the ground without tents. Everyone's sitting down. We're really tired. We've been marching. My feet don't really hurt, though. I don't know why they don't. Maybe I'm used to it."

Even though she felt good physically, MaryLynne's apprehension followed her.

"It's the evening and there are fires. I didn't build one. They were there when I woke up. Everybody's sitting around eating and chatting. It makes me worried, though. They can see you when you have a fire. I think they're closer than anyone else thinks. I think we're in

Virginia because we've walked, we haven't taken a train. It hasn't been too long since we left Washington. It's not like a camp. We'll probably have to march again.

"They are talking loud. They're crude. I don't fit in. They're older than me. I'm about seventeen. They know a lot more than I do, though. They aren't educated like me. I like to write. I'm writing something now about the march. We've been at it a while. It just goes on and on. It gets boring. I can't write when I'm walking. I'm just hanging out. I stay by myself and write and watch them.

"I saw a couple officers on horses. One has more stuff on his uniform—a sash and a fancy sword. I don't know his name. He must be visiting us. He's going to make us march again. We must be with other units. There's so many more people than before. Everyone is wearing sack coats. Some men, even in our group, have different hats."

I noticed MaryLynne wasn't showing much interest in details of the uniforms. When I asked her to move to the next important event, she said she felt as if she were alone and drifting. I suggested she move backward a little and she became anxious.

"It's daytime and I'm outside. I'm feeling panicky again. I don't know why. Lots of people are lying all over. My head hurts. My face hurts. I don't think I was hurt, though. I'm standing. I'm scared. There's no more firing. I think there was firing. I wasn't here when it happened. I don't want to stay here. My head hurts again. Maybe I should get someone to look at it. I'm a little far from others. They're all yelling and upset. Maybe they are panicking, too. I'm drifting again. I can't see anything now.

"It doesn't hurt any more. This is silly. I'm up in the air. I don't know why. It's nice. My head doesn't hurt. I can look down. I see a lot of people lying around."

I asked MaryLynne to view her body. Now she seemed totally unemotional and detached, which contrasted sharply with her last feelings of panic.

"I see my body. It's just a guy. Nothing special—tall and skinny, with brown hair. The guy who was yelling at me is looking at it. I'm moving. I'm going away. Maybe I was hit in the head. I feel fine now. My body's getting smaller. I'm just floating up. It's all gone. I see nothing now."

MaryLynne's regression had begun with a feeling of panic, the sense that something was wrong, and a lot of white light—getting brighter. She was then regressed to the beginning of that lifetime. Although MaryLynne thought that she was a woman in the first death scene, she may have just assumed that she was the same sex and was surprised to find herself a six-year-old Midwestern boy growing up without a father.

The only woman in the study, MaryLynne was the only reenactor to find a change of sex in the previous life. Some of her friends were not surprised that she recalled a male lifetime because she thought like a man, was good at plumbing, and had once wanted to be an air force pilot.

I found MaryLynne's experiences to be consistent with Dr. Ian Stevenson's research into past-life sex changes.[116] Children who remember previous lives as a member of the opposite sex always show, when they are young, traits characteristic of the former sex. Meanwhile, in her work *Many Lifetimes,* Joan Grant emphasized the importance for such individuals of not denying the instincts and intuition that had been acquired as the opposite sex.[117]

Stevenson saw a correlation between reported sex-change cases and cultural beliefs.[118] In the University of Virginia's collection of regression study cases from Burma and Thailand, approximately twenty percent were of the sex-change type. Some cultures, such as the Druse of Lebanon, Tlingits of southeastern Alaska, and Alevis of south-central Turkey, have no reported cases of sex change. Some cultures believe that it is a punishment to return as a female. In other cultures, Stevenson reports that the incidence of sex change is about five percent.

Past-life researcher Hans TenDam says the average probability of a sex change in between two subsequent incarnations is from fifteen to twenty-five percent.[119] Psychologist Helen Wambach found that she always had a fifty-fifty ratio of men and women in each time period and group she regressed.[120] In one sample, seventy-eight percent of her subjects were women. In another, forty-five percent were male and fifty-five percent female. Another past-life researcher Muller found six percent of boys and sixteen percent of girls he studied recalled sex changes.[121]

The percentage of sex changes in this study, one-twelfth or 8.3 percent, ranks slightly higher than Stevenson's average of five percent for most cultures. This also correlates with Muller's cases and

Wambach's first study of more women recalling male lives. This study, with all males maintaining the same sex, could also point to Stevenson's consideration of the possibility that one's belief or culture at the time of death may influence his or her next life.[122]

In MaryLynne's past life, she recalled growing up in the Midwest town of Hartford. There is a Hartford in both Michigan and Indiana. Later as a soldier, she recalled dying without being shot. MaryLynne could have died of a wound or of disease at a field hospital since informal hospitals were often set up outside.

After her regression, MaryLynne said that she felt she had been drafted later in the war and that perhaps she had gone on campaign to Winchester, Virginia, or Monocacy, Maryland. Although MaryLynne did not know if this was feasible, historian Brian Pohanka believes it is plausible that Midwest regiments in 1864 would have taken the train to Baltimore or Washington, D.C., and then marched to Winchester or Monocacy. Both destinations are within 100 miles of Washington and both have some hills. It is also possible that MaryLynne could have been drafted. According to the Ohio Roster Commission, several Midwestern units were composed of drafted soldiers.[123]

There were several soldiers' names, units, and lives that could correlate somewhat with MaryLynne's remembered Civil War life. According to interment records and the Ohio Roster Commission, Thomas Brady, Company F, 73rd Ohio Volunteer Infantry, died of disease and was buried in Winchester Cemetery. The same sources indicate that Private Thomas Mitchell of Company F, 122nd Ohio Volunteer Infantry, entered the service in January 1864 at the age of eighteen. (Some of the soldiers in the 122nd Ohio were drafted.) He died of disease at Brandy Station, Virginia, on April 7, 1864, and was buried at Culpeper Cemetery, Virginia. Interment records also list George Mitchell, Company D, 192nd Ohio Volunteer Infantry, as dying March 19 and being buried at Winchester Cemetery. In addition, the National Archives military records lists two soldiers, Robert Mitchell, Company B, 42nd Indiana Volunteer Infantry, and James Brady, 43rd Indiana Volunteer Infantry, who had close names and units, but their life stories didn't match up.

Could the young, refined drafted soldier who was a loner and would rather write than mix with his comrades have any relationship to a feisty contemporary woman who worked best on her own, exhibited traditionally male abilities and interests, and excelled at Civil War-era interpretation and costuming? Could it be that besides heredity and environmental factors, past lives influence our personalities, our talents, our choices, our current lives? And, if so, based on MaryLynne's experiences revealed here, what might we be like in our next lives?

10

Dale:
Richmond Burning

While attending the 125th anniversary of the Battle of First Manassas as a spectator, Dale Clarke offered his assistance to the Georgia 22nd Heavy Artillery unit. The reenactors had just built a cannon complete with a $7,000 barrel. After hauling the cannon hundreds of miles from Georgia to Virginia, the men were disappointed when it wouldn't fire. Not to worry. Dale quickly had the cannon in good working order using a power drill he had in his car. In gratitude, the troops offered Dale the opportunity of reenacting with their unit. They outfitted him with shirt, pants, and cap.

However, they forgot to tell him to keep his mouth open when the cannon was fired. Years later, Dale still remembers his teeth rattling, ears ringing, and eyes blurring when the cannon was shot. Fortunately, the artillerymen did remember to tell him not to stand in front of the tube while it was being fired. However, at one point during the reenactment, Dale stood forward of the cannon. Even though he was off to the side of it, "blow-back" flames leapt onto Dale's clothes. One cannoneer threw a "sponge bucket" of black water, which had been used to clean out the inside of the cannon barrel, over Dale and doused the fire. Dale emerged with burned suspenders, shirt, britches, and skin—and was blackened from head to toe.

At the end of the reenactment, he recalled seeing dust everywhere and hearing the sound of muffled feet as the troops marched off the battlefield. Earlier, he had seen rabbits scurrying off the field as the fighting began. It was reminiscent of what one Civil War soldier had said and probably more had thought, "Run, cottontail, run. I wish I were you." The fire incident and even the 115 degree heat didn't put Dale off. Instead, it inspired him to become a reenactor. But he never did heavy artillery again, although his fellow artillerymen later served under him in his reenactor capacity as adjutant of the Confederate military forces.

Dale, a fifty year old who labeled himself a computer guru and has had a variety of positions as branch manager and technical director of computer firms, has carried over his leadership abilities into reenacting. He moved quickly through the ranks of the 26th North Carolina Infantry, rising to the level of adjutant. Later, as adjutant of the Confederate military forces, it was his job prior to a reenactment to survey the fields, lay out the camps, and decide where headquarters and the rest of the military hierarchical organization would be. Comparing each line to a finger on a hand, he would next lay out the staff line, brigade line, battalion lines, company lines, and streets. The engineers would then physically create the camp structure, which set boundaries involving a chain of command that no one of lesser rank would bypass.

As adjutant, he also coordinated with the brigade commanders, relaying commands from the general. After a promotion, Dale became chief of staff and spoke directly for the general. When the general was not on the field, Dale was first in command and made all major decisions. These roles appeared to suit Dale since he felt more comfortable with military staff and protocol than with foot soldiers and Civil War history.

Having never been interested in the Civil War as a youngster, the Panamanian-reared reenactor preferred playing a Roman gladiator with a wooden sword instead of Reb or Yank. Like his grandfather,

Dale's father left Virginia to work on the Panama Canal. Although none of Dale's ancestors fought in the Civil War, one ancestor was said to have traveled Boone's trail with frontiersman Daniel Boone. While in Panama, Dale's parents employed a maid to help rear Dale. The housekeeper, an Obeah princess, was a practitioner of British Island voodoo. The sick would come to her for "juju" potions, herbs, and poultices. Even Dale benefited from Miss Georgia's skills when he quickly recovered from tonsillitis after gargling with an herbal concoction.

Miss Georgia prophesied that Dale would either die before thirty or live forever. Since that prediction, Dale has had thirty narrow escapes from death, including witnessing a childhood playmate get electrocuted just a few feet away, being harpooned, having a machete come within inches of decapitating him, being trapped twenty-five feet under a waterfall, being knocked unconscious and nearly drowning when a child dove off a diving board and landed on his back, being wounded by his own Civil War sword, having his foot smashed and barely avoiding being crushed by a half-track military transport vehicle, being involved in a brawl in an Irish pub, driving a screwdriver into his hand, and being clubbed by Panamanian police. Describing the incident with the billy club, he periodically lapsed into fluent Spanish as he recalled how the perpetrator was caught and lashed with a cat-o'-nine-tails.

Perhaps partially because of his exposure to the supernatural and his friendship with the Darian Indians of Panama, as a youngster Dale was given the knowledge of how to find ancient Indian graves. As a thirteen year old, he led two adult civilians from the nearby naval base to the jungle grave site. The pair, who planned to give the pre-Columbian artifacts to a museum, decided to keep the solid gold "waca" good-luck pieces, melting them down and selling the gold. That night, while sleeping in a tree for protection from the animals, Dale had a vision of an Indian adorned with a bird feather headress. The message was clear—these grave robbers had molested the spirits and everyone should leave the grave site immediately. Unable to convince the men to leave, Dale walked twenty-five miles out of the jungle. On a later trip, the grave robbers both suffocated when the graves collapsed on them.

In Civil War reenacting, Dale continued to have some unusual experiences. Once, after driving from Virginia to Bentonville, North

Carolina, he barely found the reenactment site through the darkness and thick fog. As he got out of his car and approached a house that had actually been used as a hospital where surgeons had tossed arms and legs out of the window creating "limb pits," he felt endangered by a supernatural presence. Receiving the intuitive message that someone or something was planning to scare him off the premises, Dale returned to his car and put on his Confederate coat, hat, pistol, and sword. Immediately, he felt the danger dissolve away, as if the "ghostly guard" had been Confederate.

Moving to the issue of reincarnation, the jovial father of two boys is a proponent of the genetic memory theory. "I'm a leader, and when I go into a room, that emanates from my aura," the stocky, ruddy-faced, red-haired reenactor told me. He believed that characteristics such as these were based in the genes and emitted from the brain through the blood. During my interview with him, he speculated that if we could find a "virgin brain," the memories would already have been formed by the genes. Assuming that the back of the brain holds a library composite of our genes, Dale concluded that his sons would have both his and his ancestors' memories.

Now ready to see if he could tap into his own genetic memories, Dale settled back and I led him into a hypnotic state. "The city's deserted. It's got porches and columns, wooden houses on a dirt street. A man has a lady by her arm. He saw me and let her go. He's saluting me and leaving.

"He's a skinny, young guy wearing a jacket, a waistcoat, and a frilly white shirt and cuffs. He's bareheaded with long, greasy hair and looks like a dandy. The lady adjusts her clothes, straightens out her hat, and leaves. She's got a fan hanging on her hand, black gloves, green dress with a white apron on the front, long train behind. She picks it up to walk.

"There's hitching posts to tie horses. I don't know why the town's deserted. I'm the only one here. It's like someone's coming. Imminent danger. I don't hear anything. It's quiet. The army's coming. Everyone's supposed to get out of the city. I think everyone's still here inside hiding. You were told to leave. It's Richmond. I live across the river in Manchester. It's part of Richmond below the falls. I'm here on business.

"There's a very thin, tall man in his late thirties wearing a gold-colored vest, tails, a long coat, loose black pants. The lady also was dressed up too much. Today's not a day to be dressed up because if you look prosperous, you may have problems. Another dandy. He's got a gun. I don't know what he's up to.

"I feel apprehensive. I still don't hear anything. I'll know when the danger's here by listening. I thought I was listening for guns, but it's horses. It's 1865. There's a Richmond newspaper in a store that sells newspapers and candy. A lamp post in the street seems in the way of carriages."

Now Dale moved away from the area with the houses.

"There's a boardwalk. It's still pretty deserted. Some of the store windows are broken or dusty. When I came from the houses and down the street, the road bent to the left. Then it bent back to the right about 150 feet, then goes down and up a hill.

"At the top of the hill is a road that cuts across it. That one goes way down the hill to the left. To the right it goes up the hill quite a ways. It's a very steep angle. This is a shopping area. There's some big government buildings on that hill. They go up and down the hill. On the right is a park. This is city. The road here is paved. The one in front of the houses was dirt, but this is cobblestone. It gets a lot more traffic. I live down the hill and across the river. I don't have a horse or a carriage so I must have walked.

"I have a high collar. It's white, but it's dirty and yellowed. I don't like being disheveled. The Chinese and blacks who clean the clothes have run off. They don't own their places so they don't have any reason to stay.

"I work in a store. It's got a long storefront right on the corner next to the park. It's got a flat front, like they cut the corner off by the park, and it looks dark because of the nearby trees. There's writing on the windows. I have a key.

"There's a big open room down here. There're stairs that go up to the right. A landing goes across the top of the back of the room that's two stories high. The windows are only in the bottom. There are desks. It's an accounting office. This is my place and I do very well. There's nothing here for them to take. I'm afraid they'll burn all the records and paperwork.

"Some people are drunk in the park. Farmers, some crippled soldiers. They've got bandages and one has crutches. They're rabble. Some beggars will do any kind of work, even cleaning up for a meal.

They stole that liquor from the liquor store. I told them to get out of my park. They told me it's not my park.

"I own the corner of this block—the two buildings on the left side, around the corner. My buildings overlook the park, so my people take care of it. There's nice people living in the two houses that I own. I rent them out. One is gone; the other's an older lady. She lives upstairs in the white house.

"My building is brown with yellow lettering in the window. It says something like 'Hodgkiss and Clarke.' I'm Sherbrook Clarke. I don't have a partner. Maybe he died some time ago.

"I've got a lot of money in my pocket. Our paper money's no good. You need a lot to buy anything. I haven't eaten today. I'm hungry. There's no one with food. It's been some time since I've been home. I've been to the government buildings on the hill looking for news. The government's still functioning."

Dale now began to chuckle with understanding.

"So that's what's happening. Richmond is falling. The cavalry is coming. That's what I'm listening for. The government people said they would come first. I still don't hear anything, and I can see a long way. They told me the gold was gone. Soldiers put it on the train and took it away from Richmond.

"I have a family, but I'm not worried about them. I don't think any soldiers will even go there. Soldiers are going to come here because of the government. If they burn the government buildings, they may burn mine. I'm here to try to protect it. Manchester is where I grew up. It's a poor area."

Dale now began to think of his wife the way he liked to remember her during better times and before they had their six children.

"My wife is wearing a pink and silver-blue dress. She's reclining. This gown is low cut, has a round bodice and long sleeves that are layered down to cover her hands. She's got almost white hair and very pale skin. She's heavy set.

"One son has gone to the war. He's dead. He wasn't very big or old enough to enlist. I wouldn't let him go, but he went anyway. Just like me. I never listened to my dad either. I should have; he was a smart man."

Formerly jovial in spite of impending danger, Dale's tone now became somber.

"I'm angry at my son for getting himself killed—near Richmond, on the other side of the river in a swamp in the wilderness. He was shot for nothing! They weren't defending anything, just fighting in the woods. It was John, but we called him Jack, Jacky as a boy. I called him Jack to make him mad."

Dale's voice trembled and then he composed himself.

"The relatives are OK," he said. "They live out in the county where nobody would go. It's off the beaten path and not a big house.

"I was proud my son was with Stonewall Jackson. I never had a chance to tell him. I'd call him John now, if he wanted. I don't know what unit he was in. All I know is that he was a foot soldier. He was a good shot. We used to hunt deer. He had an old, long rifle. He'd drop a deer if he could see it. There's a lot of deer on our place. I still remember the first time I showed him how to gut a deer. He didn't like getting all messy.

"I told him it doesn't matter if you have on your work clothes. You don't have to clean the clothes because it's woman's work. My wife doesn't do it. She has help from some poor cousins living with her. The blacks won't leave. She had a lady that reared her who came with her when we married. She always wears a white bonnet. She's not going anywhere.

"I've got one black man, Barney, taking care of the place. He won't let anything go wrong. I freed him, so I don't have to pay the taxes every year. It's expensive, so I freed them all. Barney and the others are house blacks. The people who worked on the farm are gone. I've lost thousands of dollars, if I don't get them back. I don't know where they went—they ran off quite a while ago, before my boy was killed.

"It seems as if it's been a long time, but it hasn't been that long. He went looking for the army in the field to enlist. He took a red horse. It wasn't his horse yet, but it would have been. He's the only boy. The five girls are young still. That's my only worry—if soldiers come. They're pretty. No road goes through there. I got a feeling I shouldn't be here in town. I should be at home. I have no way to get there."

After Dale expressed his concern for the welfare of his family, I suggested that he move forward to the next significant event, thinking that he may return home. However, he remained in Richmond.

"I see soldiers coming—Yankees on horseback. They look dingy and are covered with dust. Humm. They are flying our flag. I've always considered myself an American and that flag still stands for America. I pity the Yankees because they don't know what they're fighting for. If they knew all we wanted to do was to be left alone, they wouldn't die for it. They've been told wrong things about us. I've read stories in the Yankee newspapers—how we're mistreating Yankee prisoners and kill people on the battlefield when they're wounded. That's not in the newspaper, though. I met a wounded Yankee soldier down by the hospital. He thought they were going to kill him.

"That's where my carriage is—at the hospital. A Confederate officer said he needed it. It only carries two people and the horse threw a shoe and has a hurt foot. I bet he's going to use it to run. He looked like that kind of man. He was a fancy, clean-dressed cavalry officer. He's got a blue-gray coat. He's a first lieutenant with two stripes. I think he would have shot me if I hadn't given him up the reins. I would have given him the wagon, if it would have helped the soldiers.

"I feel sorry for them boys all shot up. They call it a hospital. It's nothing but an old barn with filthy straw piled up outside covered with blood. Flies on everything. I know one of the doctors. He's from here in Richmond. He used to be a dentist. Now he's cutting off arms and legs. He says they'll die for sure if you don't cut them off. The ones that got bullets in them, there's not much you can do. If it's down inside of them and they can't get it out, they just leave it in there. They try to heal up the outside. Most of them get hit with a bullet that just tears them apart.

"They only bring them here if it's the end of an arm or a leg that's been shot off, or if they're an officer. If they get hit anywhere else, they got to make it here themselves. Three or four days ago, wagons stopped coming."

Suddenly, Dale showed surprise and seemed to shore himself up for possible trouble.

"Ah, the Yankee soldiers are here. They're waiting for an officer to come. They are all around on their horses and I'm sitting on the front stoop. They have guns on me. They put them away now. I thought they were going to shoot me for nothing. I got a gun. They don't know I have it. It's a derringer. There are twelve or thirteen soldiers and lots more down the street checking the other buildings. They're staying on their horses. They aren't going any closer to the government buildings. They're waiting.

"There are fires down at the bottom of the hill now. They're not going past the park to the buildings. The fire is across the river. A lot of smoke. Manchester looks like it's burning.

"Oh-oh. Some of our soldiers are coming up the hill. The Yankees have got their guns out again. Cavalry's gone by, going up the hill towards the government. These guys are just hunkered down on their horses. The Yanks are outnumbered. The cavalry's gone. Had to be 100 to 150 men.

"Infantry's marching up the hill in bad shape, carrying their weapons any old way. Many are wounded. We're on a side street about 100 yards away. They can't see us. Damn. I ought to fire a shot so they could chase these Yanks off. But they'd shoot me. The soldiers say I can't go inside. Other people on the street below me got called out of their houses and shops. There are about thirty Yanks on the street.

"Our soldiers are still going by—close to a thousand men going up the hill. Four or five flags. There should be only one flag with a thousand men. They aren't looking. They're retreating. The cavalry went by fast, intent on going up the hill. They are going right by the government buildings towards the train station. Haven't been trains for weeks.

"The soldiers have all gone by. A Yankee rides up to the corner looking after them. He comes riding back. They told us to go inside. They are riding off to where they came from. More fires down by the bottom of the hill—really burning merrily now. I can see flames. Buildings are engulfed. I see the glow of flames down there. A few stragglers coming up the hill."

With the Yankees gone, Dale ventured into the street.

"I hear a horse in the park. I'm going to get it. The drunks ran through the woods when the soldiers came.

"There's a Yankee soldier. He's dead. One of our boys is dead, too. He's tangled up in the reins of the horse like he flew off. The Yank's got a sword stuck through him. Jesus. The Confederate's a young officer. I didn't hear a shot. He's got a hole in his stomach right next to the hip. Half the shoulder is blown away. There's a musket lying next to the Yankee. It's been fired and the hammer's down on the cap."

Taking in the horrifying scene, Dale gulped uncomfortably.

"Eyeballs are out of the officer. That's why I didn't hear the shot. He stuck him with the gun and pulled the trigger. It went in the hip and came out the back. I'll get him out of the rain. I'm going to take his horse and leave. He's got two pistols on the saddle. I'll leave the guns here with the officer. I put his hat over his face. He's so young. "Where'd the Yankee come from? The Yankee's infantry. I only saw Yankee cavalry. He's got an ordinary musket. He's not a sharp shooter. Maybe he's a deserter. There's a little ball of string in his pocket. I check his jacket. Enlistment papers. Can't read them. They're all sweated off."

Now, Dale laughed at the string and sweaty enlistment papers. "He's a freckle-faced boy with red hair. I'll look in his hat. 'Roger'— probably his first name. He's got a pebble in his coat and a red cloverleaf of felt on his hat. He has twenty-seven cents in his other pocket. He's from the far North because the skin underneath his shirt is all pasty. His shoes are worn out. The heels are plumb gone. I pull the sword out of him, roll him over, and neaten him up. I drag him over next to the officer.

"But for the different uniforms, they could be brothers. Both young kids. The Yankee has red hair and freckles. Our boy has light brown hair cut short—like he just got a haircut. I cover them both up. I'm going to leave all the weapons here. I'll just carry my derringer in case I get in trouble."

Now that Dale had transportation, he could finally get home.

"I'm passing the government buildings and going up my street in front of my buildings. Fires are burning the woods down at the bottom of the hill. I take one last look at my place. It looks OK. I stop and make sure Miss Custis, the widow woman, is OK. I call upstairs to her. She calls back. I tell her I'm leaving. Reckon I have to. Wish she could go. I offer her a ride on the horse. She laughs. It's not since she was a young woman that she rode a horse. She always rode in carriages.

"I check the saddlebags to make sure there are no guns. Hardtack and a German weenie. I bite the end off the weenie. It's a bit green, but tastes good and salty. I break off a piece of the hard bread and toss it inside the saddlebags. He doesn't have a canteen or haversack. On the next street is a pump. I get water for the horse, which is a light red, almost orange solid color. I got to go back and get the Yankee's canteen."

Dale returned to the pair of dead soldiers.

"There's blood all over now. When I pulled the sword out, he started leaking. A big puddle of blood on the ground. Blood on the canteen, too. I'll wash it off at the pump."

Dale chuckled at the thought of riding a soldier's horse.

"I'm going to get in trouble riding this U.S. horse. It's got a brand on it. Well, if he could ride it, I can ride it. It's got a Confederate senior officer's saddle with a gold-edged saddle blanket. He had two stripes—a first lieutenant.

"I'm getting out of here. I'm going down a dirt road parallel to the one I came up. I go out of town to the north. I have to hold my black hat on. I stop and tie it on with the Yankee's string. My shoes don't work good in these stirrups. Maybe I should have took the officer's boots."

Nearing the end of his journey, Dale was relieved to be approaching home.

"I'm almost home. There's nobody coming up the road. No footprints. I check the barn. Horses are there—the four they left us. I had to give the others up to the government. There's Barney. He's coming across the field. He's a smart fellow. He heard somebody coming so he took the girls across the creek. There's a tobacco farm over there. It's an old dilapidated one we never rebuilt. We stopped growing tobacco and started growing corn. Everybody's OK. I haven't told them what's happened yet. I don't want to alarm them. I tell Barney. He's OK. The two poor cousins left two days ago saying they'd be back.

"The corn is cut. It's fall. Trees are starting to turn. The corn's in already. It's already taken with some people's help. The government took half of the food—in the garden, too. At least they only took half. They took one of the horses, too. Barney told the officer that came to get the horses that I was a colonel. He was taking a big chance. The man could have shot him. That makes five horses and six women.

"Barney says the neighbors left a wagon. If I borrow it, where would we go? You can't outrun the cavalry in a wagon. If they catch you on the road, they're liable to do anything. If they catch you in the house, they might give you a break.

"I'm surprised the Yanks in town didn't loot. Maybe because I was there. That's one of the best parts of town. They were awfully young. The guy did speak respectful to me. Smoke is rising up from the burning in Richmond, just the way it was.

"The girls are fine. Nobody's been out here. My wife's family have gone west. They left a couple of weeks ago. They are from Chesterfield—the other side of the river."

Now Dale began reminiscing and contemplating the changing times.

"My father died a long time ago. I don't miss him. He was a mean man. He let us run ragged to school while he had plenty of money, but drank it up. He did let us go to school, though. He owned a lot of land, but sold most off and gambled it away.

"This was part of the old homestead—all I was able to save. I cut a deed to it and got him to sign it when he was drunk. I got three of my friends to witness it and take it to court. They said it had to be surveyed. This is long before the war. He never found out. He piddled away what was not deeded to someone else. It was only sixty-five acres. He never noticed it. He had thousands of acres. It was a shame. The land he owned is just fallow. Nobody to work it since he used to work tobacco.

"My mother was a little woman. The girls take after her and are all small. My wife's not fat, mind you, but big boned. Her hair has gone white. She's a lot older than I picture her. She would still look lovely if she was to dress herself up. They are all in gingham work dresses now. The girls got their nails broke tending the place. They didn't have to do it before the war. That was the job of the blacks and their cousins.

"Barney don't like me to call him 'black.' He likes 'nigger.' He says if I call him black, I'll get myself in trouble with the white folks. He don't know where he'd go if he was to leave. He was one of my father's blacks. I remember him from when I was a boy. He got a lot bigger than me. He's big boned and bald. He plucks out his hair and says it doesn't hurt. Just to show me, he pulled out one of mine. Now he wouldn't touch me unless I asked him to. He'd do most anything I asked."

Dale chuckled about the hair-pulling episode, but then got more serious as he came back to the hard reality of war.

"Now that I know the family is OK, I reckon I'll ride over and see how the neighbor's house is. Barney will do what he did before, if anybody comes. It's about five miles north to the nearest neighbor. It's a big yellow house. Yellow's a harsh color. It's clapboard siding. You got no poles or posts in front of the house, like mine. A garret on one end makes it look unbalanced. There are lots of windows. It's just not my taste.

"There's nobody there. The wagon's there. They have three or four wagons. He's a drover and owns a building company. He hauls stuff and brings the wagons here to fix. He's got a shed in the back where he works with a couple of carpenters. He's got a hell of a blacksmith, too—Snider. Big fellow. Gone, too. Two of them are gone, so I reckon he's gone for the duration. He stole the tools. They weren't his to take. I don't believe in mistreating them, but a man who steals from his master ought to be shot. They know what the law is. He paid full fare and tax on all his niggers. I don't reckon the last few years he's been paying much, but the government doesn't bother with the taxes. They're hoping we stay here and feed the city.

"The neighbor's got a lot more land than I do. Once you come off my sixty-five acres, you're in the middle of his property. He's got ten miles in front. That's not half as big as my dad's place. My dad's place is almost twenty miles in frontage and about an equal amount deep. You can see the James River from there. He owned property in Ablemarle on the other side of the river, too. I don't know where because it was gone before I was grown."

From his neighbor's house, he viewed the smoke from Richmond.

"It looks like the smoke's slowing down," he continued. "It looked like it was burning along the river. If the wind was blowing toward the river, it would stop there. We're twenty-five miles away. The city is up on a hill, but it's too far to see. It doesn't look like it's burning on the hill. I'll ride to the south and see Dad's old place. The road that the cavalry was on runs through there. I'll ride by the house to let Barney know I'm going.

"I should hitch up one of those wagons. One wheel's got a couple of spokes gone. It's probably why he brought it back here, but we aren't going to be hauling loads anywhere. I'll leave a note. I've always got pencils in my coat. I write it on a $100 bill. He'll give it back to me if it's any good. He's a good man. 'I owe you one wagon. S.C.' I slip it under his door. The door's open. How come he did that? No one answers."

Still laughing about his creative notepaper, Dale entered the house to check it out.

"I hesitate to go into the master bedroom. That's the only door upstairs that's closed. I call him. There's no answer. I bang on the doors. I hate to go in a man's bedroom. It's nice. There's nobody here. I'll check the rest of the house. "I'll check the cellar. It's a dirt room underneath the kitchen. Empty. There was a time when it would be completely full—hams, apples. I lock the front door. The horse won't let me hitch up the wagon so I saddle him back up."

Leaving his neighbor's home, Dale returned home. I then asked him to move forward to the next important occurrence.

"Yankees are in my house," he said. "There's a young cavalry officer who wants to know where I got the horse. I told him. He believes me, but he wants to take all the horses. He's leaving one horse—a walking horse. It's not any good to him. His front feet are too short. I tell him I was an accountant and that I did the books for the firms. He wanted to see the books, and I told him they were in Richmond. He says Richmond has fallen. It's late '64 or early '65. It's fall. No, it's spring. I don't know if Richmond is garrisoned. He didn't tell me. He tells me I should plant. I asked him, 'Plant with what?' He said, 'Plant with your own hands.' I said, 'That's not what I'm worried about, sir. I need seed.' He's taken aback.

"He told Barney he had to leave. Barney told him he was a free man. He told him all blacks had to leave the property. Barney told him he wasn't a black; he was a nigger. Barney's a pretty smart fellow." Dale laughs. "The officer said, 'Contraband niggers have to leave the property.' Barney said, 'I'm not a nigger. I'm black. And my master always calls me black, much to my disdain.' The officer asked me if this was true. I said, 'Yes, I did it to anger him.' That poor officer. He didn't know how to take us. He said that if anybody else came, to give them the piece of paper he gave me saying what he had taken and that I could keep what else I had."

During the month that passed, Dale's home was again invaded.

"Another officer is coming with a whole troop of cavalry. Ha! He wants my walking horse. I'm not going to let him. He's going to shoot me. I tell him, 'Over my dead body.' He's got his gun out. No. He's taken everything. I don't have anything left. It's the principle. I got a paper that says he can't take it. He says he outranks the officer who gave me the paper. He's a captain, too. All of the troopers are cocking their rifles.

"Maybe I'd better give him the horse. At least I can care for the women that way." Now, Dale laughs. "He told the troopers he could take care of the situation. The sergeant told him, 'Sir, we're not aim-ing at him. You shoot him and we'll shoot you.' He said he didn't need the damned old horse anyway, and he rode off. The horse is going to die and has only eaten parched grass. I must have reminded the Irish sergeant of his father.

"Now I don't know what to do. I don't have any horses. I can't plow the garden with this old horse. It's been about a month since the Yankee soldier told me Richmond fell. He told me not to go back there, but I'm going to go back now." He laughs. "The only saddle I got is this Confederate officer's saddle. I have to go to Richmond. I don't reckon I can get a horse, but maybe I can get a mule or at least some food. We've been eating spring onions from the garden. We have some corn left. We've been eating corn bread and venison. The deer aren't doing too well. Nobody's planting. I used to see them in the gardens."

Once again leaving his wife and daughters in Barney's expert care, Dale returned to Richmond to see what he could find and to determine the damages.

"Richmond is about the same as when I left. There are a couple of shops open. Yankees are everywhere. Miss Custis is OK. She told them she was a widow woman and they left her alone. She said she owned both the houses there. It pays to be nice to people. My office is open and the door is broke. I'll unlock it and walk in anyway. 'Hodgkiss and Clarke.' Somebody's been through all the drawers in the desks. There wasn't anything to take except paper and that's all over the place. I go upstairs. There is a safe up there. They didn't find it. Nothing in it but Confederate money. Wonder if it's any good. I don't have gold. The gold is gone. I had gone to the government building to see if I could get some, but they didn't have any.

"The bodies are gone out of the park and there's not even a stain where the blood was. The park hasn't been taken care of and it's all grown up. The wooden benches are broken.

"I'm going down the street. The bakery's open. I can smell it. There're no troops here. They're up by the government buildings. Just a few bandaged stragglers wandering around. They must be wounded. They won't tell me anything about how the war goes. They say they don't know and wouldn't tell me if they did. They don't like the looks of me and seem unfriendly. Most of the townsfolk don't look as prosperous as me.

"I stop and get bread. The lady working is one of the owner's family. She started crying and tells me the owner went to Petersburg where three of her boys were killed. She's gone there to stay and mourn and try to find their bodies. "I get some bread and pecan pie. They don't have any berry pies like usual." He laughs. "I've got a whole basement of pecans. The Yankees love pecan pies. I've got pecan trees all over. They fall on the ground and I feed them to the pigs.

"I'll go up to the government house and see if I can get some money from the Yankees with the little I've got here. Our money is worthless. They gave me twenty dollars for my gold watch. Twenty dollars will buy seed. I told them I was going to buy seed. They told me if I go to the quartermaster, he'd give it to me if I'd plant it for the Yankees. I asked him where the quartermaster was and went off in that direction. I'm not going to plant for the Yankees. There's no seed to buy. They didn't tell me much other than that Richmond had fallen and they are pursuing the army. They said the army is retreating."

Discouraged about the lack of seed, Dale sighed at the devastating news.

"Petersburg is all torn up. Everything within three blocks of the river is burned—landings, the lower part of Richmond. Hospitals are full of Yankees. Dr. Johns is there in the Richmond Hospital. He says they carted off all the Confederate wounded to prison and most die. Everybody who could walk left with the army before the Yanks arrived.

"My carriage is still here but it's smashed up. Another Confederate killed the officer who took it. Guess he deserted. Dr. Johns says he doesn't mind taking care of Yankees because 'his oath says he has to help people. It doesn't matter what side they're on.' I wonder where his oath comes from since he's a dentist. Guess he's been around doctors too long. He says they overran Petersburg and there was little resistance in Richmond. The Federals burned Richmond. He says there's food in town now. He knows where there's seed in Petersburg. It's a long trip. My horse won't make it. I can use his horse."

Grateful for the use of the doctor's horse, Dale began his ride to Petersburg in search of seed.

"There's no seed in Petersburg. It's destroyed. The fighting must have been hellacious. There are craters everywhere. Petersburg Road has been blown away. People just marched around the craters. I'm riding on that. All the buildings are burned. I saw a horse running loose. I'll see if I can catch it. I can't catch it. It rode away. There's a half-burned farmhouse. It's a corn farm and it's got seed. There's enough here to seed sixty-five acres. How do I get it back?"

Dale's hands fidget as he tried to solve his latest problem.

"I feed some to my horse. I put out some water by the trough. The pump's broke. I go downhill, take a bag of seed, and snag a gray horse. I feed him and he walks right up to me. Now, I've got a horse, too. I take twelve whole bags. That's enough to seed the farm and feed the horses. I push a log on top of the rest in case I get to come back. It's awful far, though.

"People ask me where I got the corn. I say I got it from a family farm that's been burned. It's the truth. It was somebody's family. I take Dr. Johns back his horse and ask if I can borrow it to seed my farm. He trades me for the walking horse. He doesn't need to ride it. He lives in town."

Saved by his wits, Dale planted the corn and watched it grow as time passed and the war ended.

"The corn's two feet high. The war is over. It doesn't make a difference now. Nobody's bothering me. The war wasn't here. Now Richmond isn't the capital any more. No one cares. Johnson surrendered in Tennessee. Lee surrendered some time ago. The war was lost when Lee surrendered. We didn't get far.

"The two boys next door came back. They were paroled. They were with Lee's army. Judd was one of them. I don't know the younger one's name. Snell is the last name. It's German. I don't know how to spell it, but he's a big, blond-headed kid. There were too many of them that surrendered to be taken prisoner. They told them to go home and not fight any more. When Lee surrendered, they were paroled. They were Richmond Home Guard—home grown. They were at Petersburg and retreated from there. They didn't eat for over twelve days. I don't know where their parents are. The boys are welcome to stay with us. They are remaining to take care of their house.

"They were in the trenches in Petersburg. There was shelling all the time and they couldn't get any sleep. The older boy talks about it. The younger boy doesn't talk about it."

At this point, I asked Dale to ask Judd the name of his regiment. "He doesn't know, but it's Company I. He didn't get a piece of the flag that they cut up rather than give to the Yanks. "He said that they were eating tree bark. Yankees fed them at the surrender. They said the Yankee boys weren't that tough. A lot of them cried after the surrender. They weren't very big either, when you got up close. Judd said that they should have kept on fighting and had plenty of bullets but no food."

With Dale's post-war life having become more stable and his twentieth-century time approaching midnight, we finished the session. One of the most fascinating observations one could make of Dale's regression process was that he had been unable to make minor adjustments to the scenes according to my suggestions. Three other reenactors in the study had also been unable to alter what they saw or experienced, including asking a buddy the name of their unit. Sometimes the reenactors did not want to ask questions for fear that their buddies would think they were stupid.

Another reenactor, although he had been able to make slight changes, said he wasn't able to take my suggestion, for example, to go up a hill to take a look around, because going there was off limits. Regression subject Brian Pohanka (see chapter 15) was annoyed at even being asked his name. This was surprising since he was a historian by profession. Although he appeared extremely hesitant to go forward in the regression to find out what happened in one particular scene, he hadn't been able to change his order to engage in a battle in which he knew, historically, that there had been a lot of carnage. Meanwhile, Alan McBride had not been able to move away from a wall. It was later determined that he had been a prisoner of war, possibly assisting as a guard.

Past-life researchers disagree on the significance of a subject's ability to alter events during a regression. Psychic Joan Grant suggested that the inability to alter the script was a means of discriminating between fantasy and memory.[124] In contrast, Dr. Ian Stevenson suggested that plasticity in an apparent memory does not prove it to be a fantasy.[125]

The fact that one-third of the reenactors in the study could not "change the script" even in minor ways when it was suggested and that the others could make only minor changes, some even resisting those, runs counter to the theory that hypnotized subjects are merely responding in order to please the therapist, highlighting their degree of suggestibility or nonsuggestibility. The fact that the scripts were "set," whether the reenactors liked them or not—having an arm cut off, being a prisoner or being bored, hungry, or going into a battle that might mean their death—would tend to discount any comparison to dreams, which can be changed. The fact that each Civil War past life was so tailored to the individual made me question Dale's idea of genetic memory, the collective unconscious, or even race memory.

Yet, was Dale's past life as a partner in an accounting firm in Richmond the genetic memory of an ancestor? In the post-regression interview, Dale recalled that his relative, James Clarke, owned coal pits in Richmond during the Civil War, and Clarke's partner, Pitts, owned about 100 slaves. There are similarities to Dale's owning his own company in Richmond, and slaves as well, in his regression.

Nevertheless, Dale did not have prior knowledge of the layout of the town of Richmond in 1865 or any personal details about himself or his family. The historical chronology of Dale's past-life narrative was correct, from the death of his son at Seven Pines in 1862 or Cold Harbor in 1864 to the siege of Petersburg from June 1864 to April 1865; and from the burning of Richmond in April 1865 to the surrender at Appomattox just days later.

A small detail such as Dale's mention of pecan trees was confirmed by a Richmond librarian. Dale's surprise at finding string in a dead officer's pocket correlated with another regression subject's reference to the usefulness of string (see chapter 15).

Also of interest was Dale's account of his neighbors, the Snell brothers, who were in the Richmond Home Guard. Civil War historian Brian Pohanka says that there was a battalion of young boys and old men who defended Petersburg from 1864 through 1865 and who were in the Confederate march in early April 1865.

Researching the names Hodgkiss and Clarke proved difficult. Checking the 1860 Richmond census compiled by Eugene Feslow in 1961, I located an S. B. Clarke who worked as a clerk at Merchant's Insurance Co.; a Dane Hobson who clerked with Dane Hobson & James & George, Arlington House; while clerk D. M. Hopkins worked at R & H Maury & Co. No Hodgkiss was found.[126]

Meanwhile, possible historical matches for Dale's son John include John H. Clarke, Company D, 55th Virginia Infantry, who enlisted in July 1861 and was sick at home at the end of 1861. He was killed in action at Mechanicsville, Virginia, June 26, 1862.[127] Interment records for Oakwood Cemetery for Confederates near Richmond indicate that John Clark(e), Company A, Division G, 28th Virginia, and J. C. Clark, 53rd Virginia, were both buried there. Other Clarks or Clarkes from Virginia units who died around Richmond include Thomas F. Clarke, Company A, Virginia Infantry, who enlisted May 1862 and was present until killed in action at Mechanicsville, June 21, 1862.[128] Private Alfred M. Clark, Company B, 49th Virginia Infantry, formerly Company G, 2nd Virginia, died in Richmond Hospital June 10, 1862, and was buried in nearby Hollywood Cemetery.[129] Private George W. Clark, Company B, 37th Virginia Infantry, was wounded in Spotsylvania, Virginia, hospitalized May 17, 1864, died weeks later, and was buried at Hollywood Cemetery.[130]

As for Dale's neighbors, the Snell brothers, there are several close matches. According to Civil War historian Louis Manarin,[131] there were several specific Richmond Home Guard units. The Richmond Light Guard recorded a Private James A. Snell, the Hampden Artillery had a Private George T. Snellings, and D.A. Snellings was in Parker's Battery. All three companies fought at Petersburg and surrendered at Appomattox. Although Purcell's Battery was also part of the Richmond Home Guard and included a Private William Snellings, the battery was in trenches at Petersburg, but not paroled at Appomattox.

Both D.A. Snellings and R.I. Snellings were in Company G, Farinholt's 1st Virginia, in November 1864. Also, Company K, 1st Virginia State Local, which included a Private James A. Snell, consolidated with Farinholt. In the late war, Farinholt's Reserves fell under the Department of Richmond. During the Appomattox campaign, many were captured at Sayler's Creek.[132]

In addition, the National Archives military records show a variety of Snellings who enlisted in Company I of the 47th Virginia Infantry, in Fredericksburg on July 22, 1861. They include John Snelling, Walter J. Snellings, William F. Snellings, and Benjamin S. Snellings. Private E.L. Snelling and Private James W. Snelling were both enlisted in Company B. The 47th Virginia was active in Petersburg and a few surrendered at Appomattox.[133]

Whether Dale's past life that included his family and neighbors was genetic memory or not, he wove a fascinating story of living by his wits through necessity. His resourcefulness and good will pervaded his colorful episodes. The Dale of yesteryear had endured losing his son, his business, and his livelihood and managed to retain his humor. This is much the same way in which twentieth-century Dale has survived harpoonings and clubbings and can still live life with gusto and an easygoing disposition.

11

Ed:
Food for the Soul

Ed Embrey's mother and father shared an interesting connection. Each parent had ancestors who served in the Civil War in the 9th Virginia Cavalry. Amazingly enough, both had been wagon drivers, and both had survived the war. Ed laughingly said that, being wagoners, they stayed out of trouble in back of the lines of fire. His mother's relative, Simeon Chesterfield Paytes, served throughout the entire war, while youthful William Wallace Embrey enlisted in 1863.

Another of Ed's mother's relatives, John Thompson Brown, was wounded at Cedar Creek, captured, and sent to prison at Point Lookout, Maryland. While Ed's grandmother had believed that Brown had been in Mosby's Cavalry, Ed's research indicated that Brown had served in the 13th Virginia Infantry.

While growing up, Ed was aware that he had ancestors who fought in the Civil War, but until he did research after becoming a reenactor, he didn't know their names, units, or the side on which they fought.

His ancestors' Civil War involvement, however, did not influence Ed's decision to join reenacting, nor the side on which he chose to reenact. From the time he was five, while visiting his grandmother who lived on the outskirts of Virginia's Wilderness Battlefield, Ed would play Rebs and Yanks with his cousins. Because Ed lived in Northern Virginia and his cousins lived to the south, he was forced to play the Yank. He didn't like it much back then, so, when he joined the reenactors later, he chose the Confederate side.

Ed carried his interest in the Civil War into the classroom. At the age of about twelve, he was reading heavily about the war. In college, his interest once again emerged. He became a history major and focused on American and European history.

In 1980, Ed saw his first Civil War reenactment and decided to become involved. He approached a Confederate troop that was wearing brown "butternut," rather than gray uniforms, and asked how he could get involved. One of the men stuck out his hand and said, "You already are."

When Ed asked, the men told him several reasons why some Confederate uniforms were butternut color. One is that there was a large amount of iron and copper in the dye, and when the gray uniforms would "weather," the material would "rust." Another theory was that the brown color came from crushed walnut hulls that were ground up to make a tannish-to-brown dye.

Now that Ed had his own butternut uniform and had been a reenactor in that unit for thirteen years, he appreciated how members of his unit are striving for authenticity—settling for a blanket rather than tucking into a nice Coleman® sleeping bag and foregoing the cooler of beer.

These days, he also savored reading soldiers' anecdotal accounts. In fact, Ed, a pharmacy technician and father of three boys, sometimes got "second-hand déjà vu" feelings when he read diary accounts and then would have similar experiences while reenacting. During our pre-regression interview, he said he got the "willies" when he saw troops creating a "traffic jam" while squeamishly tiptoeing across a three-inch stream during the Battle of the Wilderness. The scene, which was not preplanned, brought to life for Ed the reality of a common experience of the common soldier.

On another occasion, in the midst of a thunderstorm, Ed and his companions were sleeping in a Sibley tent, which is somewhat like a tepee. During the night, the rain and wind blew off the tent's rain cover, doused the fire in the wood stove, and created some flooding inside the tent. After rearranging the bedding, Ed picked up a reenactor newsletter that contained the text of a nineteenth-century dispatch from a Yankee. In it, the soldier referred to a gale that blew most of the tents down, but his remained intact. The next morning, when Ed poked his head out of his tent, he saw that about seventy percent of the other tents had blown down and the men had gone into a barn to get out of the elements. Ed had experienced many such "coincidences."

His most dramatic experience occurred when he was one of thousands of reenactors during the 125th anniversary of Pickett's Charge at Gettysburg, Pennsylvania, in 1988. Just like the descriptions he'd read in books, he heard deep within himself the "rattle of musketry" and the sound of gunfire "like sheets ripping in the wind." His inner experience, however, went much deeper than that which he had read. These spontaneous personal experiences lent a rich tapestry of understanding that went far beyond the written word, somehow bridging the distant past with his "hobby."

With all of his reading and reenacting experiences, Ed, thirty-five years old at the time of the regression, realized that war was nasty business. He said that, at times, he felt it was justified, while at other times questionable. When war was used for political gain, Ed was anti-war. Since to him war was conflict and life was filled with conflict, Ed believed there would always be war and that we would have to learn to deal with it. He believed that history repeats itself and that we can choose to learn or not to learn from our mistakes.

In the same way that Ed questioned human nature, he also questioned why he was a Civil War reenactor. Like Dale Clarke, Ed preferred the scientific explanation for past-life recall: cellular or genetic memory. To illustrate, he told me that while once browsing through a Civil War Time-Life Book, he located a photograph of his Civil War-era relative, Simeon Paytes. Ed was surprised to find that Paytes's facial characteristics were similar to Ed's cousin Donny. Ed theorized that maybe the mind can pass down information to descendants just like genetics passes on physical characteristics.

With these thoughts in mind, we were ready to begin Ed's regression session. Before he arrived in the Civil War time frame, Ed explored segments of several other lifetimes. In one of those, he was a fifteen-year-old boy who was bedridden. The family got word that his father, who had been away fighting in Europe for three years during World War I, had been killed. As fascinating as that was, at an opportune point, I guided him backward in time to the Civil War era where I found Ed stargazing.

"It's black," he said. "I'm about twenty. I'm wearing leather boots. I'm lying on the grass, staring at the stars. There's lots of stars. They're not bright like they should be. There could be clouds. It's blurry, hazy. I'm wearing blue pants, a shirt, and a light brown jacket with sleeves that are too short.

"I'm still lying down, holding some reins. My horse is pulling me and bobbing his head, like a game. There's a clearing on one side of the road and woods everywhere. There's the moon. It's getting clearer.

"I'm a couple of days' distance from home. I'm looking for some men. I've got to give them some papers. Colonel Johnson gave them to me. There are staff on horses not too far down the road, but I can't find them. He said, 'Give these to the chief of staff right away.' I've been riding for a couple of hours. I don't think they're down that road. I'll double back and see if I can find where they went off the road. The moon went away again. I can't see down the road. I must have missed the turn."

After his break, he decided on his course to continue his mission. He was getting his name and identifying unit.

"My name is Bob Sanders. I'm in 1st Maryland. I'm the aide to the colonel. I've got to find them."

Doubling back, Ed continued his search for the staff.

"I think I found them, but I can't tell who they are. I'll just go slow. Oh, no, I don't think that's them. I got to get away. It's not the right group. I'm not sure if they saw me. Yep, here they come. I'm riding. They're shooting. I can't stay on the road. The woods are too thick. I can't find any place to get off the road. They just keep coming. There's six or seven. I've got to go."

At this point, Ed was getting very agitated. He was feeling trapped.

"God damn it! Shoot! They caught up and surrounded me. I got nowhere to go. They took the papers. We're walking back. I'm tired. I can't believe they got me. They're taking me back to their camp."

Ed twitched and sniffed as if he were crying, miserable at the thought of being captured. After a short period in the camp, he was sent on.

"They're putting me on the train with other soldiers, some in cattle cars. I feel upset. Stupid. I shouldn't have let them see me. The colonel's going to be pissed. I don't know what information they got. "The train's rattling along. We're going to prison. I don't know where. I don't know anybody. They're all strangers." He sniffed. "We're locked in here—we can't escape."

During the train ride, Ed thought of home and reminisced.

"I just ain't going home. I want to go home. Home is Frederick, Maryland. Ma is still there. It's gonna be a long ride. I've been away two years. I haven't gotten any letters from Ma. I can't read, and Ma can't write. I learned to sign my name. I used to help Ma around the house. It was a small house. I don't think I had a job. I don't know where we got money to buy food, but we always had enough. When I got paid, I used to send it home. Guess I can't send any now.

"The train's stopping in Pennsylvania. We're not getting off. They keep moving us. I don't know where we're going."

Ed was eventually transferred from the train to a prison where he observed the other prisoners and the situation.

"I'm sitting on some blankets in the barracks looking around. Some fellows are sleeping or talking; some are playing checkers. It's crowded. There's some room in the corner. Some fellows from over there died. They buried them. I don't know what happened. Someone will take it. I got my spot. They say the name of this place is Elmira. It's a Federal prison in New York.

"I'm hungry. I haven't eaten for a day or two. I had some crackers, and a carrot a girl threw from the wall. I caught it. The people on the wall are laughing at us. Damn it! It ain't funny. They are looking up over the top of the wall. These folks are pretty mean, watching us chase for food. Never mind the food. I just wish they'd stop laughing. I hate them! I'd never do that to them. Piss on them!

"I don't much care for the Federals. These guards ain't worth shit. They're acting so high and mighty. They're probably not real soldiers. They're mean to everybody. They laugh about our clothes and the way some of the boys talk. They're ornery.

"I just talk to fellows and dream about food. We have crackers and bad meat sometimes. Sometimes just rice. Quite a few are dy-

ing. Yah, I ain't sick like them. I'm just hungry."
   Ed went from hungry to not being able to keep anything down.
"It hurts. My gut. I can't eat. It don't stay down. I don't know what it
is. I don't see a doctor."
   Ed was now crying. He seemed to be in pain and frightened.
"I'm in the hospital. Nobody comes out of here. What did they
put me in here for? I wish the pain would just go away. It hurts."
   When Ed began to cry harder, I told him that he could rise above
the scene and observe. He appeared relieved.
   "Fellows are lying there. Most of them are dead. I guess this is it. I
don't feel anything. I'm lying there looking up at the ceiling and wait-
ing for them to come and get me. They haven't come yet. I feel tired
and lonely. I don't think I'll know when they come for me."
   Ed sighed a big sigh. He continued.
   "I feel weak. I want to go to sleep. It's just dark."
   Since these images are typical of death scenes, I suggested that
Ed rise up and look down at his body. There was no response. After
Ed surfaced from the regression, he told me that the colors he had
seen during his death-memory experience had changed from light
to dark. He claimed that he never remembered experiencing such
darkness before and said it felt like being in a void—like being at the
beginning of something. His memory of the death process was
reminiscent of a recurring "dream" in which Ed would float out of
his body and look down at it. He'd had the same kind of floating
sensation at his death, except that it was dark and he didn't see anything.
   Ed's prison existence had been dismal, and he died a bleak death.
He'd had to scramble for a carrot and dreamt of food. Being hungry
was one of the common threads running through the lifetimes of
the other reenactors. As soldiers, they were often hungry, thirsty,
tired, and their feet hurt.
   In fact, ninety percent of the soldiers in the study said that they
were hungry or thirsty, ninety percent said they didn't know where
they were going, and eighty percent said they were tired. Seven of
eight who were marching complained of their feet hurting. Only
one, who had been an officer, never complained. In addition, soldiers and even the officers were never informed of their destinations.
   The physical deprivation of the reenactors indicates the recalled

lifetimes were not very attractive. In addition, only one of the ten soldiers wasn't wounded, only four lived, six died, and three were prisoners.

These experiences are similar to regressions of Dr. Edith Fiore's clients.[134] Her patients and subjects most often encounter lives that are dreary and totally lacking in glamour. Dr. Raymond Moody's work and research concurs that most past lives are mundane.[135]

War can be tedious and terrorizing. Even so, Ed had also recalled a life in which his father died in World War I. Other reenactors had other lives in other wars. Paul Jones recalled being a youngster in 1941 and being excited at seeing a battleship docked in the harbor (see chapter 14). Tom Galleher's Civil War regression started out with the Mexican War (see chapter 12). In David Morse's first regression, he was wearing a bearskin cap and walking toward a fort in Albany with some "Red Coats" who were wearing white pants and black hats (see chapter 13).

One possible reason for their recall of other wars is that I suggested they "go to a lifetime that gave them insight into their current reenactment interests." The Civil War was not specified, so as not to influence them.

Nine of these reenactors have interests in other wars, weapons, and historical periods. A few are also reenactors in other wars. Their interests range from the Napoleonic period to the Zulu wars and from gladiators to the Three Musketeers. Others are engrossed in the French-Indian War, the British Civil War, the two World Wars, and Vietnam.

One of Edgar Cayce's psychic readings told of a seventeen year old who had a love of firearms. The readings saw the boy as a navigator in the English navy in a previous life. In another life he was second in command of the Bedouins who fought the invading Grecian forces (circa 900 B.C.).[136]

Although Ed had not served in the military, four of twelve reenactors had served in the military and one worked for the Department of Defense. The one woman in the study, MaryLynne Bauer, had considered a career as a pilot in the air force.

The twelve adults in my study who made a hobby of "playing war" had a variety of views on war. One was a pacifist and one felt comfortable with war. Other convictions ranged from war being a necessary evil to being disastrous. Some were resigned that there would always be wars or that wars were really an expansion of politics. Two acknowledged that there were some good and some bad wars.

Ed, who was resigned to the inevitability of war, said he had never heard nor seen any descriptions of Elmira Prison, didn't know when it opened, or that it was strictly for transfer prisoners.

Before getting on the train to Elmira, he recalled feeling that he wanted to go back to Point Lookout Prison in Maryland. Perhaps he had first been placed at Point Lookout, but, because he felt confused, he didn't mention this in his regression. Elmira opened later in the war and took only transfer prisoners, mostly from Point Lookout.

After the regression, Ed went to Fredericksburg, Virginia, looking for a book on prisons. Not having any luck, he picked up a book entitled *The Photographic History of the Civil War.*[137] The book fell open to an explanation of Elmira Prison. During the regression, Ed had been confused as to how people could have looked down on the prisoners over a twelve-foot wall, but the book showed the picture of a walkway on the outside of the prison wall. Soldiers charged civilians ten cents to climb up and see the prisoners. In addition, historian Brian Pohanka said that it was common for Civil War prisoners to die of intestinal problems. Nearly 45,000 Union soldiers alone died of diarrhea and dysentery. There were twice as many deaths from disease as from hostile bullets.[138]

About a year after his regression, Ed acted as a Union prisoner in the movie *Andersonville.* While there, he toured the Visitor's Center. He was touched by a large drawing made by a prisoner. Around the borders were vignettes of various ways to die at Andersonville Prison. There were illustrations of soldiers with dysentery, diarrhea, and nausea. When Ed saw this, he described feeling "kicked in the pants." His emotions had registered a major response to the death scenes in the vignettes, forcing Ed's mind back to how in his regression he had recalled dying.

Interestingly, as a reenactor, Ed always felt that he saw Pickett's Charge looking through the Union line at Gettysburg. This puzzled him because he reenacts as a Confederate. Even though he didn't recall Pickett's Charge during his regression, his research following the regression indicated that the "Maryland line" was engaged at Culp's Hill, which would have given him a view through the "J-shaped" Union line. First Maryland, a Confederate unit, would have looked over the Union line from the Confederate west. Ed felt that his past life as a soldier in lst Maryland could explain why he had always visualized the battle from the Union perspective, while fighting for the South. Was it possible that Ed's past-life personality could have been present at Gettysburg before his capture?

Coincidentally, about twelve months after his regression, Ed, whose first name is William, was shaken when he stumbled across an account of a Mosby Ranger with his exact name who had been killed during an ambush in Newtown, Virginia, in May 1864.[139] Ed was additionally amazed that the cavalryman had transferred from the 8th Virginia Infantry, his reenacting unit, prior to the incident.[140]

Previously, Ed had mentally twitched each time he replayed his regression scenario of figures on horseback gaining on him, evoking feelings of being trapped. For him, it was now almost too close for comfort that a cavalryman named William E. Embrey may have experienced similar feelings of desperation upon finding himself surrounded by the enemy.

I felt that my research into the name Saunders yielded some strong possible identities for Ed's past-life persona. There were two Saunderses who were captured and died of diarrhea in Elmira Prison. William R. Saunders, 44th Virginia, from Louisa County, was captured at Spotsylvania on May 12, 1864. Five days later, he was sent to Point Lookout. In less than three months, William was transferred to Elmira. He died of chronic diarrhea the following January and was buried in Woodlawn National Cemetery in Elmira, New York. Saunders, whose middle name could have been Robert, could have lived in Frederick County or Fredericksburg, Virginia, and was sent to Maryland to prison.[141] Perhaps that's why Ed remembered Maryland as a unit.

Vincent H. Saunders, Company K, 50th Virginia, was captured at Wilderness, taken to Point Lookout, and transferred to Elmira Prison where he died October 1864 of diarrhea.[142]

According to the National Archives prison list, T.C. Saunders, Company G, 15th South Carolina Cavalry, also died in Elmira Prison in mid-February 1865.

In addition, National Archives military records mention two R. Sanderses who were in the cavalry: R. Sanders in Company F, Wade's 8th Cavalry, and Major R. W. Sanders in Taylor's Cavalry.

As I mentally assembled all of Ed's Civil War connections, I flashed back to the stories of his relatives in the cavalry and the one who had been captured and sent to Point Lookout. I pondered whether we weren't coming full circle and whether there hadn't been something to Ed's theory of genetic memory. But clearly, both Ed and I were touched by his past-life remembrance of a dismal prison life, one lacking in not only pomp and circumstance, but dignity. Long after his Civil War regression took place, Ed would still mentally twitch at the thought of being captured. Whatever the explanation for Ed's recalled life, his humiliation at being caught, his anger at how he was treated as a prisoner, and his painful death now seemed to be seared into his twentieth-century emotional makeup.

A Connection to the Past

Left: David Purschwitz is a Civil War reenactor whose past-life regression narrative is recounted in chapter 6. His narrative revealed many details about a life he lived during the Civil War.

Above: Purschwitz's past-life regression revealed that he had lived as his own great-grandfather, James McNally, shown here in civilian clothes in 1862 at age twenty-one. He served in the 8th U.S. Infantry and later in the 5th New York Heavy Artillery.

Above: The only other available photo shows James McNally as he appeared in 1911 at the age of sixty-nine. When he was a prisoner of war, McNally's left arm had been amputated, and Purschwitz's memory of that event was revealed during the session.

1

Past-Life Regression Subjects in Reenactors' Uniforms

Left: (Captain) David H. Morse, commanding officer of Company F, 8th Virginia Infantry reenactor's group. He is shown here wearing a dress frock coat with gauntlets and foraging cap (see chapter 13).

PHOTO BY DAVE BARTLEY.

PHOTO BY CLAUDE LEVET.

Right: Brian Pohanka portrayed Union general Alexander S. Webb in the Turner Entertainment motion picture *Gettysburg*. He is shown in the general's uniform wearing a sack coat and slouch hat with officer's hat cord and the trefoil insignia of the 2nd Corps (see chapter 15).

Reenactors on the Set of the Motion Picture *Gettysburg*

A photo taken during the filming of *Gettysburg* depicts three of the author's past-life regression subjects with the Fauquier Artillery Battery at Gettysburg, Pennsylvania. *1st from left:* Captain David H. Morse (see chapter 13); *2nd from left:* Private Dallas Bare (see chapter 8); *5th from left:* Private William Embrey (see chapter 11).

PHOTO BY DAVID MORSE.

Civil War-Era Fashion Experts

Left: MaryLynne Bauer, a living historian and historical costume consultant, makes her own Civil War-era ensembles. She takes care never to be seen in public without her bonnet and gloves. MaryLynne feels comfortable in hoop skirts and has climbed over rocks in them (see chapter 9).

Right: Robert Lee Hodge was the only kid wearing a Confederate kepi in his first grade class picture. Since then, he has made an avocation of perfecting his Civil War look. Attired as a junior Confederate officer, Rob wears a jean shell jacket and jean cloth trousers (see chapter 7).

Colorful Zouaves

Just as the French Zouave units caught the American imagination in the mid-nineteeth century, the uniforms continue to entice both Yank and Reb Civil War reenactors. Although uniform colors vary, the 5th New York wears blue jackets with red trim, red trousers, and fez.

PHOTO BY BARBARA LANE.

PHOTO BY BARBARA LANE.

Left: With fixed bayonet and turban, Corporal Stephen Melko, 5th New York, is ready for anything. In his past-life session, he also recalled being a Union noncommissioned officer (see chapter 4).

Above: A relative newcomer to reenacting, Alan McBride, Company A, 5th New York Volunteer Infantry, takes his appearance and his drill seriously. In his past life, he recalled being among a disheveled group of Federal prisoners (see chapter 5).

PHOTO BY BARBARA LANE.

Right: A captain in the 5th New York, Brian Pohanka leads his company on parade through the streets of historic Alexandria. During his past-life sessions, he recalled climbing the ranks to become an officer for a New York regiment (see chapter 15).

Regression Subjects Reenact for the North and the South

Left: Paul Jones, seen in his 1st Delaware Volunteer Infantry regimental uniform, owns about fifteen uniforms. The first-generation Virginian has also reenacted as a Southerner (see chapter 14).

Right: Born into a military family, Thomas Galleher, Jr., currently reenacts on both sides. His mid-war impression includes a dark gray wool Richmond depot shell jacket, light brown civilian trousers, and an 1842 Springfield musket (see chapter 12).

Reenactors and Family Involvement

Left: Photo of Dave Morse and his wife, Jane, who sews Dave's uniforms and her own ballgowns. She says reenactors' obsession with the Civil War puts stress on some marriages (see chapter 13).

Right: By the time Dale Clarke's son Ian was eight years old, he had survived 125-degree heat at the 125th anniversary of Gettysburg (pictured here) and 20 degrees below zero at a reenactment at Fort Fisher, North Carolina. The hardships discouraged Ian from continued involvement in "the hobby." Interestingly, in Dale's regression, his then young son was killed in the Civil War (see chapter 10).

From the National Archives

Though inconclusive, evidence of the subjects' past lives, revealed by the author's search, led to these and other documents that are convincing testimony to the facts revealed in the narratives.

Left: The past-life regression narrative of Civil War reenactor Alan McBride led the author to this declaration of pension for illness sustained to Edward White of the 13th Pennsylvania Cavalry while in Salisbury Prison (see chapter 5).

Right: This casualty sheet, dated September 17, 1862, ties into details revealed in the past-life regression of Stephen Melko, who recalls in detail his death at a battle that matches historical descriptions of the Battle of Sharpsburg (Antietam), Maryland (see chapter 4).

12

Tom:
An Officer and a Gentleman

Both Thomas Galleher and his wife Jennifer grew up with fathers who had been infantry colonels. Being in military families, they both enjoyed the regimental traditions, military structure, and hearing war stories. As a youngster, Tom heard about General "Black Jack" Pershing being best man at his grandfather's wedding. His grandfather had commanded the 24th Infantry in the 1920s when the division was all black and the officers were all white.

Tom's and Jennifer's families traveled extensively and lived in a variety of states and countries. When Tom's father was stationed in Europe, Tom was sent to a private high school in Switzerland. There, he was mesmerized with history as it had been taught to him by a fascinating teacher. For several weeks the class gathered around huge maps of the battlesite of Waterloo and followed the hour-by-hour troop movements. After interacting on such an intimate basis with the 1815 Belgian battle which was the scene of Emperor Napoleon

Bonaparte's final defeat, the impressionable teenager became addicted to military strategy and history, particularly the Napoleonic period.

Since childhood, Tom considered himself a history buff. With no brothers or sisters, he happily occupied himself reading history books, drawing war cartoons, and playing war with other children on base. Through the years, Tom, forty-three at the time of my study, had read everything in English that he could find on the Napoleonic armies. He even took French classes so that he could read the books that hadn't yet been translated into English. He once offered to pay a French teacher to translate them for him.

Taking second place to Napoleon was Tom's interest in the Victorian period, World War I, and the Civil War. Besides Civil War reenacting, which he had done for more than seven years, he read extensively on military strategy and collected war movies, board games, and miniatures.

Tom's love of history led him in the direction of becoming a history teacher, but after over two years of college and too much partying, he dropped out of school and got married soon after.

Even though he loved military structure and strategy, he protested the Vietnam War and recalled marching on Washington, D.C., wearing a black armband and chanting, "Hell, no, we won't go."

Tom said that he was not anti-war, but did not agree with U.S. politics involving Southeast Asia. He did, however, agree in principle with Desert Storm and considered volunteering even though he was about forty years old and married.

At the time of our pre-regression interview, after nearly twenty-three years as a civilian working for the army, Tom was in charge of Total Quality Management coordination and instruction. Just to get to work, he drove 100 miles round trip each day, but much of the rest of the 35,000 miles he put on his car each year was spent going to reenactments.

After bargaining with Jennifer to spend a weekend away from home, he would leave her with their cats and dogs, which have numbered as high as eighteen. He would pack, trim and wax his moustache, roll his own cigarettes, and then begin his drive to a reenactment or living history event. Because these affairs were often out of his state of Virginia, Tom would think of his driving time like being in a time capsule, helping him make the transition back to the 1860s. He would play the soundtrack from the film *Glory* or some nineteenth-century Irish songs, and his mind-set would slowly move back 130 years. After reenactments, he would use the drive home to review the events, critique himself, and break the Civil War spell, while slowly stepping back into the twentieth century. But the transition into the 1990s wasn't always easy for Tom, who jokingly said, "I was born 150 years too late."

Drawn to the romantic, chivalrous, agrarian image of the Civil War South, Tom couldn't fathom dressing as a Federal for the first five years of his reenacting experience. Although he grew up in California and considered himself neutral in relationship to the Civil War, he found the Confederate uniforms "spiffy" and Jennifer adored each of the nine swirling ballgowns she'd made for the historical, candlelit cotillions that the pair attended. But during the last few years, aside from his Virginian unit forming up with other units to re-create the Stonewall Brigade, Tom had ventured for the first time into a Union Iron Brigade uniform.

Tom and his family had done some impressive genealogical research into the time of the Civil War. An Irish horse-thieving relative of Tom's settled in New Orleans and made a fortune in slaves and liquor. Too old to wear a Civil War uniform, he put his wealth into the Confederate cause while his son became the city's third Episcopalian bishop. About a year after his regression, Tom's family found that this ancestral bishop, John Nicholas Galleher, had been baptized by Bishop General Polk and later became adjutant general to Confederate General Simon Buckner. After the war, the bishop became sheriff of Memphis, and, near the end of his life, he gave the last rites to Confederate President Jefferson Davis. Meanwhile, Jennifer's great-great-grandfather had worked for the War Department throughout the Civil War, and the couple still had his retirement gift—a lithograph of President Lincoln, which hung in their home.

Turning to other topics in our interview, Tom shared his excitement about having portrayed a 1st Sergeant, his normal rank, in the motion picture *Gettysburg*. Like the other reenactors, he was conscious of interpreting his role as accurately as possible, as the group, collectively, pressed the film's director for the same level of historical authenticity throughout the filming.

Regarding his philosophical views, Tom admitted that he trusted in God and in an afterlife and expressed high hopes that he would recall a Civil War past life during the regression. While reenacting, he had often wondered if he would have had the guts to fight in a real battle.

Tom was now prepared to find out. On a wintery afternoon, he came dressed in his English kersey wool uniform and accoutrements and armed with hand-rolled cigarettes. After relaxation and visualization exercises, he slipped into a hypnotic state.

"I'm barefoot and wearing dark blue, scratchy trousers," he started. "I'm very hot. I'm wearing a white shirt and something on my shoulder that looks like a strap for a canteen. My hat is black, beat up, and sweaty. The other men are laughing at me. Everybody's dressed different. They say I don't have any shoes. I haven't gotten mine yet. I don't like them laughing at me. I'm the new man. I've just been here a couple of days. I don't know anybody. I wanna go home. I'm not sure where I'm at. It's a big field with some houses and barns.

"Other people farther away are dressed brighter and more colorful. They look like everybody else. They're watching us. The men have their backs to them and they're looking at me. We're soldiers in the army. I'm younger than the rest. I'm twenty, and it's about 1840. I'd have to look at a newspaper to tell.

"It's time to eat. They're telling me to come eat. My last meal was last night. We had chicken. It was pretty good, but not much of it. I was still hungry. I don't have a cup. When it gets to be my turn, I can ask the man by the fire to borrow one.

"I'm moving up in line but there are 100 men in front of me. Everybody's talking and laughing and joking about how the food's not very good, how it's not very much. They say the men at the back—where I am—may not get any. It smells bad and I don't know if I want any. It looks like a big soup. I am hungry, so I'll probably eat. Maybe I'll just hold my breath. That way, I won't taste it. Maybe I'll just drink it real quick.

"There's a man up front, not in line, asking me where my cup is. He's giving me one and tells me to keep it. It's dirty and greasy. I think somebody else already ate out of it. They are making us sit together in groups on the ground. The ground is wet and cold. I wish I had my blanket but must have left it back at camp. It's about an hour's walk. I found my shoes. They were right where we're sitting. I must have taken them off. Somebody could have stolen them. They're too tight. My feet hurt and that's why I took them off.

"I have a friend. His name is Nathan. He's also twenty. We came into the service together. I can't remember where we're from. I think it's in the South and east of where we are now. I could ask Nathan. He's talking to somebody about girls. Do I want to interrupt? 'Nathan, where are we from?' I don't think it's stupid. He says 'Louisiana.'

"My father is real strict. I always have to say, 'Yes, sir, and no, sir,' and wait to be spoken to. I don't think he's stricter than most fathers. Nathan's father is just as strict. That's why we wanted to go in the army. The parents were all very angry. I think we made a mistake. They are worse here than at home. We wanted to see a Mexican. I told Nathan if we went in the army, we'd get a fancy uniform and get to see Mexico.

"We're not in Mexico. That's a desert. This is a big green field. It's an army camp. Now that we've finished eating, we're supposed to go back to camp. It's about an hour away. Everybody's really tired because we were marching."

Seizing the opportunity, I asked Tom to consult his friend Nathan about the year.

"'Nathan, what year is it?' '1840 or 1846.' It's been so long ago since we were home. It's been months and months.

"At home, I have a father, mother, and a dog. He's brown, he's got long hair and he's really old. I got him when I was a boy. He's my buddy. I miss him. We live on a farm in 'Mary-land.' 'Mary-land' is right near Virginia. I don't live in Louisiana. That's where they sent us. There's rumors that we are going to leave Louisiana pretty soon. We're going to get on a ship and head south as soon as the general shows up.

"Nathan calls me John. My real name is Jonathan. Isn't that funny, I can't think of my last name. It begins with a C—A-T-E-S. That's my name. 'Jonathan Cates.'

"My feet have been blistering and I don't have any socks. Nathan told me I could take someone else's stockings off the line after they were washed. I don't want to get in trouble, but my feet hurt. Every time I tell somebody something, they tell me I either lost it or broke it. They make you pay for it. Nathan has given me good advice. I don't have any money."

Now Tom's demeanor changed. He became more serious and spoke in hushed tones.

"Everybody's standing at attention. The officer is reading something. You have to be very quiet or you'll get in trouble. He's talking about General Scott coming to visit us. He doesn't know me, but everybody knows the general. He's very famous for fighting the Indians in Florida. He wrote a book. Everybody has to drill or march by his methods. When he gets here, we're going to Mexico. I'll believe it when I see it. That's why we've been here for so long. We have to clean up our equipment and be ready to strike the tents and our camp at a moment's notice.

"There's a flag of our country. We're the militia and so is the officer. I don't know him very well, but I think his name is John Stewart. He's new. He's not from our village, Upper Maryland—Springs, right next to Pennsylvania. It's north, right near the National Road. We're called 'The Rifles.'"

Tom coughed. "I'm real thirsty from that long march. All we do is walk around. So much dust. My canteen leaks. I drink out of Nathan's. 'Nathan, what's our company?' He says the 'Frederick Rifles.' Frederick is a town south of the Springs."   After resting up from the march, Tom's unit awaited the general's visit which came all too quickly. I suspected that Tom could shortly become involved in the Mexican War, which predated the Civil War.

"The general comes. That means we're going to go to war. Mexico. I'm scared. Nathan and I never shot anything more than a rabbit or deer. Everybody's going. That's why we came down here. We're going to teach them a lesson. The paper said the Mexicans wouldn't talk with our government. You know how those politicians are. They want to make California part of our country. Mexico won't let us. They even gave them money. It didn't make any difference. The country's got to grow.

"Everybody's running around packing up. They say we're going to march tomorrow morning. We are all getting on a boat. I'm excited. Nathan feels the same way. As long as we can be together. There wasn't nothing to do in Maryland except be a farmer or a merchant. I did that my whole life, and I didn't want to do it any more. I'm looking forward to this adventure. If you trust in God and have a good friend, you'll be all right.

"I've never been on a boat before. If you can see land and the wind ain't blowing hard, it'll probably be all right. When we sail away, I bet plenty of the boys get sick."

Tom's prediction was accurate.

"We're on the ship. Everybody's sick. It's everywhere. There's no place to stand. There's more men than I can imagine. God, I hope we don't sink. I can't swim. Everybody just stands and sits. The boat rocks back and forth. I want to go back to Louisiana. I wasn't sick there. "We're going to Mexico to invade. We're not a very big army. As long as the general is leading us, there's nothing to worry about. Everybody's worried about doing their part; not being a coward. It's strange. You could be far away from home in Mexico and do something wrong. Your family could be all the way in Maryland, and they could pay the price for your mistake because I'm my father's son. I wish we'd hurry up and fight."

Tom got his wish and quickly moved into his first battle in Mexico. "It's glorious. We're winning. Mexicans don't fight good. They don't shoot well. It's just like they told us. 'Take your time, pay attention, listen to the orders.' Everybody's doing what they're told. A few men get hurt. In minutes, they run away. Everybody was afraid, but they're afraid of us."

Tom laughed, and then continued with an air of newfound confidence and relief after completing his first battle.

"That noise is really strange. When someone shoots at you, it sounds like an angry bee. You can tell if it's way up high or way down low by how loud it is. When the cannon balls come bouncing along, it's easy to get out of their way. Everybody's being very deliberate and slow. It's nothing like I imagined.

"We won. It was just a pass, way up in the mountains. We had to get through it to get to Mexico City. If they fight, there will be a battle there. I can't believe they would just give us California. If we get to Mexico City and win the war, Nathan says we'll be heroes. We'll probably be pretty good with the ladies, don't you think? But not if they saw us."

Back on the march, soldiering no longer seemed so glamorous.

"My shoes fell apart and I can't get another pair until we get to Mexico City. You take a piece of leather and tie it on your foot. It comes apart, but you just tie it on again. You just don't want to run. Nathan and I'll go back where the artillery's leather saddles and bridles are and cut a big piece of leather when nobody's looking. The ground is hot and full of sharp pebbles. It's easy to cut your feet. I thought we'd marched a lot in Louisiana, but it's nothing like here.

"We landed at Vera Cruz. It's a famous town. We took it away from them. I thought the war was going to end. The general said we had to go to Mexico City and dictate terms. We keep waiting. I think the men would go anywhere.

"I saw the general. He's very handsome and sits on a white horse. He's got gold all over his uniform and it's not ripped and torn. He wears a big plume. He knows what he's doing.

"You can't hit nothing with our muskets far away. The general takes us real close and, when we get fifty feet away, gives the order to shoot. Hell, you can't miss. They run. It's worked so far. That's why we keep winning. When we come on the field and those Mexican boys start shooting, hardly anybody gets hurt. When you get close to their cannons, men get killed."

Just as Tom was getting the hang of fighting, he contracted an illness and never reached Mexico City. Instead, he was sent back to Louisiana by boat.

"Many of us got a horrible sickness. Your belly swells up and you get real thirsty. You can't keep nothing down. I haven't seen Nathan in a couple of weeks. They sent me back with others. I was really angry. I didn't want to leave Nathan. We had come so far and I wanted to see Mexico City. I don't know if I'll ever go back. We couldn't stay in Vera Cruz because we'd get sick there, too. We're going back to Louisiana. Getting out of that heat, dust, and flies, and fresh air will do us good.

"Everybody's going to get sick on the boat. I don't know why I'm laughing. I was right last time, and I got so sick. Now I don't feel good, and I'm going to get even sicker. But they're right about the fresh air. As long as the wind doesn't blow, I'll be all right if it's smooth sailing. I've done it before. The sailor boys say every time it gets easier. I'm hoping.

"I only got a little sick. Maybe I'll join the navy. They don't have to march and the sailors say the navy issues rum or grog. It didn't taste good, but made me forget being sick."

Tom is sent back to Louisiana to recuperate. Now, he seemed to be enjoying it more the second time around.

"I feel much better now that I'm back in Louisiana. It's nice to be able to talk to people. When we were in Mexico, I don't speak no Spanish, and they don't speak American. Now, it's fun to be back. Will I be a hero when I go back to Maryland? The surgeon says we're going home in a couple of weeks.

"They gave us our discharge papers. We can go wherever we

want. I'll wait for Nathan. They don't know when they'll be back. We have to wait a couple of days for the next boat. I'll need to get some work in the meantime.

"I can work a plow, but they got the darkies to do that. I'll probably look around in town. Maybe I can find a job reading or writing. I can teach youngsters. I'm not real good, but I'm better than most. If a man's enterprising and willing to sweat, he can do anything. Of course, having money doesn't hurt. They gave us our army money. It wasn't much, but I bought shoes, a walking stick, a new shirt, and a real fine hat."

His youthful optimism was dashed when Tom found out the bad news about his buddy Nathan.

"Nathan and a bunch of boys were killed storming a gate in Mexico City. That damned Mexican artillery! I don't want to go to Maryland and face everybody's families."

Determined not to go home, Tom searched the New Orleans area. With his diligence, he soon landed a job.

"Well, I talked to a fellow down by the docks who's hiring able-bodied men who didn't get sick. I figured after three times I could handle it. So, I'm thinking about sailing. When we were young, they told us pirate stories. The boat is going to go to the British Islands off Florida. From there, you could get to Europe. I can't believe my best friend is gone and I wasn't there. I don't want to stay here."

After being hired as a crew member, Tom embarked on another adventure.

"We're on the ocean. It's pretty good pay and the shipmaster is a good fellow. After the army, this isn't bad. I'm in the cabins below and sleep and eat with the crew. We sailed up the coast to Charleston. I never went to Charleston before. It's a big, busy port, hot and expensive. They talk slow and are hard to understand. When the ship comes into the port, you see beautiful homes. They must have a lot of rich people.

"From Charleston, we cross the ocean to Liverpool, England. We're taking huge bales of cotton. It takes several men and a lot of work to load them. The whole aft of the ship is full. We get wages plus a percentage, if the ship arrives safely. The English don't grow cotton any more, but get it from Egypt and India. I'd like to go to India."

Tom enjoyed his new trade and lifestyle, until an accident changed his direction once again.

"I fell from the riggings during rough weather. It's my left leg. There's no surgeon on the boat, just a fellow that has some knowledge. They say I may never be able to walk on it. It broke in several places and it hurts. They give you laudanum. It makes the hurt go away for a while. If it's going to hurt that bad, I don't want to keep it. They tried to set it. I don't think it's working. We get to England soon enough. Doctors there can treat me. Oh, God, it hurts."

With his excruciating leg pain, Tom had new reason to get to port. Meanwhile, I was thinking that with Tom's badly damaged leg and his relocation to England, he would never be able to participate in the Civil War.

"I'm in England," he continued. "The doctor had to rebreak my leg and reset my bones. My leg looks funny. It's bent. I limp. Nobody wants to look like a beggar on the streets. You can always tell the men who went to war. They sit without their legs and arms, depending on generosity. That's not what I want to do.

"The ship's gone. The master paid me off. The crew took up a collection. The captain paid for the doctor bills. I don't know what I'm going to do. I don't talk like them. I thought they talked funny in the South. They're so uppity here. I can't afford passage back to the States. Unless somebody will hire me, I have to stay. At least they have the same Protestant religion."

After spending some time in England doing odd jobs and tutoring, Tom saved his money and booked passage back to America. During his stay, he changed his opinion about the British.

"They weren't so uppity. They were pretty nice. I had to come back because there's a great Civil War going on. The Rebels fired on Fort Sumter. That means we're going to fight for sure. President Lincoln has called for volunteers to put down the rebellion. I'm going to volunteer. I still walk with a limp, but I can ride a horse. They are going to need somebody who knows what it's like in the army. I have experience.

"I didn't go back to Maryland—too many memories. I moved into Pennsylvania and enlisted with the 71st Pennsylvania. I command a company. I'm a captain. We're joking about how they must be desperate to hire some older, crippled men to show them how it's done. I feel old, like I'm in my late forties or early fifties.

"Some boys can't even shave. They're so young, I feel like a father. I have to watch out for them. I remember Nathan and Louisiana. We were so green. Experience makes a difference."

After his reenlistment, I suggested that Tom move forward to his first major battle.

"Oh, God, it's horrible. It's just like Mexico. People are dead. There's blood everywhere. You can smell it. Everybody's scared. I'm real scared, but I'm more scared for my boys.

"We're in Pennsylvania again. They marched us all the way up here. General Lee brought his army of Rebels across the Potomac. We had to follow. We've been marching for hours. It's hot. The boys are really tired. They keep telling us we can't stop. Here comes this crossroad. We're sitting on a hill that's not very big. It's the second day. They were fighting yesterday.

"I don't know the name of the town, but I can ask. It's 'Gettysburg.' I never heard of it before. They address me, 'Sir.' The sergeant addresses me by my Christian name. I don't mind.

"You could smell death while we were marching in. Death. Blood. Horses. Sweat. You think you're going to get used to it, but you don't. We marched in right past some of the hospitals. I told them to keep their eyes forward and keep marching. If we don't stop soon, I won't have many left. I sent the lieutenant and two corporals to clean up all the stragglers.

"We weren't in the battle yesterday. The walking made my leg hurt. It hadn't been stiff like that in a long time. I can't get a horse. Captains don't get horses. I could ask to ride in the wagons. Once you up give up your company, you may not get it back. Yeah, everybody thinks we're going to fight tomorrow. We'll be ready for them. Maybe if I put my leg on a rock and lie down, I'd be all right."

At this point, Tom, who had been favoring his left knee while on the couch, rested it on a pillow and proceeded.

"They're putting our brigade next to a stone wall. It's not very high. Some of the boys think I'm crazy. They say the Rebels aren't coming, that they've had enough. I think they'll fight. They came all this way. How could they go home now? If they leave, they didn't win. Wouldn't everybody be proud if we win? It would be the greatest victory. We haven't had many victories. We've been in fighting before. You never see more than a couple of yards either way. This fight counts because the Rebels are in Maryland and Pennsylvania. If they win, where can we go? We have to push them back and show we're stronger.

"Cannons. Noise. Men running all over. The colonel ordered everybody to lie down. The Confederates are shelling us. We're shooting back. God, I've never seen a place like this. Men are blown up. Those cannon balls don't look slow any more. They make a God-awful noise. You can hear them pass right over. Sometimes, there's a thud. It's hit somebody. Everybody looks around. You don't want to act scared, so you act nonchalant.

"The shelling's been going on for a while. I can't believe it would go on much longer. Several of my guys have been hurt. A couple ran away. I don't blame them. I would if I could. There's no glory, no adventure, just death.

"The Rebels are coming. There's thousands of them. I've never seen nothing like that before—as far as the eye can see. That's OK. We'll be ready for them. If every man does his duty, we'll be all right. We'll show them. I'm telling the guys to wait—not to shoot. The Rebels still have a long way to go. I want everybody to be prepared. Men are kneeling; some are lying. They keep getting closer. You can almost see their faces. So many are dying. I don't see how any man in his right mind would cross that field. And we haven't even fired yet. Everybody has to be brave. This is the fight that counts.

"I want to stand up. That way my men can see me. They see me. Oh, God. What a foolish thing to do! I have to do something because you can see it in their eyes. They're scared. They want someone to show them. I guess that's what I'm a captain for. You can hear the shooting. God, it's so loud. It's deafening. You can't draw breath. It's one noise after another. Somebody's screaming. They're getting closer.

"I've been shot. I got hit in the stomach. A couple of the men want to pull me off, but I send them back. It's an old soldier's trick. If somebody's shot, men will try to carry him off the field. I'm not going to let my boys do that.

"I take a sip of water from a canteen. It burns going down. I never thought I would have it happen. I never thought I wouldn't want water. I wish now I hadn't stood up.

"That's strange. I just saw Nathan before me. He's beckoning to me. It's getting very dark. I hurt so bad. My insides are on fire. I can hear commotion. It's like nobody sees me any more. Nathan is there. I can't see anything any more. It's very dark."

At this point, I suggested that Tom rise up out of his body and look down on it.

"I'm all curled up. There's blood all over the place. There's smoke. I'm not moving. I'll get up in a minute after the pain goes away. Nobody's paying attention to me. They're all too busy. My boys had to fall back from the wall. General Webb came up and has the brigade under control. My boys are shot to hell and can't hold their ground. They're going to leave me.

"I can't see or hear anything. It's deathly quiet. I call my name out. I don't think anybody will hear me. I think I'm dying. I keep bleeding, and it hurts. I hear nothing and yet I know there's fighting all around me.

"This must be what it's like. It seems so peaceful. I thought it would be so horrible. That's what I thought happened to Nathan and the boys in Mexico. I've seen so many men die. They scream and jump around. They beg for their mamas, give you their letters and keepsakes, and ask you to tell their friends.

"It's like a soft light, a candle that's just barely flickering. My leg doesn't hurt any more. I wonder why. I must look terrible, all covered in blood, like my insides were coming out. Why do men yell, scream, holler, and carry on?"

There was a long pause.

"It's so quiet. I don't see Nathan any more. I can't see me any more. It's just a candle. I feel so sleepy. Maybe if I just close my eyes for a while."

Tom's was one of three regressions that began significantly before the Civil War and one of two to take us back to the time of another war, namely, the war with Mexico. In this narrative, we were given a privileged peek at life and wartime prior to the Civil War and were able to follow a soldier not only through battle in the war with Mexico, but on his life aboard ship to England, his accident, and return to America with an injury. In fact, his injured left leg was stiff during hypnosis and continued to hurt even after he returned to full consciousness.

What was also different about Tom's regression, however, was that he was one of only two soldiers in the study to recall having been an officer, while a third soldier clearly recalled having been a noncommissioned officer. I found this significant since some past-life skeptics have a misperception that people tend to believe they were famous before.

Although Tom was a private when he enlisted for the Mexican-American War, he was later commissioned when he reenlisted as a veteran. Another reenactor remembered coming up through the ranks with the appropriate duty changes and uniform enhancements. In their modern-day reenacting, there were twice as many officers as in the regressions. Five subjects in my study had been officers in reenacting, while three were noncommissioned officers.

In addition, two reenactors had been told they resemble famous Civil War generals today: Rob Hodge looked like Confederate General Nathan Bedford Forest. Dave Morse (see next chapter) looked like Confederate General Ambrose Powell Hill. And yet, even those who looked like generals in this life were not officers in their regression narratives.

In psychologist-researcher Helen Wambach's study of 1,088 reported past lives recounted in *Reliving Past Lives: The Evidence Under Hypnosis,* few had been in positions of leadership or wealth in those lives.[143] In the eleven historical time periods she charted, past lives reported in the upper class always accounted for less than ten percent. In categorizing the subjects she found who were soldiers, those with no authority she put in the lower class, while those with some authority she relegated to middle class. Comparing the twelve past lives of my subjects to Wambach's standards, twenty-five percent of these reenactors, including commissioned and noncommissioned officers, would have been considered middle class. Additionally, Brian Pohanka (one of the officers) and MaryLynne Bauer indicated they were from families that were financially comfortable, while Dale Clarke owned his own business. Wambach would have also categorized them middle class.

In addition, Wambach found that none of her subjects reported a past life as a famous historical personage. Author Noel Langley, in *Edgar Cayce on Reincarnation,* made it clear that the "celebrities" of history also represented a very small minority of Edgar Cayce's life readings.[144] In fact, the Edgar Cayce psychic readings suggest that most souls make their greatest spiritual advances while living obscure, uneventful lives.

The fact that none of the reenactors were famous and only two were officers in their past lives conforms to the findings of reincarnation research, such as Wambach's, and literature, such as Langley's.

This result contradicts some opponents of the reincarnation theory who point to a trend that many who believe in past lives seem to believe that they were well known.

As he was a sergeant in reenacting, Tom's area of interest involved tactics and military strategy. He had never read soldiers' diaries or focused on personal lives, nor had he done much research on the Union. He was surprised to find intimate details and feelings of friendship, protection, pain, and fear in his regression experience.

Interestingly, according to historian Brian Pohanka, Tom's recalled unit, 71st Pennsylvania, was known as the California Regiment. It was engaged on the second and third days at Gettysburg, just as Tom described. Colonel Edward D. Baker, who had started the unit, was a veteran of the Mexican War, and General Webb did command the 71st Pennsylvania in his brigade at Gettysburg.

In regard to the Mexican army, General Winfield Scott was its senior commander, and he did win skirmishes before the advance on Mexico City where many American lives were lost. Scott's tactics were used in the war which began in 1846. It was also a fact that soldiers sometimes didn't have shoes or would use a piece of leather as a replacement.[145]

According to the historical compilations of John Busey in *These Honored Dead,*[146] there was a captain and a sergeant from the 71st Pennsylvania Volunteer Infantry both killed in action at Gettysburg: Captain John Steffan, Company A, 71st Pennsylvania Volunteer Infantry, and Sergeant Thomas Cosgrove, Company K, 71st Pennsylvania Volunteer Infantry. Private James Kay, Company E, 73rd Pennsylvania Volunteer Infantry, Private John Cain, Company D, 81st Pennsylvania Volunteer Infantry, and eighteen-year-old Sergeant George F. Cate of Company A, 20th Massachusetts Volunteer Infantry, also died in battle at Gettysburg. National Archives military and pension records list a forty-five-year-old Private Edward Kales in Company K, 73rd Pennsylvania Volunteer Infantry, who was discharged in 1862 for disability.

Whether Tom's past-life character was disabled or killed, he does know one thing. Under hypnosis, he felt the pain of a leg injury so acutely that he wished it would be cut off. Even after coming out of the regression, his "injured" knee still felt painful and stiff. As the son of an army colonel and a lover of military strategy, Tom is now fascinated with the human interest aspects of war—especially after having lived it through his regression.

13

David:
Living Death

Jokingly, reenactor David Morse would sometimes tell his friends that if he had lived during the Civil War, he must have died by 1863 or before, because, deep down, he found a strange familiarity with the early battles, but didn't relate emotionally to the last half of the war.

Dressed in a red artilleryman's shirt, the thin, wiry reenactor told me of his unusual affinity for firearms. His father was a mechanical engineer for a company that built tanks, so he had been able to visit the arsenal as a youngster. Perhaps he had found the rumbling clap of thunder at the moment of his birth on New Year's Day in 1948 exciting. Later, when he was a youngster, David's attitude was "the bigger the bang, the better." Although his primary Civil War reenacting unit was an infantry company, he had also enlisted in Cuttshaw's Artillery Battery, which utilized a six-pound M-1841 howitzer. He even had an ancestor, Samuel F.B. Morse, who had been the inventor of Morse rifles, Morse code, and the telegraph. After serving ten years in the army, David admitted to a strange sense of easiness around war. While photographing officers who were being decorated for working behind desks in Saigon, he decided he'd do what he could to give credit to the common soldiers who were risking their lives in the Vietnam bush. He volunteered to go into the jungles as a combat photographer and was amazed to find he wasn't afraid, but only cautious. Even today, David, who physically resembled Confederate General Ambrose Powell Hill, preferred to read personal diaries of Civil War soldiers than the "bland" accounts of officers and their narratives of battles and maneuvers.

After his Vietnam experience, David vowed that he would never again fight another country's war, but if the U.S. were attacked, he would rise to the occasion. Still, he got a rush of exhilaration as a Civil War reenactor, which allowed him to vicariously express his role as "warrior."

"A man who has never been in battle is like a woman who has never given childbirth" is how his wife, Jane, philosophically justifies David's warrior compulsion. David, now a medical photographer, met his wife of twenty-two years when she came to his studio for some photographs. In the early years of her husband's reenacting, Jane was on her way to becoming a "war widow" until she put her sewing skills to work making period clothing for both of them. She has realized that reenactors' obsessions may cause marital problems by leaving families neglected. A newswriter and editor, she accompanied David to the regression session and explained "the hobby" to me by saying that it's a manifestation of the "big-boy game" and an escape from frustrating, dull lives. "These men can go to war in glory and fight without getting hurt," observed Jane, who also served in the military and lived with David in Korea for several years.

More than fifteen years before, David had observed a Union reenactor unit at a living-history event and became quite intrigued. Several weeks later, David was invited by a friend to try out another unit. Since he didn't care whether he reenacted as a Northerner or Southerner, he donned a Confederate uniform and joined his friend's unit for the weekend experience. Before the event was over, he had enlisted. Since then, he's risen to adjutant and has spent six years as the unit's commander.

Before becoming a part of my study, David was mesmerized, at his unit's 1994 Christmas party, by three comrades' descriptions of the past-life regressions they had just undertaken with me. All three—Dave Purschwitz, Buddy Bare, and Ed Embrey—described seeing vivid black and white images. I found this fact, relayed to me by David, interesting, since many of my regression subjects describe seeing in color and, additionally, I had not read about any other research on the topic.

Buddy's story intrigued David because of the small details Buddy couldn't have known without doing research. Although passionate about reenacting, Buddy was not known for having an interest in reading details of war. David was also fascinated with Buddy's vivid description of his own death scene and how, when asked to view his body, could describe his face and see a hole blown through his abdomen.

Ed, a reenactor who was well read, impressed David with his past-life recall of sensations such as burning, searing pain, and chills, although he was physically healthy and had been in a warm room during the regression. Last was the third reenactor, Dave Purschwitz, who recalled the heart-wrenching account of losing his arm and the pain that ensued.

The morning after the party, David called me and volunteered for the study. He was more open to the idea of reincarnation than most of the others, considering it to be plausible and finding it intensely interesting. He was curious about whether he had known his current family in another life. Although he had vaguely heard about ancestors from Michigan and Massachusetts who lived at the time of the Civil War, David was more interested in how his notable ancestor Samuel Morse who, in addition to inventing rifles, had taught the famous Civil War photographer Matthew Brady his photography skills. David was eager to see if he, too, had participated in the Civil War.

As we wrapped up the interview and prepared for the regression, my eager participant put out his pipe and quoted General George Patton by saying, "I was a warrior in past lives and I'm a warrior now." Patton, you may recall, had believed in past lives and claimed to have "known" exactly where Caesar had pitched his tent in Langres, France.[147] Once, after being kicked by a horse, Patton had a flashback of a Viking lifetime. For another lifetime, he recalled himself as a Tunisian, drinking urine out of a helmet and cursing the Romans. Patton spoke of the impact of these experiences as "searing to the soul." When he was wounded in World War I, Patton had a vision of his grandfather and grand-uncle who had both died in the Civil War.[148] Perhaps David felt that he was in good company.

Using the same hypnotic regression techniques I had used on his colleagues, I saw David's eyes flutter and knew that he was ready to begin.

David immediately found himself to be a twenty-year-old man having sore legs, an empty stomach, and feeling very cold. He was tired of walking, and his shoulders hurt from carrying something heavy. He saw smoke and people running away from a village. Cone-shaped buildings were on fire. He was impressed with the vision of a horror-stricken face, perhaps someone frightened by the destruction. He observed that the men he was walking with wore red coats with gold buttons, black bearskin hats, and white pants. However, David felt that he was wearing brown pants and shirt. Perhaps he was a scout or volunteer. Seeing the pointed logs of a stockade, he surmised it to be an eighteenth-century fort and knew its location to be Albany, New York.

David's first regression session took about ninety minutes. When he came out of hypnosis, he was nursing his aching shoulders, calves, and feet. Meanwhile, his wife, who had observed the regression, said that his descriptions were reminiscent of David's interest in the French and Indian War and one of his favorite movies, *Drums Along the Mohawk*. When he was fully awake, David disagreed with his wife and identified the scene of the fort as pre-French and Indian War, a period prior to that depicted in the movie.

Although we were all a little weary, we decided to try again. After having David slip back into a hypnotic state, I suggested that he move on to a different time frame.

"I see wheels," he began. "I'm looking out the back of the wagon."

At this point, David's body jerked so violently he awoke. He was so shaken by his memory of an explosion that he was unable to continue the regression.

About a week later, David returned to see if we could pick up where he left off. This time, his wife did not accompany him.

"There's nothing on my feet," he said. "I'm wearing trousers that

feel warm and something light on top. My arms are covered. I'm
male. I see rail fencès, a gate, a stone building two stories high. It's
my home. There's a gable and black shutters on the windows. It's a
rural area.

"I'm in the kitchen. I seem to be alone. There's a fireplace, a table,
a cupboard, and a hutch. A shining lamp is hanging on the wall. I'm
twenty-eight. It's 1858. Maybe I'm a farmer."

Now that David was settled in the mid-1800s, we move forward
in time a bit. At least now I knew that we were in the Civil War era.

"I'm outside with many others. I have heavy shoes on, warm trousers, and something light covering my arms. There's a big open area
and dark houses with white window frames. Maybe it's a town.

"I see a woman's face. I don't know her. The face looks like a relief
carving, as if chiseled out of stone. It's a three-quarter view. The
woman's eyes might be closed. She has a straight nose. It's like a bust
with shadowing. It looks like a filigree oval around the face."

Changing his focus away from the face, David noticed that the
scene seemed to shift.

"It looks like a parade field—a large open field," he said. "There
are tall, multifloored buildings on two sides, one long side and one
short side. I'm standing on that field with others. Cows and cattle
there look like little statues."

I asked David to move forward to the next significant event.
"There's a red clapboard house behind the fence, like a New England cottage with two columns and outbuildings. There's a porch
on the front. Just ducks and geese around. We're walking by on a
road. I sense others—black masses but no detail.

"It's daytime. I see trees at a distance. It's flat. There's a long line of
pointy things in the air—like bayonets. I see a column marching
and dark uniform jackets. Men are wearing small dark hats like kepis
or bummer forage caps. The pants are not as dark as the coats. We're
marching at shoulder arms. Bayonets are on the guns, muskets on
the left shoulder. The barrels are shiny. We're using Gilham's manual.
The road's dusty. My mouth's dry. I don't know where we're going.

"There's an explosion. Dirt and smoke are flying up in the air."

Suddenly, while still under hypnosis, David jerked, opened his
eyes, and reached for his heart. He jerked a second and third time
and reopened his eyes. His hand then came to rest on his chest.

"I suddenly feel hot," he continued. "My heart is beating hard. It's whatever caused the convulsion. It seems like I can't stop it. Just the other night, in my first regression, was the first time I ever experienced these convulsions. I'm sure about this. My legs feel numb. I can't stop shaking."

I recalled how David was so shaken by the explosion in his last regression that he jerked himself awake and couldn't return to a hypnotic state. But this time he didn't awaken, even though his left eye was partially open. I directed him to become relaxed when I touched his shoulder. The jerks lessened. Although I was monitoring David's every move and knew that everything was under control, I was glad that Jane wasn't present because she may have become needlessly alarmed. Such reactions during regression work can sometimes be expected and are not harmful to the subject.

"I saw explosions and smoke," he said. "It looked like something was exploding on the ground, and then there was a profusion of explosions. It's like we marched into an artillery barrage. I can't stop shaking."

I again touched his shoulder and calmed him with suggestions. The jerks stopped.

"I feel like there's another tremor or two to come." I guided him to pass beyond the tremors, and then he said, "I can't feel my legs. When I was having spasms, they felt like little tremors. Now I can't see or feel anything."

At this point, I suggested that David rise above his body and observe it.

"I'm lying on my chest. I have a clean-shaven face and light hair. I can see half of it. I can't see a wound—no perforation from the back. I'm just lying there. The legs are askew. There's no movement. I'm not breathing. I don't think I'm alive. There are other bodies."

With David dying, this was my last chance to ask him his name and unit, and he had an answer right away.

"George Henderson, Company K, 2nd Rhode Island. I get the sense it's early in the war."

When David came back to full awareness, he couldn't feel anything from the waist down. He had to literally pick up his legs in order to get them to move again.

As a photographer in Vietnam, he had witnessed soldiers die after going through a process called "chain-stoking," during which their hearts pounded, breathing became rapid, and they broke out in sweats and convulsions. Interestingly, during David's own death scene, he experienced rapid, hard breathing, a pounding heart, the sensation of convulsions, and felt hot as though he were breaking out in a sweat. Later, after describing the conditions of his dramatic past-life death experience to three experts, two physicians and a pathologist, they all indicated that David was, in fact, describing "chain-stoking" conditions.

The feeling of tremors would only stop when I put my hand on his shoulder and gave him the suggestion that they would stop. He said he felt that two more spasms would have come if there had not been an intervention.

David's dramatic physical and emotional sensations, as well as those described in the other reenactors' narratives, could be helpful in discerning the validity of their past lives. As Civil War soldiers, some reenactors remembered being bored, confused, or embarrassed, while at least nine remembered being fearful or panicky. Three-fourths experienced physical pain, those who traveled by boat in their regressions had seasickness, and several men even cried. I believe that the eleven males and one female, whose ages ranged from twenty-seven to fifty-one years, would probably have been reluctant to have fabricated and expressed these feelings, especially to a female hypnotherapist they had never met before.

Several past-life researchers have placed importance on emotional and physical sensations expressed in past lives. In the *Journal of the American Society for Psychical Research,* Dr. Ian Stevenson cited an incident in which emotional recollections reproduced actual bleeding wounds at the site of the original wound.[149] Of less severity, reenactors David Morse and Tom Galleher experienced pain that lingered upon returning from their regressions. In *You Have Been Here Before,* Dr. Edith Fiore highlighted the importance of emotional and physical past-life expressions.[150] "The tears, shaking, flinching, smiling, gasping for breath, groaning, sweating, and other physical manifestations are all too real." In her book, *Reliving Past Lives: The Evidence Under Hypnosis,* psychologist Helen Wambach considered her subjects' ability to report feelings the most significant aspect of hypnosis.[151] Her subjects tended to believe the emotions came from deeper levels than the visual experiences.

Another significant element that researchers believe helpful in discerning the legitimacy of past lives involves the vividness of descriptions. Each reenactor in my study reported vivid descriptions of his or her regression experiences, surroundings, people, and events. Many descriptions included sound—bugles, music, explosions. Camps, cities, prisons, hospitals, train rides, fighting tactics, uniforms, and homecomings were all described in brilliant detail. In fact, the lifelike, realistic quality of the reenactors' recalled memories led them to question where they got the detailed information. The vividness, coupled with the emotions, led them to rate their regression experiences an average of eighty-five percent for realism and to raise their belief in the possibility of reincarnation by nearly twenty percent.

Interestingly, five reenactors even gave physical descriptions of their Civil War appearance, all differing from their current looks. In fact, today David is one of two reenactors who resemble generals and one of several who look like they just stepped out of a Civil War movie. In David's regression, he was surprised to find his beard gone and his hair considerably lighter. Most of the reenactors also found they were younger in their Civil War experience.

Vivid descriptions were a focus for Dr. Raymond Moody, whose regression subjects discussed in his book, *Coming Back,* said that their images were more vivid and real than in ordinary dreams.[152]

Ian Stevenson also looked at vividness as a possible marker of paranormality in dreams.[153] In a study of 125 precognitive dreams, forty-five percent were described as vivid or realistic. Stevenson says most dreams are not vivid.

The vividness of detail, coupled with emotional and physical sensations the reenactors experienced in their regressions, help to support, as past-life researchers and authors suggest, the legitimacy of their regression narratives.

Turning to the potential historical validity of David's Civil War life, he claimed to be unaware of Company K of the 2nd Rhode Island. According to Civil War historian Brian Pohanka, the 2nd Rhode Island was one of the first regiments to leave the state. It was heavily engaged in the Battle of Bull Run—on Matthews Hill in July 1861—and sustained heavy losses. David could have been killed in the first battle.

In a description not unlike David's, Civil War diarist Elisha Hunt Rhodes described the 2nd Rhode Island marching down a road to the Gettysburg battlefield.[154] Just as they reached a house used as a headquarters for General Meade, there was an explosion of shellfire. Thirty men from the brigade were killed or wounded, all from the 2nd Rhode Island. Unfortunately, there are no Hendersons from the 2nd Rhode Island reported killed at Gettysburg in July 1863.[155] Although David reenacted as a Confederate, he had an affinity for the North. Deep down, he suspected that he could have been Union. In fact, he would have joined a Yankee unit if a friend hadn't influenced him to join the Confederates. Only in a blue uniform twice, once for the filming of *Gettysburg*, he felt strange when he put it on.

David related only to early battles, had a fascination for war, and loved firearms. At the time of the study, he reenacted as an artilleryman. While regressed, he recalled riding on the back of a wagon and could have been from a heavy artillery unit. Joseph G. Henderson, 5th Rhode Island Heavy Artillery, enlisted in October 1862. His assignment was not known since there was no further record.[156] Since his name was never taken up on the muster roll, this could mean that he either never showed up or that records are lost.

Hendersons who died early in the war and were buried in Richmond area cemeteries, according to interment records, are Private William Henderson, Jr., 3rd Vermont Volunteer Infantry, who died October 8, 1864; Private S. Henderson, U.S. Colored Troop, who died November 14, 1864; and Private J.J. Henderson, Company D, 12th New York Volunteer Infantry. The Rhode Island State Archives and the National Archives military records list a 1st Lieutenant George Henderson, 3rd Rhode Island Cavalry, who was a quartermaster in Louisiana and mustered out after the war.

Despite no firm match in the Civil War records, David's regression experience explained strange feelings he's had in his current life. As a reenactor, he has had an eerie feeling of familiarity in the early battles of the war, but no emotional involvement with the later battles. According to David's regression, it could be entirely possible that he died early in the war. Even as a youngster, David had an unusual fascination with firearms. In his regression, he recalled riding on the back of a wagon, which could easily have been used for heavy artillery. As a photographer in Vietnam, David, unlike many of his comrades, had an unexplained sense of ease around combat.

In fact, he had identified strongly with General Patton's belief that he had been a warrior in past lives and that he was a warrior now. David's regression experience proved to him that this was the case.

14

Paul:
Home to Alexandria

In Paul Jones's closet you would have found a complete wardrobe of historical uniforms that number, counting components, about fifteen different kinds. He owned Revolutionary War, Civil War, and World War II attire. His Civil War uniforms alone ranged from early and late war to fatigues, generic, special and dress uniforms, winter coats, and accoutrements for a variety of impressions and scenarios.

Actually, battles were the least meaningful part of reenacting, according to Paul. Although he had reenacted in all three time periods, he viewed the military structures as only focal points for reliving history. He preferred camp life, routines, and living-history events to re-creating battles. For one thing, Paul found some of the reenactment battles mismanaged. Primarily, he enjoyed re-creating civilian life. For example, one highlight in Civil War reenacting had, for him, been the portrayal of the pre-war 1860 Election Day.

In fact, that was one reason why this thirty-five year old decided to become a Union reenactor, because Federalists historically filled a wide range of functions besides fighting. Paul's reenactment unit, the 1st Delaware Volunteer Infantry, served as an honor guard for the 125th anniversary of President Lincoln's Second Inauguration, as well as for various functions at Ford's Theatre in Washington, D.C. The 1st Delaware also participated in living-history events at Harper's Ferry, Antietam, and other park sites.

Besides the variety of living-history opportunities available to the 1st Delaware reenactor's group, the real unit had actually been active until the end of the Civil War. While doing garrison duty for the first two years of war, the soldiers became competent in drilling. Because of their extensive training, they were later used consistently as skirmishers and on the front line throughout most of the major battles. At the end of the war there remained fewer than fifty soldiers out of the original 750 at the unit's inception.

Most of today's 1st Delaware soldiers' residences were evenly split between Northern and Southern states, while Paul humorously identified himself as a "first-generation Southerner." He has lived in Virginia and his family was from Massachusetts. Claiming he had no leanings to either the Northern or Southern Civil War cause, the first unit he joined was Confederate. After about a year, he changed to the Union side, primarily for "modern reasons" such as better opportunities. He admitted to feeling more comfortable with his Federal buddies, enjoyed the humor, and had formed fast friendships during his five years of participation. Historically, Paul understood the political and ideological causes of both sides. While he found the idea of slavery insufferable, he believed the Declaration of Independence gave the South the right to secede.

Whichever side he was on, Paul attempted to re-create the events as accurately as possible using documented "props" and appropriate clothing. Especially enjoying the day-to-day life, Paul savored marching on a hot day or sleeping in a tent in a rainstorm. With an appreciation for the general ambience, the more mundane activities rang true to him.

For Paul, who serviced swimming pools for a profession after several years of college specializing in fine art, history was his main hobby. Interested in the subject since he was a child, he also took it seriously as an adult. A history teacher's dream, he always found the subject filled with all the drama, adventure, and mystery of life. Reenacting gave him the chance to get a personal perspective on the war and "to walk a mile in another's shoes." It also allowed him to escape from the twentieth century, enjoy camaraderie, have fun, and share educational opportunities with his wife and two daughters.

Meanwhile, in checking the genealogical history of his family, Paul learned second-hand about an ancestor who was a Union soldier who was court-martialed for stealing government property. Strangely coincidental was that, like David Morse, Paul was also related to inventor Samuel F. B. Morse. Neither David nor Paul knew each other.

Moving on to Paul's perception of war, he said that he believed there was nothing more influential to the course of history or more liable to create dramatic changes than war. This concept, however, never induced him to join the service. He said that he found modern wars lacking in taste, style, and a clear definition, while results were often ineffective.

Another of his philosophical positions supported the genetic memory theory of how regressions yield apparent historical insights. Although he considered the theory of reincarnation implausible, Paul pointed to the migration patterns of animals as a possible illustration of genetic memory being passed through heredity, believing that it worked the same way in human society. Now, Paul was ready to embark on his own mind's journey back into time. Once under hypnosis, at my suggestion he moved to a lifetime that correlated with his interest in reenacting. He began by describing a scene.

"There are lots of pines trees, a woodline, a forest, and a field. It's spring or fall and I'm wearing something substantial. I don't live around here. I feel alone, content, and I'm lying down, looking up. Out of my peripheral view, I see certain hills that feel familiar. I feel dead—not moving—and I couldn't get up if I tried. I don't feel a part of the scene but am not disturbed and am just observing.

"There are people whom I think I know. I had the impression of a few people moving by, going somewhere in a hurry.

"It's dark in the woods, and they don't notice me even though they are close enough. They just passed by and they're gone. It's curious and confusing. I feel more comfortable in the woods than in the field where I feel lost or away from where I should be. I'm lying down, looking up and over my shoulder and can't move. I'm not where I'm supposed to be. Someone expects me somewhere.

"My wife is not far. She's on the other side of the woods. I could yell and she probably wouldn't hear me. I'm hurt. I can't move my left leg; it feels heavy. I can't get up. I feel like I know which way to go, but I can't move that much. It seems sad in a way."

Sensing that he was dying, I quickly asked him his name.

"Henry, I—1889—Connecticut. I'm thinking about getting up and moving towards the woods. I'm feeling frustrated. It's a late afternoon in the fall, and the grass is tall and brown. I'm moving closer to the woods. . ."

By now, I understood that Paul had died. It was unclear as to whether he had hurt himself on his own family's farmland. It was also unclear if he had only envisioned his wife while he was dying. Also the name and date were sketchy at best and came out with his dying breath. Could this have actually been the end of his Civil War-era life? I suggested that Paul move to another scene. A "still life" photo flashed before him.

"There's a battleship a couple of streets away and houses in between. I'm up on a hill, looking down on the tile roofs, and the gray battleship is docked at the harbor. I'm eleven years old, it's 1941, and I'm excited about the novelty of this unusual happening. It looks like Pennsylvania Harbor."

Realizing that we had arrived at a different century, I decided to see if Paul would move back to the Civil War era. He easily made the transition.

"It's 1840 and I saw a sewing machine. It's a black machine on a wooden table. I'm in a shop. My father works there. It feels good to visit—like a privilege. I think he makes them. I'm a young boy. My name begins with a 'C'. Bedford is the town. I can picture it. It's nothing remarkable. There's a mixture of homes and shops. I see windows with diamond-shaped glass and lead in between. I see a woman. She doesn't feel like my mom."

At this point, Paul had been regressed for several hours and was tired. Bringing him back from memories of Bedford, Massachusetts, into full waking consciousness, I set another appointment to see if I could get some more information. About a week later, Paul returned and we endeavored to pick up where we had left off.

"It's daytime and I'm outside. I'm male and I'm with my sister. She's a few years older than I. I'm in my twenties. We're waiting for something. A train. We're in the hallway of the train station, near the tracks. We're waiting for the president."

At this point, Paul sounded surprised, like this must have been wrong information. He hesitantly continued.

"It doesn't seem like a lot of people there. There are scattered buildings across the way. Maybe I live here, I'm not sure. There are baggage-handler types around.

"I'm dressed up fairly well. I'm in a frock coat and hat. My sister is dressed up. She has on a light-colored dress. It's a long, full hoop skirt. She doesn't have real long hair."

Paul now felt he was getting a mental block and questioned the information he was getting. After I told him it's normal to doubt what comes up, he relaxed. Slowly, he proceeded.

"It's a brick station. I get the impression of a short guy who's balding. He doesn't have a hat on. Otherwise, he's well dressed. I'm not sure if he was on the train. I'm not sure I'm waiting for anyone. Maybe I'm there on business. He's not a relation. Maybe I'm supposed to be meeting him. I think he's supposed to be staying with us. I don't work with him, but we've met before. I feel I work in a hotel. I also live at the hotel. I think I'm taking him to the hotel.

"We loaded baggage and then we're at the hotel. The hotel lobby is just like an ordinary parlor, not like a front desk. It doesn't seem like a formal hotel. Maybe it's a rooming house. It doesn't seem like a business. It's just a two-story, white- or light-colored house. It's a strange feeling. It feels like I know exactly where I am, but I don't know where that is. It's like I have a sense of what's around me.

"Outside, there's no trees. It seems like a lot of dirt. The landscape seems white, but snow doesn't seem right. There's a large stream a ways away—not right behind the building. There's a road right in front. The tracks go by on the other side of the road a little ways. We're down from the station. There're hills on either side. It's like we're in a large stream-valley. It's a low area. It looks kind of—not industrial exactly—but well trampled over the years. I get the feeling it's Alexandria or near Alexandria. This is strange. I get the feeling I could point to it on a map or even go there if I'm right.

"Humm. I don't think it was a train station. I think it was a business by the tracks. It's brick or dark wood. There's a camp of soldiers up the street. I don't feel I have anything to do with them except that they're there.

"I got a real clear image in my head. It's lots of detail, but no one detail stands out. There are a lot of tracks merging together not far up—just past the soldier's camp. The camp's on the right. There's a picket fence along the road near the soldiers' camp. There are a number of trains around. I can just see the tents up the road. I can't seem to change my point of perspective. It's strange. I can look around. I feel as though I should draw it.

"All of a sudden, my vantage point seems a lot farther away from the hotel. Now, I'm across the tracks. The Federals are more to my left now, and I see more of the camp. I also see more of a landscape than anything I'm near to. It's as if I'm looking out across a long way. I'm not close to it. I'm by myself now." At this point, Paul once again berated himself for thinking too hard. He then composed himself and continued:

"I see men in shirt sleeves," he observed. "It looks like they're digging, but it seems more like they're working on a wooden wall or a large gate. The gate goes across the tracks. The men are just workers. They are civilians and their clothes are dirty. Two officers are nearby. They seem to be either supervising or just taking a look. They are in dark blue coats and trousers. They're both wearing hats. They're junior-grade officers. One's younger with a moustache and a kepi-type hat. The other's older with long whiskers and sideburns. The guys seem nice enough. It's surprising that they'd seem nice.

"I'm still at the wall. I feel like something's happened. They're getting back to work on the wall that they had started a while back because of some recent threat, maybe a threat to the train yard."

Although he could picture the scene, Paul told me that he was unable to control the experience. Like many people who are regressed to past lives, he questioned whether he was imagining all this, because what he was seeing was how he would have expected it to look.

"It's definitely Alexandria," he said. "I can picture it vividly. It just feels strange. I'm looking down the street towards the water. There's lots of boats right about where the marker is on King Street. It's strange. It seems like a photo and I can't manipulate it.

"Now I understand. I wasn't waiting for the president. It was the president's funeral car. President Lincoln. They're putting it together in the yard or working on it. I feel like I just found out. I feel like I'm going to cry. I feel angry at the soldiers for some reason—like they seemed somehow to blame for it. The rail car is draped."

With the war over and Paul frustrated due to the painstaking regression process, we completed the session without getting a name for his former self. Upon returning to full waking consciousness, Paul said he was relieved to have had some strong visual images and sensations that indicated a Civil War-era lifetime.

What I found particularly intriguing about Paul's regression, as with the other reenactors in the study, was the concept of continuing where you left off—in Paul's case both geographically and philosophically. With my interest in metaphysics and the law of karma, I had often wondered whether a Yankee would return to live in the South, while a Rebel would have a Northern experience in his next life.

Interestingly, Paul had moved to Alexandria in both his current and Civil War lives. In the regression session, he lived in Massachusetts as a boy, while in this life his family was from Massachusetts. As an adult during the Civil War era, Paul had lived in the occupied city of Alexandria, Virginia, and was understandably wary of the Union soldiers. At the time of the regression, he reenacted as both a Northerner and a Southerner and claimed to have no particular allegiance. Although he grew up in Virginia, he felt more comfortable with Northerners and enjoyed their humor. But his growing frustration with the government made him appreciate the Southern viewpoint, perhaps even more than the Northern ideology. Paul's basic neutrality seemed to be consistent with both his upbringing, living in Virginia with family loyalties to the North, and his past-life recall. A secondary factor could be that he was not a soldier and, therefore, did not harbor such strong feelings.

Paul's lack of strong loyalty to one side or the other was not unlike Tom's, who grew up in a military family in California. Tom also reenacted as both a Confederate and Union soldier.

This information made me curious about the other reenactors and where their loyalties may have originated. Seven of the twelve participants' affinity to reenact a particular side in the Civil War correlated positively with the sympathies held in the area in which they grew up. Of the other five, Buddy and Rob grew up in the North, but their fathers were from the South. Also, in Buddy's case, Washington, D.C., was just minutes away from Virginia. Dale grew up in Panama, but his relatives were Southern. David was from Michigan and initially thought about joining a Union troop. He considered himself neutral. Only Alan held a firm allegiance to the Union for ideological reasons in spite of his geographical upbringing or family influence.

In addition, half of the group gave ideological reasons for their current alignment with the North or South. Three said they were influenced by their family, one said he developed his loyalties as a child, and two said they didn't have any particular allegiance.

Since the geography of their births has had an impact on Civil War reenactors, my thoughts returned to Dale, who had been reared in Panama and had never had any curiosity in the Civil War prior to his lengthy involvement in reenactments. Although I knew that Civil War interest has never waned in the South, I was surprised to find nearly as many units in California as in the Carolinas today. In Florida, reenactments have taken place on beaches with palm trees.

Amazingly, there has even been interest for the American Civil War outside the country. There's a Southern Skirmish Association in Britain, a Confederate Headquarters of Europe in Zurich, and a Lincoln Society of the China Academy that has gathered in Taiwan to learn more about the Union's leader.[157]

Meanwhile, Civil War reenactors have come from as far away as Germany and Australia to immerse themselves in American history. Because some of them did not have American ancestors, these people should not have been prone to the influence of genetic memory or even the race memory of Americans.

Inquisitiveness got the best of me. Why, I wondered, did non-Americans care so much about a past war that was not their own? I found what I thought could be one possible explanation in psychologist Helen Wambach's research book, *Reliving Past Lives: The Evidence Under Hypnosis.*[158] In her regression of 213 subjects, mainly California residents, to the 1850 time period, fifty percent went to lifetimes in the U.S., thirty-two percent to Europe, nine percent to Asia, five percent to South America, three percent to Africa, and one percent to the Near East. Therefore, I reasoned, if there was any validity to this, the converse could also be true: people living today in other countries could have lived in America during the Civil War.

But, leaving geographical issues behind, I turned my focus to comparing whether the reenactors found themselves fighting on their chosen side in reenacting. I found it interesting that only two of the twelve had past-life recall as soldiers on the opposite side, and both of those had extenuating circumstances. Of those, David Morse rated himself as neutral and said he has considered joining a Union troop in the past. Only in Dave Purschwitz's case was he 100 percent committed to the Confederate cause, and yet found himself in a Union uniform in his past life. His case was unusual, however, because he recalled being his own great-grandfather.

These reenactors, for the most part, felt very strongly about the side they had chosen. The ten people who found themselves on the same side in both lifetimes rated their intensity of conviction at over eighty percent. Even though Rob, from Ohio, and Ed currently reenacted on both sides, the Confederate cause was their strong favorite. Both had recalled memories as Southern soldiers.

I now speculated that one possible reason for this intense commitment to a 130-year-old cause may be found in the high correlation to remembered past lives—fighting, being wounded or taken prisoner, or even having died for that cause.

Turning to reincarnation and past-life therapy literature for support, I found that it had, indeed, reinforced my findings that ten of twelve recalled past lives were on the same side as their current loyalties. The therapists—such as Fiore, Lucas, Goldberg, and Netherton—had all emphasized recurring thought and behavior patterns rather than more drastic shifts.[159]

Gina Cerminara, in her book *Many Mansions*, said a way of thinking or acting was probably the result of an energy pattern, and changing it would take much time.[160] She gave an instance of one of Dr. Fred Reinhold's patients who suffered violence from men in this lifetime and showed a similar pattern of being victimized in other lives. Thus, perhaps the concept that someone who is abused in this life was an abuser in the last is not only an oversimplification, but a misperception of some of the facets of the concept of karma and the law of cause and effect.

In his research with children, Dr. Ian Stevenson found only weak indications of karma (in the sense of reward, punishment, retribution, or compensation) in only four cases out of 106.[161]

In her book *Reincarnation: Claiming Your Past, Creating Your Future*, Lynn Sparrow explained the Edgar Cayce readings' position on the law of continuation.[162] Cayce suggested that there is a tendency for our actions, choices, traits, biases, prejudices, and tastes to have a momentum that continues from lifetime to lifetime. "The karmic law of cause and effect reflects our tendency to carry on in a new setting and under new circumstances, much the same old things."

Whether it was the law of continuation at work or not, Paul recalled a vivid view of the layout of 1865 Alexandria and its wharf, and felt that some of the details were new to him. Not being consciously aware that Lincoln's funeral car had been built in Alexandria, he was pleased to hear that it was indeed built on Duke Street in Alexandria.[163] Although Paul thought it was incorrect, historian Brian Pohanka confirmed that sewing machines were coming into use in the 1840s.

The law of continuation may have drawn Paul back to the old seaport town of Alexandria to somehow pick up where he left off in his recalled Civil War lifetime. While many of the original buildings of Old Town still remain, some have been refurbished while maintaining their historical integrity. So, too, with Paul. Although his education, career, lifestyle, and dress are clearly that of the twentieth century, his mind-set and feelings may have felt the tug of another century. Northern roots from both lifetimes may have given him the sense of neutrality he has felt for the Civil War. Perhaps the whispers of the past have left him more connected to the civilian aspects of the Civil War era than the soldiering he may never have experienced.

15

Brian:
A Historian's Heart

At the young age of twelve, Brian Pohanka could be found in the awe-inspiring halls of the National Archives in the nation's capital, poring over authentic military and pension records of Civil War soldiers. In fact, he was such an ardent student of the Civil War that he conducted his own research using original records.

While still in elementary school, he read Bruce Catton's first well-known Civil War trilogy: *Mr. Lincoln's Army, Glory Road,* and *Stillness at Appomattox.* He also convinced his father to drive him to the Civil War battlesites at Fredericksburg and Gettysburg. By the age of eight or nine, the Civil War had developed into a serious pursuit for him.

Early on, Brian instinctively knew something that many of us forget: history is biography. He had never forgotten that history is really about people. As an adult, he had a strong impulse to keep history alive and honor the *people* of the past. He even researched all the former owners of his turn-of-the-century townhome. For several years, he had paid out of his own pocket to keep up the grave sites of the parents of one of the home's original owners. Committed to the preservation of Civil War battlesites, which he sees as "sacred ground," Brian gave talks and became involved in fund-raisers. He also worked with Civil War commemorative groups throughout the country to memorialize some of the war's fallen heroes by marking their unmarked graves.

At the time of the regression, Brian made his living as a historical consultant and writer. He reviewed movies for their historical accuracy, appeared regularly on Civil War documentaries, and had written articles and worked on historical texts. The thirty-eight year old had parlayed his love of history into a successful career.

Incorporating his knowledge of history into Civil War reenacting, Brian eventually became captain and commander of his Zouave unit. With more than fifteen years of reenacting under his belt, he constantly strove for higher levels of authenticity and respected the competency and the efforts others made in this regard. Although he said that the level of correct clothing has improved in reenacting, he also liked to see the military structure and attitudes, drill, and military tactics upheld in order "to keep the illusion" of nineteenth-century military lifestyle. As a "living historian," he saw reenacting as a tool for educating people about the Civil War.

Born in Washington, D.C., Brian grew up in Maryland and went to college in Pennsylvania. His parents were both from the North as were his Civil War ancestors. A great-great-grandfather served for ninety days in the 8th New York Militia, helping to quell the draft riots, while a great-great-granduncle had served as a captain in the 51st Pennsylvania Volunteer Infantry. Still, Brian said that this didn't influence him to join a Federal unit. Instead, he was aligned with the morality and philosophy of the North—the Union, the flag, and freedom. Although when he was young he had a romantic attachment to the South, he now said that he wouldn't choose to fight as a Confederate.

Of all his reenacting experiences, the 125th anniversary of the Battle of Gettysburg was the most impressive to him because of the sheer numbers—some 10,000 reenactors—who participated. The most exhilarating time he ever had was during the filming of the night attack on Fort Wagner for the movie *Glory.* As Brian and other reenactors charged across the moat, splashing into the water in the darkness, explosions flashed overhead and smoke permeated the air. Soldiers were hollering and were swept up in the realistically created sense of danger.

Moving to an overview of the Civil War, Brian viewed it as a decisive watershed in American history and culture. He believed the Civil War was the most important event to happen to America as a nation, in part because it addressed issues of slavery and states rights that had been left unaddressed by the Founding Fathers. Brian compared the situation to an alcoholic who was in denial until the problem reached a boiling point. Since nearly every American was to some extent involved in the Civil War, it served as a rallying point, as well as a crucible or test, of the American people.

War in general was inevitable, according to Brian. Whether somebody took their aggressions out on a football field or hit someone over the head with a baseball bat, it was instinctive. Brian viewed many wars as petty feuds among men. What he found so awful about war was not just the deaths, but also the cultural destruction. Although humans were resilient and regenerate, inspired and treasured cathedrals, art and architecture were often destroyed, particularly in Europe during both World Wars. Nevertheless, Brian acknowledged that other times looked more romantic than our own. Even the soldiers of the Civil War, in shedding blood for their beliefs, transcended themselves and became a part of something more important and beyond the physical. Today, this connection to the Civil War soldiers and their sense of compelling patriotism has elevated "the hobby" to spiritual levels that fulfill some reenactors' inner quests.

The transcendence of Civil War soldiers' ideals and the need to escape the frustration of everyday life without another frontier available were two reasons why Brian concluded that people were drawn to reenacting. He speculated that that's why some people look transculturally to, for example, Buddhists in Tibetan monasteries, and emulate them, knowing that they wouldn't be able to re-create all of the transcendent elements themselves. He saw this spiritual search, in which people look for a connection outside themselves, as a search for the frontier, a vehicle for transcendence like Civil War reenacting can become for those who participate.

Saying that he tries to be open minded, Brian still admitted his skepticism about the possibility of reincarnation. He looked at the concept of past lives as a genetic or cultural memory, or perhaps as a controllable form of dreaming.

Concerned that he was "unregressible," he nevertheless was willing to give it a try. Braving the elements, Brian arrived for his first regression session on a snowy wintry night. Moving beyond his apprehension at being "unhypnotizable," he allowed himself to become relaxed. As we began preliminary visualization exercises, I couldn't help but be impressed with his moustache and beard, as well as his semiformal air. I was easily able to envision him as a Civil War officer. Even though he thought he couldn't be regressed, I was excited about the possibility of sending an historian back in time to relive the Civil War. Shortly after the regression began, I wasn't disappointed because as soon as Brian reached a deep hypnotic state, he jumped, startled awake.

"There was an explosion—a flash—really close—near the woods," he said excitedly. "It scared me. I was looking down at my feet moving. There was a road and people marching. I was marching with them. I don't know if it hit me or how close it was. Like a big cloud going out. I don't know if it was the smoke or the light.

"I see thick, dark woods and green leaves on trees. Silver-like muskets are on right shoulder shift, moving to the woods.

"There's apprehension. We're in close and pushing through the woods pretty quick. Men with their hands out. The ones in front are in a column. I see the forage cap of the man in front of me. I think he's a Federal. My arm is almost on his shoulder. Troops are moving on the right. I hear rustling.

"An officer raises binoculars and looks. We're stopped. There's no fighting. Other people have moved past. Men were kneeling, resting in place with muskets in their right hands."

Brian relaxed a little and then appeared to be moving onto another scene. His head jerked and then he began again.

"It's hot and sunny. It's a camp. There're logs for a cabin. To the left there's a tent on top of a cabin—like a winter hut. You could almost touch it—the cut logs sideways; tent on top. It's on a hill that drops off to the right.

"Four men are putting logs down, bending over, piling it up. Men are hunched over a campfire. The sky's open and trees are chopped down. Men are in dark clothes. They must be Union."

Feeling hot, Brian asked me to bring him to a more conscious level. Realizing that it was only the summer climate in his mental experience, I kept him at his present regression level. Moving to the next scene, he smiled. "Two men are seated on logs, talking. There's a fire with a log smoking nearby. The one on the left uses his hands when he talks, has a beard, dark hair, and light suspenders. The other is younger with a shorter beard and darker suspenders that cross in the back of his shirt. Their trousers have the V-shaped cut in the back. I know them. We're in conversation and I feel happy.

"It's peaceful. We're at the edge of camp. Trees are blowing, leaves are fluttering. It's summer. A young guy with sleeves rolled up is carrying water with a wooden bucket.

"There's bright sun hitting the fields—like dried grass. It's pretty hot, but shady along the creek. I don't know what's on the other side. The woods cut it off.

"People are passing back and forth to the creek. The men's pants are light blue, faded, dusty. The field's trampled.

"I would have thought they'd be swimming. They're hunched down along the bank, some washing, splashing with their hands. A tall, thin guy is holding his wet shirt. Everybody's glad to be here and taking it easy.

"Everybody's in their shirts except for the drummer boy. He's a little guy with a kepi, very young and fat with a round face. Everyone else is skinny. He's seated and not part of the group. Everyone treats him good, though.

"The whole army's resting. Men are in light-colored shirts. They're sewing a button or going through their clothes. One has a long beard, shirt sleeves rolled up. He's sitting cross-legged hunting for lice, and the men are kidding him."

He chuckled. "Some men have caps on, one with the company letter 'A' or 'K' on it. I have a simple wooden pipe in my hand. I'm standing with my left hand in my pocket. I have boots, forage cap, and unbuttoned coat on. I think I may be a sergeant. Maybe you have to wear that to set a good example.

"I don't know if I'm supposed to keep an eye on them, but the creek is down away from where the camp is. I can't leave.

"White canvas pup tents are scattered up the hill to the right that goes up away from the creek. A ridge runs all the way along the back.

There's a stack of muskets and soldiers lying in front of the tents, which aren't laid out to regulations, but look more like an army on campaign."

Now Brian told me that this was a very recognizable place. He saw it as if he were there, but he couldn't leave his position. I realized that it may have been military orders that prevented him from leaving.

"Around the trees that stick out, there must be a tent for an officer. A big ridge really slopes up. There's at least a brigade here.

"This creek isn't that wide. It might be Malvern Hill, but it's real open. The fighting's done for now."

I was now realizing that Brian's vast storehouse of Civil War knowledge and reenacting had given him the awareness to observe and recall an incredible depth of detail during his regression. Leaving the camp, we moved ahead in time.

"A young musician's playing a fife and has blue ribbing on his shell jacket. Behind the fifer, a soldier is holding a stick, pretending to be a drum major. He's going up and down the street making fun of the boy. Two soldiers sitting in front of a hut are laughing. The boy goes into a hut, acting pissed off.

"The tall man pretending to be the drum major stamps his foot after he does the routine and jokes. He's got a long black beard and a long unbuttoned frock coat. He's the only one wearing a Hardee hat, folded up on the side without a plume. He might have been the one who was talking with his hands earlier. He uses mannerisms and puts his hands on his hips when he talks."

I was fascinated at the description of colorful, humorous personalities Brian was encountering. Now, he turned his attention to his surroundings. This time, the huts were laid out neatly in rows to regulation. Brian identified them as winter quarters that looked like the defenses of Washington. A white, dilapidated two-story house with a fieldstone chimney served as a staff headquarters.

Now, Brian told me his arms were tired and asked to be brought up a little. Actually, I was pleased because this was a sign that Brian was in a deep hypnotic state. Once again, I asked him to continue without bringing him up.

"In front of the house, I see two horses—a black one and a butterscotch one. The darker one with a black mane is wearing a saddle and switching its tail.

"The brigadier general's in the house. A sword hangs from the darker horse's saddle. I don't know the general's name. He's got brown curly hair and a moustache. He looks like General Stoughton, but this general's hair is light brown. He might be General Chipman, but he looks younger than Chipman's photographs.

"He likes good horses, and he's very dapper. He has a riding crop. He has a burnside hat—sometimes with a feather in the side. He's a dandy. He's short; not fat, but compact.

"A clean-shaven young orderly with a long face is wearing a kepi and a short jacket. He's on a black horse that moves impatiently. He's not carrying a flag. Maybe he's the general's orderly. He's got a high collar and yellow trim, like cavalry. He looks real snappy and like he's pretty full of himself. He's got a narrow waist and is a good-looking soldier.

"His horse is a very dark bay with brown hooves. The butterscotch horse still flicking its tail may be the general's horse because it's got a blue saddle blanket and sword. A covering of evergreens keeps the horses dry.

"It gets dark early and it's overcast. You can see yellow light from inside the window. Candles may be lit.

"On the right of the street, a cabin has a barrel chimney with smoke coming out. It's probably the sergeant's because the others don't have chimneys.

"It's a big, muddy camp. We're stamping feet and wiping soles on the wooden sidewalk, holding onto the rails. If you don't stomp the mud, it won't splash all over. When your feet hit the mud, you hear a sucking sound.

"It's boring, the same thing day after day. The weather's getting better. I think they're more comfortable in the general's house.

"I don't know if this is before or after the valley scene, but we've been there a while. It might be November. I get the feeling we haven't seen lots of fighting. We're well supplied."

Once again, Brian tried to identify the location of the camp, possibly near Washington or Fairfax, Virginia. He now focused in on his own uniform.

"I have sergeant's chevrons on. I have to sneak up on myself to see this. I see boots, sleeves, a vest, and dark-blue unbuttoned coat, a forage cap, and a blue stripe down my trousers. I'm younger than I am now and round faced. It doesn't look like me. I'm medium build with light, sandy brown hair, a little chin beard, and slight moustache. My face is smooth on the sides.

"The name Edward comes to mind. My last name may begin with 'M,' like 'Mor'—, 'Morris'—but longer. I think it's got a 'd' in it. The unit could have an 'eight' in it."

Although Brian seemed very comfortable with camp life, I decided it was time to see some action. I asked him to move on to another significant event.

"We're on an embankment, packed in like sardines. Beyond the road are brambly fields and woods. I'm standing up like an officer and smacking a stick on my boot to be tough and set a good example. Two officers are pointing. One is a bearded, older man. The whole regiment's there. When a shell goes off in the air behind the woods, it sounds like a whip cracking.

"It's funny! The men have fixed bayonets, but they shouldn't. They're lying prone on the right of the road. A caisson's rumbling off down to the left. We're in reserve. The men have short shell jackets and square packs."

Now, Brian expressed his concern about the possibility of his unit being involved in risky maneuvers.

"I don't want to go down in those smoky oak woods. If we go down in there, it's not going to be good. You're not supposed to act scared, but you are. You might die. There's artillery. The Rebs may be down there. Let someone else do the fighting. I'd happily spend the whole battle right here. Maybe that was something somebody said, and I'm agreeing with them inside my head. Everybody feels like it, from the colonel on down.

"We're moving forward; people are tripping. I hear bullets—it's a funny sound. I'm pushing the man in front. It's not real cold, maybe fall. Shells go off leaving a cloud of smoke. They don't look like they'd kill you, but they pull the air out of the sky. There's fighting ahead.

"I must be an officer—just the way I had to act. I have my sword in my right hand now at shoulder arms, and I'm to the left of the company. The men look really sharp even with all the brush. Their step is even down towards the woods.

"The creek is spongy. As we cross, people are stumbling. You cut your hands on briars and thorns. People curse and help each other through this boggy place. You push the man in front.

"There was fire coming out of the woods. It sounds like a spitting bee, but you could tell it was metal from the sound. Everything is all messed up because it's thick. Branches hit your face and everybody's pushing. They shouldn't be at shoulder arms—it's stupid. They have fixed bayonets, too. They are going to get their bayonets caught in the branches.

"We're in the woods. It's dark. Another regiment came in on the left. This is confusing, and I don't want us shooting at each other. It seems stupid. They should have sent out skirmishers. Maybe they did, but we could walk right into them.

"Some general really put us in it this time. I don't know if I'm thinking that or the men are saying it. We're pushing forward. I'd like to stop this, but I can't.

"They're strange woods because the brush is all on the outside. It's more open on the inside—no underbrush. Inside, these trees hold the smoke low.

"They're firing right into us. You can see their hats above the smoke and hear their yell. Men are falling, and we're firing back. Branches are falling. You can see the saplings quivering. We're yelling, 'Pour it into them!' and 'Blaze away!' I'm behind the left of the line, keeping an eye on them. I don't have a musket but a sword in my right hand.

"A man in a frock coat is shot. There's wet, red blood on his face and he looks startled. I don't think he's dead. He dropped his musket. We're firing at him.

"One young officer's really yelling, waving his sword. All the companies are firing. There's flames shooting out.

"Some men are in frock coats—there's a real mixture of coats. When they fire, the musket jerks back and slams them in the shoulder. They're just firing and firing. You think nobody can live. Who can stand it?

"Now the sun comes out. As it goes in and out of the clouds, light filters down. The sun catches through the trees on the ramrods as they ram the bullets down. Other troops came in on the left. They keep advancing and might be pushing the Rebs. We're standing there firing. Everybody's yelling.

"Little trees move when bullets hit them. Now you can't see anything, just a lot of smoke. They should say, 'Cease fire,' stop firing, and keep moving. I don't want to fire on our own men moving in on the left.

"Now, we're moving again. They stopped firing. 'Right shoulder shift.' We're pushing forward through really thick smoke—it smells bad. Bodies of dead Confederates on the ground look like lumps with their faces down. Nobody's paying much attention. They all looked the same color. We're past them. Everybody's cheering. I guess we won. We whipped 'em.

"The Rebs have pulled back. I hear that crack again. The shells exploding. Branches are coming down. I don't know how they could keep track of anybody in the woods. At least, it's fairly level and not cut up with ravines where they could hide a brigade. We're nearing the end of the woods; there's a field ahead.

"There may be some Confederates and more shelling up there. Wounded Confederates are lying down and leaning on trees by the edge of the woods. They've pulled out of the woods. We're right at the edge. They're dressed all in dark gray and slouch hats. Men are pulling the wounded Rebs back like prisoners.

"We pushed them out of the woods, but we aren't cheering. Everybody's tired, but feels good. It's not a hot day, but that was a battle going through there with our packs. There's a sense of the regiment, of group pride, of accomplishment.

"I want it to be over, but it's not. Our troops are on the left, kneeling. The woods are almost a horseshoe shape. Where they took the Reb prisoners is like an indentation in the woods. It goes farther on both sides. We're facing a field. Nobody wants to go out onto the field without orders.

"Now they're getting their wind, and they're proud. This one young Reb they took back looked like a scared, skinny kid with black hair and black slouch hat. The Rebs are pretty well dressed. It's that dark grayish type—maybe like a Richmond depot jacket. He looks so young.

"Others are still lying there. They must be badly wounded or dead. They should move them out of the way. Maybe we'll pass them. They are right at the edge of the woods. You could throw a stone and hit them. Their men left them. They must have been pulled back. Maybe we shot more than we thought."

Pausing momentarily, Brian now began to reflect on the battle's happenings.

"Except for that one place where you could see the Rebs through the smoke, the dead ones didn't have any weapons or packs on.

Maybe their men grabbed their weapons. I was surprised there wasn't more debris. The dead guy close to me fell forward on his face and wasn't as mangled as I would have thought."

New troop movements brought Brian back to the moment. "Now the troops on our left are going to move forward and keep pushing. We are staying where we are. One of our batteries moved up in the field. There's smoke coming from artillery.

"It's a stalemate—like that was our fight, and I didn't get killed. Everybody's happy. We're full of ourselves. I saw a few men fall out of line farther down, but we are fortunate. We didn't lose too many. The men are talking and point to the ones on the left who have moved up. Somehow, we must have gotten some guns up there that are firing.

"My hands were scratched up pretty bad going through the brambles. Burrs are in my pants down around my boots. It's better than a bullet—an ounce of lead."

Brian was proud, happy, and animated. Upon returning to full waking consciousness, he admitted that the last scene was scary. He questioned where some of the faces he had seen came from and was amazed at how very heavy his arms still felt. Since Brian's regression had lasted several hours, we decided to call it a night. A week later, he returned to learn the rest of his fate, and he went into a hypnotic state more rapidly.

This time he found his company on campaign—shuffling their feet as they marched, being careful of the ruts in the dusty road. Brian marched to the left of the company and fiddled with his pack straps, which dug into his shoulders, and wondered where the men he knew had gone. At my suggestion, he then moved forward to another event of significance.

"When night comes, men look orange from the fire. I've been here for so long. You go from one camp and one march to the next. You don't know where you're going. Time's passed. The war goes on. Drudgery, monotony, boredom. Everybody's quiet—not much talking or boasting. I don't feel as attached to these people. They bring in a lot of drafted men, new men, bounty men.

"If we've held out this long, we're in pretty good shape. It's down to very practical regulation uniforms. Those who have been there a long time are strong. They're not getting sick and dying of colds and illness.

"Men get food when they can. Somebody got vegetables and shared with friends. They steal everything—they have cheese. You never have enough food, but they take good care of us.

"At night when we camp, we wear overcoats. I wear a dark blue overcoat like an officer, and a slouch hat. The men have light blue overcoats. I wear a frock coat, boots, sword, belt. My hair is shorter with just a moustache now. I like to lie down, rest, and put my feet up by a fire. It's hard to get string to tie up bedrolls and hitch everything up.

"I observe the men and don't say much, because an officer's not supposed to talk to them. I don't feel like I have another officer with me. It could be that I'm the company commander now, and there're not that many of the old men left. But everybody's working together. It's fall or early spring. When they are marching, they often wear overcoats. There is an officer who comes up on horseback sometimes and gives instructions. He's probably a major. He wears gauntlets."

After what seemed to be a long time on campaign in the Shenandoah Valley and with the end of the war drawing near, Brian's regiment got a reprieve. They settled into a big encampment near Richmond where tents were laid out in company streets. Brian handed over the morning report to the adjutant and then observed an officer getting a shave in a camp chair as he walked into his Wall tent. It had a white cot and tables. From a peg, he took his sword and kepi with embroidered bugle horn.

"Having a Wall tent, I might be senior captain or acting as major. I'm better dressed now with a well-made frock coat, nice coat, nicer boots, black leather gloves. People salute me. I've risen pretty high and I'm proud.

"I want to say I'm in the 121st New York. One officer has a red cross on the side of a hat. It's the symbol of the 6th Corps. I was in Company A. Many of these men are pretty seedy. My name seems like Edward Henry Mergen or Morgan.

"We're breaking camp. Everybody's packing up. The men are falling in. They take their muskets, always by the drum. I don't like a lot of yelling. They bring wagons up, and the servants help to pack the tents and baggage. It just takes seconds to break the camp down. The men have learned to travel light. Many of them have blanket rolls. They tuck their trousers into their socks, blousing the pants, and keeping chiggers out of the ankles. There's lots of sack coats now; a few frock coats. You don't see short jackets any more.

"I'm on foot and take my place at the end of the company. There are not a lot of men in the regiment. The sergeant steps back. Two officers are on horseback. An officer rode up, and he's talking to a thick-set officer with a dark beard. That guy might be the acting commander. He had light-colored hair, a slouch hat on, and an imperial goatee.

"We must have come out of winter camp recently, because we're in good shape and well supplied. The sun's in the grayish sky. It's a very early spring. These fields are level.

"Looking down the line, you see this long column—men on horseback, field officers, square canvas-covered wagons after each regiment. We're near the head of the brigade.

"We're on a road or farm track. The fields on either side are open. One guy is smoking a pipe and pointing like a sightseer, talking about what happened here earlier in the war.

"You go where fate takes you. Maybe when they transferred us, I stayed and reenlisted with a few others and got a veteran's furlough. Most others went home when their three-year term ran out. When I was promoted, I was given Company D and haven't commanded it that long. Maybe because I was on leave, I got a quality uniform.

"The men sing and joke. It must be near the end of the war. There's not as much apprehension now—probably because we don't know where the enemy is. Everybody feels the enemy's all bottled up, and we're going to win—it's just a matter of time. We're proud to be there near the end. It must be late 1864 or spring of 1865."

Brian's musings were abruptly interrupted by the sound of gunfire ahead. The marching was halted as men took cover.

"Union artillery is firing up ahead on top of a ridge. I hear the shriek the shells make and the enemy firing back. Artillerymen jerk the lanyards, the guns recoil, and men push them back. Others carry ammunition. We're supporting the artillery.

"The men are lying down; I'm kneeling. The ground is wet and spongy from rain. My knees are muddy. Everybody ducks instinctively when shells come over, although they're not right over us. I don't think the enemy has much artillery left. Our brigade captured some guns. When the artillery fires, there's a concussion and clouds of smoke. Behind us, a barn's on fire.

"Other troops lying down in column of division are massed to our left. It's a different regiment. Everybody's packed in. We should spread out more, or they could get more casualties.

"Officers are kneeling or standing. One young field officer with a double row of buttons on his coat is writing an order or sketching. They hand a message to our commander.

"They're retreating, and we're shelling them. We've been pushing them for the last few weeks, but now we're really after them. Shells overhead, like loud rockets, are overshooting us. Our troops have come out of some woods. Our regiment's guns are firing. Horses are pretty close to the guns, and they're trying to hold them. This battle must have come on quick. A horse reared up and neighed—maybe it was wounded. The driver is trying to control it so it doesn't turn the caisson around.

"The staff of the brigade commander is off to the left—the flag and the horsemen. We're near the right of the brigade. The thick-set officer with the dark hair, moustache, and a short chin beard is tall with a double-breasted frock coat. The colonel is talking to the men to boost morale. He's a good officer.

"Explosions in the brigade to the left cause the mud to geyser up, hitting chunks of dirt or maybe having hit some men.

"Now, the Union's bringing in some guns over to the left. The main artillery is to our front and right. They're unlimbering. I have great admiration for them. They're wheeling the guns up—the right gun, the left, the first section, then the next. We're so close to the guns. If one of those caissons went off, it would cause damage. They go up and load it. We watch the choreography to keep our minds off of what's going on.

"Smoke blows back over us. It's been raining. It hugs the ground and drifts back. You start to choke from the sulphur.

"Along the crest, officers on horseback are looking through field glasses. The brigade commander and his staff are talking to the artillery commander and pointing. The staff's right there on the skyline. They are going to take some fire if they're not careful. Their horses are nervous when the guns fire.

"It looks like war. Everybody's professional now—they've been in the service so long. They've sent staff officers off—maybe to get instructions. It looks like the Battle of Sayler's Creek—it's the 6th Corps and there's artillery on a ridge.

"The brigadier commander may be Joseph Hamblin—he looks like him, but younger than I thought Hamblin did. He's got the same style beard. All these guys are young.

"Everybody stands up, still with their packs on. 'All right, boys.' He sent his staff officer over. They brought a dark horse up for the field officer. I feel he's been away for a while, and the stocky guy has been acting as the regimental commander.

"We really want it to be over with, but we don't want to be the last ones to get killed. I don't know if we're going to advance or not, but it sure looks like it. How are we going to get through the guns? 'Shoulder arms.' I walk down to the front of the company. 'Forward march.'"

First Brian's unit and then the rest of the brigade began to march forward.

"The officer on horseback came up in front. We're moving forward and will deploy on the center and pass between the two batteries. It's our company and the color company (flag-bearing company).

"The others are falling in behind us as we move. You can feel the concussion and the smoke come through. We are passing through the batteries. I pull my sword out. It's at shoulder arms. You look down the line and see the clenched jaws.

"There're woods and fences that disorganize the troops on the left. They have to keep the line dressed. The enemy may have pulled back. The ground is bad ground—it's cut up. There's a swell, then it rises up again on the right. You can't see too clearly. There are trees and the land is like a funnel. Where we are is more open, but then it narrows towards these woods.

"There aren't many leaves on the trees. It's spring. You can see where the leaves will be coming out. There're a few evergreens and it's still wintery looking.

"Their skirmishers are firing at us. We still don't have skirmishers out—just like last time. That's crazy. There's firing in the woods anyway—you can hear the echo. Maybe we do have skirmishers in the woods. Off to the left, there's some hay piled up in shocks. There's a barn or log outbuilding for the cattle. The men are pushing around those obstructions."

Now Brian's company got the dangerous assignment of moving ahead into the woods as skirmishers.

"The officer rode up and pointed. We're going out as skirmishers.

We may have skirmishers in there from some other organization. We're moving forward in skirmish intervals.

"Another fight in the woods. I tell an officer to keep an eye on the left; I'll keep an eye on the right. One guy fired. It's mushy. There are dead leaves. You can hear some firing.

"Other skirmishers are bringing back this prisoner. He's scared, and his hands are in the air. He doesn't have any hat on, his coat's unbuttoned, he's disheveled looking. He has a blanket roll, gray jacket, and pants. They're taking him to the rear.

"We do have other skirmishers there—so we shouldn't be firing. A thin officer with a moustache from another company says there are skirmishers out already, and the main forces are to our left. He sent a man to tell the colonel.

"I don't know what's up ahead. It looks like more woods. I can't tell the lay of the land. It's confusing. We've halted the skirmish line until we get new orders. They've captured some Rebs. Maybe they're just pulling back, and it's the rear guard of their army. The artillery isn't firing any more."

Brian now got orders for his men to move, so they complied.

"Somebody came back from where the colonel was. We are moving off to the left, still in single file, like skirmishers, climbing over logs. Wet is coming off the branches. It must have rained recently. We're still in the woods, but it's more open. If we're going to catch up with them, we've got to move up. Now there's troops in line of battle up there. After they sent us out, they probably had them move to the left. Everybody's tired, climbing up the hill.

"We're going back in our proper place. They have to give way and let us in there, because we're in the center. I don't know how the commander will ride his horse through there—maybe leave it behind. The racket of musketry is off to the left.

"They're bringing in more prisoners. It looks like the Rebs are just giving up. They're in bad shape, not in rags, but really disheveled. Acting like they're beaten, they have their hands up in the air and are being pushed along.

"We move forward again. The men are at trail arms. Their bayonets are unfixed—which is good. They shouldn't be fixed in the woods. There's a clearing up ahead, out of the woods. 'Right shoulder shift.' The right flank is still in the woods, but most of us are now in an overgrown field. A few fruit trees are dead, gnarled, or fallen over. There's a dead Confederate sunk in the grass. There's been some fighting here.

"Reb skirmishers on the ridge ahead are falling back, turning, and firing over their shoulders at us. They're not hitting anybody. They dropped down over the ridge.

"We're cheering. Everybody's keyed up. The men are trying to pick up the pace, and the officers are saying, 'No, keep the line dressed.' Everybody's confident.

"Our guns are moving on the left. We got them on the run down this slope. Now we're going at a 'double-quick.' We're almost laughing because we're chasing them.

"We're out of the woods. It's rolling country and fences. The Rebs are pulling back everyplace. They aren't even shooting straight. To the right our troops are coming out of the woods. There was firing with white smoke by where the Rebs would be.

"Our cavalry is all up and down along these wagons out of formation. They're corralling these guys by the hair, by the ear. This one sergeant has his sword out and is dragging a Reb alongside his horse. The Reb dropped his musket. They're being rounded up. Confederates are running. It's disorganized.

"There's an old gray, abandoned wooden house with fences. We're moving to the left, toward, and past it. Everybody's out of breath. We're climbing over a rail fence with a cross support. Men are jumping over the side and helping the guys coming over.

"We are pushing on. We're not even dressing the line any more. If we push on, we'll get them. It must be the rear guard of Lee's army. There's more Confederate prisoners being brought. Cavalry and infantry are guarding them. We must have gotten into this battle late. The enemy has gone to pieces."

Now Brian got orders to have his troops stop, while the brigade reorganized. Meanwhile, he reassessed what was happening.

"Everybody's talking and happy," he observed smiling. "It wasn't much of a battle, but we beat them everyplace. They've got a whole company of Rebel prisoners. It's been a very confused battle. It's more like a big skirmish where the Rebs are just giving up.

"These guys are marching past. In front, there's a Reb officer with a beard who looks like a hot potato and is trying to be defiant. Others are trudging along. Many have their hands in their pockets. Their weapons have been taken away.

"The Rebs have pulled back across this road. We're so disorganized. There are other troops coming up; our cavalry is out ahead
after them. There're guns moving up there. Everybody's on horseback, moving fast—chasing them. The Rebs are 'off the map.' It must
be almost the end of the war. Everybody's real glad. You feel sorry for
those who are killed. Most of them are just surrendering. They're
not even putting up much of a fight.

"This battle is confusing. Everywhere there's movement. We have
a lot more men. We're hitting them from all different sides. The cavalry is great—just corralling the Confederates. They yell at them and
bully them, and they're just giving up.

"Not one Confederate has a knapsack, but blanket rolls instead.
Their uniforms are gray and greenish gray. The dead guy had yel-
lowish brown pants and a gray jacket. No two look alike. They're all
pretty lean. Seeing them this close, you realize they're people. Men
talk in the ranks about it. You don't usually get to see that many Rebs
surrendering.

"Staff comes riding up. There's the lieutenant again—looking
through binoculars. I don't think it's Sayler's Creek because it's not
that heavy fighting. It might be just before Appomattox. Our men
are cheering. More cavalry and artillery are going out. I don't want
to fight any more. I think that's it. I think we've won. No one wants to
get shot at the end."

Getting the command to move again, Brian's company re-formed
quickly into a big column.

"Now we're marching off to the right following other troops in a
column. Passing the gray house, we go down a swell and up another
side. They're shifting us to the right to hook up with the other infantry over there. Other troops came out of the woods where the heavier
fighting was.

"There're about nine dead Rebs on the crest of this ridge to the
left. One guy's got his knee up, he's on his back. There're some dead
Rebs by this partial wall. One guy is propped against it. He's got
blood all over his face and coat; his hand is on the wall, his head's
back. One guy has a musket lying next to him. He's lying on his face.

"They made a stand there. I bet that's the smoke we saw earlier.
They must have carried off the wounded or we captured them. Cartridge papers are lying around.

"I don't see many of our guys dead. One or two of our men are with a surgeon on the left, in this field."

Confident that the battle was over, I asked Brian to move to another event. What he envisioned next was a welcomed surprise. "I hear a train whistle. The band is playing polkas and *The Star-Spangled Banner* faster than we play it now. I see people with families. A portly man hugs a lieutenant as he gets off the train. We're back in town—Ogdensburg, New York.

"There's an indoor market. To the right you can see row houses and a church. Soldiers in blue with knapsacks look like islands with people around them. It's a train station. I'm trying to talk to a lot of people at once. People have brought things to drink and eat. Soldiers are outside, officers inside.

"There's a recreation hall with bunting on the beams. There are lots of ladies. I'm hugging my sister. She has dark hair and is wearing a pale lemon dress with black trim and hoop skirt. She's the best-dressed girl there. She's all coiffed up, and her dress is of nice fabric. My sister goes to a girl's school. I'm proud of her. My parents may have died.

"An old lady kisses me on both cheeks. Maybe she's my grandmother. Her hair is pulled back, and her fashion is out of date. There're tables of food prepared by matronly cooks—delicacies like tongue, bread, cakes with powdered sugar. I'm holding a punch glass. I have a red sash on and a sword.

"People are jabbering. There's a lady on my left, a girl on my right. Officers, civilians. It's afternoon. One of the color sergeants (flag bearer) is holding a baby wearing a long white dress up in the air. His wife is there. It's a big festival.

"There are Civil War instruments—kids with horns, drumming. There's too much going on. One bald officer with brown side whiskers and a frock coat makes a toast. 'To the Union.' Soldiers are hugging each other and dancing.

"I'm really happy. I'm proud to be alive, but sad about Lincoln. It was terrible when he got shot. A picture of President Lincoln is draped in black. We are wearing armbands because of his death. There's a picture of Andrew Johnson there. No one knows how Johnson will do.

"A church bell's ringing. It's a brick building in a business area. It's getting dark. Lamps are on. Outside, teenagers with short jackets and caps are practicing with horns. It's cool, the air is fresh, and it's going to be a beautiful evening."

When his lengthy regression session was finished, Brian was astounded at the completely authentic nature of everything he had seen, heard, and experienced in his past life.

Brian, like most of the reenactors who were regressed, took "the hobby" very seriously. They described themselves as "hard core" or "sticklers for authenticity." Some admitted to feelings of disdain for reenactors who make no effort to maintain the military structure or historic period in character. Brian and several of these reenactors had actually been in the vanguard of upgrading the authenticity of the movement. Most expressed a "reverence" for authenticity and felt a sense of spirituality related to the Civil War.

Within this framework is one of the most telling statistics—the reenactors' rating of the realism of their regressions in relationship to the realism of the reenacting experience. Of course, the re-creation of the 1860s in the 1990s cannot be perfect. There are Kodak® cameras, beer cans, and Broncos, especially apparent to the observers of a reenactment. The reenactors in my study—as a whole and individually—rate themselves in the top third of all reenactors in their concern for authenticity. And for some, this is a conservative estimate, because they are diehards in their zeal for re-creating history as perfectly as possible.

These fastidious subjects overwhelmingly rated their regression experiences as more realistic than reenacting by an average of thirty percent. Two scores were particularly noteworthy. Brian, the Civil War historian, agreed that his experience was 100 percent "farb free," while he rated his reenacting experiences as only fifty percent in realism. The other was Rob Hodge, who was so "fanatical" about authenticity that he dieted, just because Civil War soldiers were thin. He also was elated that his hypnosis experience had been nearly 100 percent authentic. Although both Brian and Rob were regressed for more than five hours each, neither had been able to find one detail from their regression material that was historically incorrect.

However Brian may have received his prior historical knowledge, he was astonished at finding that every detail in his regression was historically accurate. In addition, he couldn't account for knowing some of the information that he had retrieved, nor could he account for the personalities he'd described or the feelings he had experienced.

He was interested in the good construction of the huts in the winter quarters, which was possibly Falmouth Winter Camp, Virginia. The logs were tight, and there were windows and chimney barrels. He was surprised to discover railings and sidewalks—like corduroy roads of logs—for the mud. Brian said that the camp and lodgings had been constructed by the book. William Price, in his *Civil War Handbook*, confirms that log cabins often replaced tents during the winter months when armies settled down.[164]

Because of geographical details such as hills, woods, bogs, a river, and the time of year, Brian thought his first battle may have been part of the Seven Days Battles—possibly Gaines's Mill or Malvern Hill near the James River. Brian observed no one wearing corps badges, and corps badges were not worn in the early war. Since the Battle on the Peninsula had taken place during the summer of 1862, he surmised that this was another probable location.

Another location, the train station in Ogdensburg, New York, was the scene of Brian's victory celebration. Although Brian had heard of the town prior to his regression, he had never been there, nor had he any idea of what the town looked like.

There were other powerful impressions that Brian couldn't discount in his regression experiences. One was the sense of time passing and his moving through the ranks—first as a noncommissioned officer with stripes; later, as an officer with different uniforms. During one march, Brian found himself standing behind the left of the line. Because the captain stands on the right, he may have been a 1st lieutenant. He also conferred with officers on several occasions.

He remembered feeling very proud of his last uniform and his tight black leather gloves. In this lifetime, he sometimes wore white cotton gloves for full-dress affairs. In the regression, as an officer Brian wore his canteen and haversack on his left. In reenacting, he always wears them on the right.

The sound of live shells exploding was unlike anything Brian had experienced in either movies or reenacting. He described the sound of shells exploding like a metallic crack—like the end of a bullwhip. Also, seeing soldiers die was completely real and unduplicated in reenacting or in the filming of movies.

Brian saw many troops in shell jackets. This could have been a New York unit. He also saw entire regiments with packs on and bayonets fixed. Although these details were historically correct, Brian remarked that it was not like reenactors to wear packs in reenactments. The differences between reenacting and Brian's own regression experiences served to enhance his belief in the credibility of his own narrative.

Another observation surprised him—that there were soldiers who were not as short as he thought average Civil War soldiers to be. The average soldier he saw in his regression he guessed to be around five feet, nine inches.

Even as a historian, there were things Brian couldn't have known, such as his own fate at Sayler's Creek. Due to his prior knowledge of the Battle of Sayler's Creek, in which he felt he was about to become engaged, he anticipated a bloody battle and feared his own death and the death of his troops. Instead, however, he was greatly relieved to be coming in on the end of the battle, while the Confederates were surrendering en masse.

Brian wondered how he had perceived the varied personalities of the men he had never known, as well as the human interest sequences that unfolded. Some of the men even reappeared older in his second regression.

Meanwhile, at the victory party, he described a woman who accompanied him. She had on a lemon yellow hoop dress with black trim. This would not have been one of his preferred colors. MaryLynne Bauer, a Civil War costume expert (see chapter 9), said this color was popular during the Civil War. Brian had not known this.

Even though Brian didn't bring forth a complete name during his regression, I checked the National Archives military records for possible matches to his past life. They showed a Lieutenant Henry E. Munger, of the 18th New York, who mustered in as a sergeant in Albany and was promoted to 2nd and 1st lieutenant. Although one record[165] indicated that Munger mustered out in 1863, another archives record dated April 30, 1863, showed him mustering in November 1 in Alexandria for two years. Brian's regression personality had appeared to reenlist and change units. There are no further records to document this, nor any further information from Brian's hypnosis narrative. Other National Archives military records show a 1st Lieutenant Samuel Maurice Morgan, Company F, 86th New York Volunteer Infantry, who mustered in as a 1st lieutenant, was promoted to captain, spent time in a camp near Falmouth, Virginia, and served as an aide to a general. (There was no mention of this in the regression either.)

Information compiled by Phisterer in 1909 made mention of Captain Byron B. Morris, of the 81st New York Volunteer Infantry, who mustered in as a private in Company I. He was promoted to corporal and reenlisted as lst lieutenant in Company F in 1864. He fought in Virginia and was present through the end of the war.[166] First Lieutenant Charles B. Morrill, of the 60th New York Volunteer Infantry, enrolled in Ogdensburg, New York, as a private in Company D, was promoted to corporal and sergeant. A lst lieutenant in Company B, he mustered out with his company (possibly to Ogdensburg).[167] Phisterer also mentioned a Michael Nolan, of the 60th New York Volunteer Infantry, who mustered in at Ogdensburg as lst sergeant in Company F. He was later promoted to 2nd and lst lieutenant in Company I and then captain of Company D. His company fought in the Virginia area. Nolan mustered out with his company (possibly to Ogdensburg) after the end of the war in July 1865.[168]

A perfect name and unit match, although not a viable life match, was Lieutenant James H. Morgan, 18th New York Volunteer Infantry, who mustered in as a 1st lieutenant and resigned September 1861 because of back pain. He later served in the 7th New York Heavy Artillery and died in Salisbury Prison.[169] Interestingly, Brian had back problems in this life.

Whether or not a perfect match was found, what was equally as important was that with Brian's expertise as a Civil War historian, he verified that every detail he experienced in both his regressions was 100 percent accurate and far more realistic than reenacting. In addition, the historical consultant, who gets paid to scrutinize major movies for their authenticity, was additionally impressed when he learned that the other reenactors' regressions were also historically accurate—even when they thought that what they had experienced was incorrect.

Since he was a youngster, Brian had compiled a wealth of information about the Civil War. That knowledge and the writing he's done on the subject lent a literary richness to his vivid descriptions. His attention to detail helped him articulate his narrative while under hypnosis, so that my role as facilitator was greatly eased.

Brian's love of history might allow us to conjecture that he—and others like him—may actually be the very people among us who remember past lives without knowing it. For them, it seems, history comes alive in their imagination. One could even suspect that historians who specialize in a specific period might well have lived at that time. Perhaps the freshness of their memory is what even leads them to fall in love with history.

Through Brian's firsthand past-life experience, he now was consciously aware of a fresh perspective and new insights that moved beyond statistical knowledge, merging with it and bringing forward additional understanding from the heart.

16

Echoes Revisited

The late afternoon sun shone through the trees on a warm day in late March 1995 as I searched for the weather-worn headstones of two Civil War soldiers buried at Antietam, Maryland. Modern computers at the entrance to the park had helped to narrow the search to two clusters of graves, arranged by states. Although some names had been washed away by time, my friends helped me locate the soldiers whose military lives I had already reviewed at the National Archives. As I stood in front of their graves, I got an eerie sensation as I contemplated the possibility that one of the men buried there may have been a match with the personality that Stephen Melko had recalled during his regression. If that were the case, then how would Steve feel if he were to stand here, as I was doing, peering at a grave that could have been his own in another life? I stopped to ponder what this could mean about death, rebirth, and the meaning of the soul. Were our bodies and personalities like costumes and roles that we assumed?

Standing in the battlefield cemetery, I recalled the fear the reenactors had expressed as they faced death during their regressions. Momentarily, the hours of research I had done at National Archives microfiche machines flooded into mind. Could the lives the men and women recalled under hypnosis have been genuine past-life memories?

Admittedly, the reenactors had rated themselves high in their knowledge of the Civil War, extremely high in their knowledge of reenacting, and above average in their ability to perform first-person dialogues in character. Their knowledge gave them the ability to observe a great depth of detail during their regressions. They were often surprised by what they didn't know, couldn't have known, or were relieved when what they anticipated would happen didn't.

Most historical data, even small details brought forth by the regressions, turned out to be accurate. Amazingly, the regression material was determined to be accurate when reenactors' preconceived notions or knowledge was proved wrong. One of the most easily traced past-life characters was Alan McBride's, a reenactor who had little scholarly knowledge of the war. Though he did not care much for historical details, Buddy Bare's belief in the possibility of reincarnation burgeoned after the details of his regression proved to be historically accurate.

During my study, I was astonished by how passionate the participants felt about re-creating Civil War life and battles. It was obvious that the nineteenth century had seeped into nearly every area of their contemporary lives. At Buddy's wedding, the entire wedding party was dressed in Civil War-era attire. Meanwhile, Rob Hodge said he'd lay down his life for the historical preservation of the battlefields. He worked odd jobs that gave him the flexibility to be seriously involved in reenacting, while carving a career niche in Civil War movies and screenwriting. Dave Purschwitz's home was like a Civil War museum. He made his own Civil War-period furniture, flags, and clothing. Tom Galleher rolled his own cigarettes. MaryLynne Bauer was a consultant for Civil War clothing design. And, according to Dave Morse's wife, dedication to "the hobby" could even jeopardize relationships!

Several of the reenactors even looked as if they had just stepped out of the 1850s and confessed that they'd be more comfortable if the clock were turned back 130 years. Dave Morse and Rob Hodge have been told they look like Civil War notables. Besides Rob's Civil War appearance, he was named after Robert E. Lee and was born on Stonewall Jackson's birthday.

Rob and Dave are like nearly all the other reenactors in the study who are so concerned about authenticity that they don't use sleeping bags or take igloo coolers to reenactments. All have at least one authentic uniform complete with required equipment. Some even wear period underwear. Paul Jones has twelve to fifteen uniforms that include the Revolutionary War and World War II.

Overall, the reenactors rated themselves a ninety percent in their desire for authenticity in reenacting, and I was elated when they overwhelmingly rated the regression experience far more realistic than reenacting. Both Brian Pohanka, a Civil War historian, and Rob Hodge, who had lost weight to match the weight of the average Civil War soldier, rated their regression experiences nearly 100 percent "farb free." Neither could find even one detail, in nearly six hours of continuous regression material, that was not historically correct.

Following the regression experience, three-fourths raised their belief in the possibility of reincarnation by nearly twenty percent. Over half said that it changed their view of reenacting, and half agreed that the experience had affected them personally.

Although most past-life regression literature claims difficulty in recalling names and other concrete details, in this study eleven out of the twelve reenactors recalled names, and all the soldiers were able to supply a unit name. David Purschwitz's recalled life as his own great-grandfather was a dramatic match. Five other possible matches closely conformed to real lifetimes and data, while six had some conformity.

Besides possible name matches and the bulk of the regression contents being historically accurate, I observed other interesting correlations.

One-third of the group was so passionate about the Civil War they were making careers in the field. One-fourth had worked or was working on a degree in history. These statistics on career choices and educational interests correlate with Edgar Cayce's philosophy of a continuity principle—that individuals bring forward talents and interests from other lifetimes.

This is further borne out by one-half having an interest in the military. In addition, four served in the military, one worked for the Department of Defense, and one had considered a career as an air force pilot. Three-fourths were interested in other wars, periods of history, or weapons. The Edgar Cayce readings reveal that military past lives are often connected with clients who, in their twentieth-century lives, had a love of firearms or an interest in wars.

Nine of my subjects were "hooked" on the Civil War by the time they were in elementary school. This was consistent with Dr. Ian Stevenson's findings of children who spontaneously remembered past lives and identified with the old personality until the age of seven. Brian Pohanka had done serious Civil War research at the age of twelve; at nine, Rob Hodge had started a letter-writing campaign to join a unit of reenactors.

Most joined "the hobby" after having attended or participated in a reenactment or having a friend in "the hobby." The battles, sites, familiar situations, or people often become subconscious triggers for the spontaneous recall of past lives.

Three-fourths had had some sort of déjà vu, spiritual, paranormal, or unexplainable experience. David Purschwitz experienced déjà vu while reenacting at the Battle of Piedmont. It was there that he, as his great-grandfather, got shot in the arm and was taken prisoner.

Although the reenactors had individually experienced particularly stirring battles, sites, or events in the course of their reenacting, Rob was the only one to recall actually having fought in one such battle during his regression.

Because reenacting was meeting so many personal needs for those who participated in the study, they have cumulatively spent more than 167 years in "the hobby," or an average of fourteen years each. For them, I found that reenacting met multidimensional needs, ranging from paying homage to the past and to the dead, to living history and educating others, to camping with friends and escaping their current life's pressures.

Predictably, most of the reenactors' current alignment to the Union or Confederate side correlated positively with sympathies held in the area in which they grew up or held by their families. Only Alan McBride held a firm allegiance to the Union for ideological reasons in spite of his geographical upbringing or family influence. Of the seven who changed their units, only MaryLynne Bauer changed for ideological reasons.

One of the most intriguing facts to result from the study was that only two had past-life recall as soldiers on the opposite side of their preference in reenacting. Of the pair, David Morse considered himself neutral, and David Purschwitz, who was 100 percent committed to the Confederate cause, had previous memories as his Yankee great-grandfather. The intensity of conviction for his current alignment was over eighty percent, as was the level of commitment of the ten reenactors who were on the same side in both lifetimes. One possible explanation could be that fighting, being wounded, or even dying on that side could affirm a strong commitment. This was in line with the theory, borne out in the Edgar Cayce readings, that—like our talents—our actions, biases, and prejudices continue from lifetime to lifetime. It is also consistent with past-life therapy literature which highlights the importance of recurring thought and behavior patterns.

All reenactors experienced emotions and physical feelings during the regressions. They all vividly described what they saw, felt, or heard. Nine of ten soldiers expressed frustration at not knowing where they were going. Nine were hungry or thirsty, eight were tired, and seven complained that their feet hurt. Only two were officers; one a corporal. In this regard, it's significant that the recalled lifetimes were not glamorous. Only one soldier didn't recall being wounded. Only four soldiers survived the war, six died, and three were prisoners.

Of the six deaths experienced, all had exhibited some of the near-death characteristics described by Raymond Moody, M.D. Five reported pain and then its release; four viewed the body; four saw a light. Interestingly, even when the men were wounded and didn't die, most experienced similar NDE characteristics.

Of the deaths or woundings, three cases can possibly correlate to health problems today. Buddy Bare has had heart surgery in this life, while in his regression death experience he realized he had probably been shot in the chest. Stephen Melko had asthma in his present life and recalled being wounded in the chest. MaryLynne Bauer had experienced sensations of panic upon recalling darkness before her Civil War death and sometimes still felt uncomfortable in the dark.

Of the twelve reenactors, only David Purschwitz recalled being his great-grandfather and only MaryLynne recalled a past-life sex change. These statistics, eight percent, correlate closely with Stevenson's findings of five to ten percent for ancestral return and five percent for sex changes.

Three-fourths of the group reached the level of processing past-life memories as if the information were running as a continuous film. Seven could make minimal adjustments to the "script" when asked. The fact that others could not alter the scene indicates they were not unduly influenced by the therapist's suggestions.

There is no doubt that the Civil War had a profound impact on the lives of these reenactors, all of whom experienced past-life memories of the era. They have given many years of their lives and thousands of dollars to "the hobby," and to the study of the Civil War. It's clear to me that further study could be done on this population.

One area of concentration for further research could be to focus on and track physical or emotional problems related to the Civil War and any emotional healing resulting from the regression work. It may also be of interest to track reenactors at various time intervals after the regression to see if their intense interest in the Civil War continues, lessens, or heightens and what the findings may mean.

Further study could be done utilizing regression work with large groups of reenactors. Perhaps if regressions are utilized, any resulting healing may help individuals and possibly the group as a whole begin to break the cycle of emotional ties to war. Perhaps the roots of soldiering lifetimes could be traced to their origins and, when understood on a soul level, the patterns could be released. Conceivably, some individual and group karma could be transmuted. In turn, this may make an impact on beginning to heal the devastating wounds the Civil War left on the country—a war that was the ultimate in fratricide. Such research could also make a positive impact on beginning to heal current issues of racism.

More than 620,000 soldiers perished in the Civil War, and evidence would indicate that most souls have continued on to live other lives. We have no idea how many of those are alive now, perhaps suffering inwardly from more than a century-old form of post-traumatic shock syndrome. Still other souls, however, linger at the battlefields and around individuals. Through spirit releasement techniques, these earthbound entities could be liberated.

Another interesting past-life regression study would be one with a group of people who are currently at war. Any correlations that emerge may give insight into war itself and into its possible healing and prevention in the future. In the case of this study, the recall of past lives in the Civil War era of all twelve reenactors may be one possible answer to questions some reenactors ask themselves. Why are they so passionate about a war and lifestyle that occurred more than 130 years ago? Why do they devote so much time, energy, and money to "the hobby"? Whether the passion resulted from a former lifetime, from sensitivity to genetic memories, or whether the passion created the memories may never be successfully determined. But the fact that all twelve reenactors recalled Civil War lifetimes that were consistent with the results of other regression studies and literature and had some historical validity as well may lead to speculation and further study.

While these regressions don't prove that reincarnation exists, the beliefs of those who participated in the study changed dramatically after their regressions because what was revealed to them during the regressions was far more vivid and realistic than what they had previously known. Could their emotional past-life experiences have been an indication of the immortality of the soul?

In terms of the United States, the watermark on the Washington Monument, where construction stopped as the Civil War loomed, stands as a reminder of the break between the states. The indelible stain is reminiscent of a deep scar on the American psyche of a time in the not-too-distant past where brother took up arms against brother. Perhaps the reenactors' "hobby" reminds us of the time when we were divided, while the regressions reveal something indomitable, constant, and indestructible in the American spirit. When listening carefully, one can hear the messages that emerge from the lingering echoes from the battlefield.

"In great deeds something abides. On great fields something stays. Forms change and pass, bodies disappear—but spirits linger, to consecrate ground for the vision-place of souls.

"And reverent men and women from afar and generations that know us not and that we know not of, heart-drawn to see where and by whom great things were suffered and done to them, shall come to this deathless field, to ponder and dream. And lo! The shadow of a mighty presence shall wrap them in its bosom, and the power of the vision pass into their souls."

Major General Joshua Lawrence Chamberlain
Gettysburg, 1889

Endnotes

1
Echoes in the Mist

1. *Civil War Handbook,* William H. Price, p. 14.
2. *Ibid.,* p. 14.

2
Do We Live Again?

3. *Exploring Reincarnation,* Hans TenDam, p. 7.
4. *The Search for Bridey Murphy,* Morey Bernstein, p. 244.
5. *Have You Lived Before This Life?* L. Ron Hubbard, p. 50.
6. See *Past Lives Therapy* by Morris Netherton.
7. *Many Lifetimes,* Denys Kelsey and Joan Grant, p. 53.
8. See *Past Lives, Future Loves* by Dick Sutphen.
9. See *Many Lives, Many Masters* and *Through Time into Healing,* both by Brian Weiss, M.D.
10. *You Have Been Here Before,* Edith Fiore, p. 6.
11. See *Reliving Past Lives: The Evidence Under Hypnosis* by Helen Wambach.
12. See *Regression Therapy: A Handbook for Professionals, Vols. I and II,* by Winafred Blake Lucas.
13. See *Mind-Probe Hypnosis* by Irene Hickman.
14. *Through Time into Healing, op. cit.,* p. 25.
15. *Many Mansions,* Gina Cerminara, p. 42.
16. *Edgar Cayce on Reincarnation,* Noel Langley, p. 84.
17. *Ibid.*
18. *Children Who Remember Previous Lives: A Question of Reincarnation,* Ian Stevenson, M.D., p. 180.
19. *Many Mansions, op. cit.,* p. 89.
20. *Children Who Remember Previous Lives: A Question of Reincarnation, op. cit.,* p. 180.
21. *You Have Been Here Before, op. cit.,* p. 8.
22. *Exploring Reincarnation, op. cit.,* p. 226.
23. *Many Mansions, op. cit.,* p. 184.
24. See *Your Past Lives: A Reincarnation Handbook* by Michael Talbot.

25. *Edgar Cayce on Reincarnation, op. cit.,* pp. 179-201.

26. *Beyond the Ashes: Cases of Reincarnation from the Holocaust,* Rabbi Yonassan Gershom, pp. xix, 304.

27. "Reincarnation: Field Studies and Theoretical Issues," Ian Stevenson, M.D., *Handbook of Parapsychology,* p. 632.

28. "Reincarnation," Benjamin Walker, *Man, Myth, and Magic,* pp. 2346-2350.

29. See *Reincarnation: Fact or Fallacy?* by Geoffrey Hodson.

30. See *Reincarnation in World Thought* by Joseph Head and S.L. Cranston.

31. *Whispers of the Mind,* Elaine Stephens, p. 3.

32. "An Unusual Case of Hypnotic Regression with Some Unexplained Contents," Linda Tarazi, *Journal of the American Society for Psychical Research,* Vol. 84, October 1990, pp. 315-335.

33. *Modern Hypnosis: Theory and Practice,* Masud Ansari, p. 26.

34. "Investigative Hypnosis: A Developing Specialty," M. Reiser and M. Neilsen, *American Journal of Clinical Hypnosis,* Vol. 23, 1980, pp. 75-84.

35. See "Hypermnesia and Reminiscence in Recall: A Historical and Empirical Review," David G. Payne, *Psychological Bulletin,* Vol. 101 (1), 1987, pp. 5-27; "Hypnosis and the Learning and Recall of Visually Presented Material," Gordon L. Stager and Richard M. Lundy, *International Journal of Clinical and Experimental Hypnosis,* Vol. 33, 1985, pp. 27-39; "Eyewitness Memory Enhancement in the Police Interview: Cognitive Retrieval Mnemonics Versus Hypnosis," R. Edward Geiselman, *et al., Journal of Applied Psychology,* Vol. 70, 1985, pp. 401-412; and "Hypnotic Effects of Hypermnesia," Patricia A. Register and John F. Kihlstrom, *International Journal of Clinical and Experimental Hypnosis,* Vol. 35, 1987, pp. 155-170.

36. *Ibid.,* pp. 155-170. Also see "Use of Hypnosis as an Aid to Eyewitness Memory," John C. Yuille and N. Hope McEwan, *Journal of Applied Psychology,* Vol. 70, May 1985, pp. 398-400.

37. "Truth in Memory: Ramifications for Psychotherapy and Hypnotherapy," Steven Jay Lynn and Michael R. Nash, *American Journal of Clinical Hypnosis,* Vol. 36, 1994, pp. 194-207.

38. "10 Q & A Past-Lives Regression," Wilson and Barber's 1983 study in Perry, Campbell, *et al.,* pp. 50-59.

39. "Hypnotic Age Regression in an Experimental and Clinical Context," Philip Spinhoven and Jorrit van Wijk, *American Journal of*

Clinical Hypnosis, Vol. 35(1), July 1992, pp. 41- 45.

40. "Hypnotic Age Regression and the Autokinetic Effect," Eric J. Van Denburg, *American Journal of Clinical Hypnosis,* Vol. 33, 1991, pp. 51-55.

41. See "Cognitive Stage Regression Through Hypnosis: Are Earlier Cognitive Stages Retrievable?" by Paul S. Silverman and Paul D. Retzlaff, *International Journal of Clinical and Experimental Hypnosis,* Vol. 34, 1986.

42. "10 Q & A Past-Lives Regression," *op. cit.,* pp. 50-59.

43. *Ibid.,* pp. 50-59. Also see "A Case of the Psychotherapist's Fallacy: Hypnotic Regression to Previous Lives" by Ian Stevenson, *American Journal of Clinical Hypnosis,* Vol. 36(3), January 1994; "Divided Consciousness in Hypnosis: The Implications of the Hidden Observer" by E.R. Hilgard, *Hypnosis: Developments in Research and New Perspectives;* and "Past-Life Hypnotic Regression: A Critical View," Nicholas Spanos, *The Hundredth Monkey and Other Paradigms of the Paranormal: A Skeptical Inquirer Collection,* pp. 78-84.

44. *Ibid.,* pp. 78-84.

45. *Ibid.,* pp. 78-84.

46. "10 Q & A Past-Lives Regression," *op. cit.,* pp. 50-59.

47. "The Effect of Hypnosis on Long Delayed Recall," J.M. Stalnaker and E.E. Riddle, *Journal of General Psychology,* Vol. 6, 1932, pp. 429-440.

48. *Exploring Reincarnation, op. cit.,* p. 23.

49. *All in the Mind: Reincarnation, Hypnotic Regression, Stigmata, Multiple Personality, and Other Little-Understood Powers of the Mind,* Ian Wilson, p. 59.

50. "Past-Life Regression: The Grand Illusion," Kampman in Melvin Harris's *Not Necessarily the New Age: Critical Essays,* pp. 135-136.

51. *The Unquiet Dead,* Edith Fiore, pp. 119-123.

52. See *Spirit Releasement Therapy: A Technique Manual,* William Baldwin, p. 211. Also see *Life After Life* by Raymond A. Moody, Jr.

53. *The Unquiet Dead, op. cit.*

54. *Regression Therapy: A Handbook for Professionals, op. cit.,* p. 17.

55. *Twenty Cases Suggestive of Reincarnation,* Ian Stevenson, M.D., p. 343.

56. *Man and His Symbols*, Carl G. Jung, *et al.*, p. 107.

57. See "Can Our Memories Survive the Death of Our Brains?" Rupert Sheldrake, *What Survives? Contemporary Explorations of Life After Death*, pp. 111-121; *The Rebirth of Nature: The Greening of Science and God* by Rupert Sheldrake; and also *Quantum Healing*, Deepak Chopra, M.D., p. 87.

3
A Short Course in Reenacting and Civil War Buzz Words

58. See "Letters from Today's Civil War," Gary D. Ford, *Southern Living*, March 1993, pp. 94-96; and "126 Years After the Real Battle of Cedar Creek, Men in Blue and Grey Fight a Much More Civil War," Michael Neill and Bill Shaw, *People*, November 12, 1990, pp. 173-175.

59. See *Reenactor's Journal: For Civil War Military and Civilian Reenactors* by Rick Keating; *Camp Chase Gazette: The Voice of Civil War Reenacting* by Grant MacMeans; and *The Civil War News* by C. Peter Jorgensen.

60. See *Rifle and Light Infantry Tactics: For the Exercise and Manoeuvres of Troops When Acting as Light Infantry and Riflemen* by William Joseph Hardee.

61. See *Infantry Tactics: For the Instruction, Exercise, and Manoeuvres of the Soldier, A Company, Line of Skirmishers, Battalion, Brigade, or Corps D'Armee* by Silas Casey.

62. "In the Grip of the Civil War," Lew Lord, *U.S. News and World Report*, August 15, 1988, p. 50.

63. *Ibid.*, pp. 48-59.

64. See *Gilham's School of the Soldier and School of the Company; For Infantry and Rifle Drill* by William Gilham.

65. *Civil War Handbook*, William H. Price, pp. 12-16.

66. *Ibid.*, p. 11.

4
Steve: The Soldier Returns

67. See *Life After Life* and *The Light Beyond*, both by Raymond Moody, Jr.

68. *Children Who Remember Previous Lives: A Question of Rein-*

carnation, Ian Stevenson, M.D., p. 183.

69. See *Regression Therapy: A Handbook for Professionals, Vols. I and II,* by Winafred Blake Lucas.

70. *Reliving Past Lives: The Evidence Under Hypnosis,* Helen Wambach, p. 142.

71. *Exploring Reincarnation,* Hans TenDam, p. 177.

72. *Edgar Cayce on Reincarnation,* Noel Langley, p. 109.

73. See *Many Lifetimes* by Denys Kelsey and Joan Grant.

74. Historical interview, Brian Pohanka.

5
Alan: Beginner's Luck

75. Historical interview, Brian Pohanka.

76. *Civil War Prisons: A Study of War Psychology,* William B. Hasseltine, p. 152.

77. *Ibid.,* p. 152.

78. *Ibid.,* p. 145.

79. *Ibid.,* p. 152.

80. Historical interview, Brian Pohanka.

81. See *The Salisbury Prison: A Case Study of Confederate Military Prisons,* Louis A. Brown.

82. *Ibid.* Also see National Archives military and pension records.

83. *Ibid.* Also see *The Salisbury Prison: A Case Study of Confederate Military Prisons, op. cit.,* p. 272.

84. *The Southern Side: Or Andersonville Prison,* R. Randolph Stevenson, M.D., p. 382.

6
Dave: Strange Coincidences

85. *Civil War Handbook,* William H. Price, p. 57.

86. *Exploring Reincarnation,* Hans TenDam, p. 120.

87. "Reincarnation: Field Studies and Theoretical Issues," Ian Stevenson, M.D., *Handbook of Parapsychology,* p. 656.

88. See source material compiled by Dave Purschwitz that includes: National Archives military and pension records, the New York State Archives, official records of the Union and Confederate

Armies, the Time-Life Civil War Series, records from the New York City Library and records from the Augusta County Library in Fisherville, Virginia.

7
Rob: Out of the Mouths of Babes

89. *Children Who Remember Previous Lives: A Question of Reincarnation*, Ian Stevenson, M.D., p. 182.

90. See *Twenty Cases Suggestive of Reincarnation* by Ian Stevenson, M.D.; and "Reincarnation: Field Studies and Theoretical Issues" by Ian Stevenson, M.D., *Handbook of Parapsychology*.

91. *Units of the Confederate Army*, Joseph Crute, Jr., p. 28.

92. *Ibid.*, p. 30.

93. *Civil War Handbook*, William H. Price, p. 13.

94. Historical interview, Brian Pohanka.

95. *Civil War Handbook*, *op. cit.*, p. 16.

96. Historical interview, Brian Pohanka.

97. *Civil War Handbook*, *op. cit.*, p. 13.

98. Historical interview, Brian Pohanka.

99. *Ibid.*

100. *Ibid.*

101. *Ibid.*

102. *Ibid.*

8
Buddy: Heart Problems

103. See *Pickett's Charge* by George R. Stewart.

104. *Civil War Handbook*, William H. Price, p. 12.

105. Historical interview, Brian Pohanka.

106. *Ibid.*

107. *Units of the Confederate Army*, Joseph Crute, Jr., p. 87.

108. Historical interview, Brian Pohanka.

109. *Ibid.*

110. See *The 7th Virginia Regimental History Series* by David Riggs.

111. *The 17th Virginia Regimental History Series*, Lee A. Wallace, p. 105.

112. *The 58th Virginia Regimental History Series,* Robert Driver, Jr., p. 94.

113. See *The 40th Virginia Regimental History Series* by Robert E. Krick.

114. See *History of the 49th Virginia Infantry CSA: Extra Billy Smith's Boys* by Laura Hale and Stanley Phillips.

115. See *The 33rd Virginia Regimental History Series* by Lowell Reidenbaugh; and interment records from Spotsylvania National Cemetery.

9
MaryLynne: A Hoop Skirt for a Gun

116. *Children Who Remember Previous Lives: A Question of Reincarnation,* Ian Stevenson, M.D., p. 185.

117. *Many Lifetimes,* Denys Kelsey and Joan Grant, p. 21.

118. "Reincarnation: Field Studies and Theoretical Issues," Ian Stevenson, M.D., *Handbook of Parapsychology,* p. 655.

119. *Exploring Reincarnation,* Hans TenDam, p. 297.

120. *Reliving Past Lives: The Evidence Under Hypnosis,* Helen Wambach, p. 124.

121. *Exploring Reincarnation, op. cit.,* p. 122.

122. "Reincarnation: Field Studies and Theoretical Issues," *op. cit.,* p. 656.

123. See *Roster of Ohio Soldiers, 1861-1866: War of the Rebellion* by Ohio Roster Commission.

10
Dale: Richmond Burning

124. "The Evidence for Survival from Claimed Memories of Former Incarnations, Part 1: Review of the Data. Part 2: Analysis of the Data and Suggestions for Further Investigations," Ian Stevenson, *Journal of the American Society for Psychical Research,* April and October 1960, p. 114.

125. *Ibid.,* p. 114.

126. See "Second Annual Directory of the City of Richmond for 1860" by W. Eugene Ferslow, *Series of Bibliographies of American Directories.*

127. See *The 55th Virginia Regimental History Series* by Richard O'Sullivan.

128. *Ibid.*

129. See *History of the 49th Virginia Infantry CSA: Extra Billy Smith's Boys* by Laura Hale and Stanley Phillips.

130. See *The 37th Virginia Regimental History Series* by Thomas Rankin.

131. See *Richmond Volunteers: The Volunteer Companies of the City of Richmond and Henrico County, Virginia, 1861-65,* by Louis H. Manarin and Lee A. Wallace, Jr.

132. See National Archives military records; and *Units of the Confederate Army* by Joseph Crute, Jr., p. 350.

133. *Ibid.,* p. 386.

11
Ed: Food for the Soul

134. *You Have Been Here Before,* Edith Fiore, p. 240.

135. *Coming Back,* Raymond A. Moody, Jr., p. 45.

136. *Edgar Cayce on Reincarnation,* Noel Langley, p. 115.

137. *The Photographic History of the Civil War,* pp. 76-81.

138. *Civil War Handbook,* William H. Price, p. 13.

139. See *Mosby's Rangers* by James J. Williamson. (Note: The incident was described as a planned ambush of a Union supply wagon train by Mosby's Cavalry on the valley pike near Newtown, Virginia. When the cavalry began to charge, they realized the wagons were supported by infantry and cavalry. The Rangers turned back, but only after the Yankees had fired a volley and killed a soldier named William E. Embrey.)

140. See *The 43rd Battalion Virginia Cavalry, Mosby's Command Regimental History* by Hugh G. Keen.

141. See National Archives prison list; and National Park Service, Point Lookout, Maryland.

142. See *The 40th Virginia Regimental History Series,* Robert Krick, p. 97; and National Archives military records.

12
Tom: An Officer and a Gentleman

143. *Reliving Past Lives: The Evidence Under Hypnosis*, Helen Wambach, p. 114.

144. *Edgar Cayce on Reincarnation*, Noel Langley, p. 104.

145. Historical interview, Brian Pohanka.

146. See *These Honored Dead: The Union Casualties at Gettysburg* by John Busey.

13
David: Living Death

147. *Whispers of the Mind*, Elaine Stephens, p. 3.

148. See *The Pattons: A Personal History of an American Family* by Robert H. Patton.

149. "The Evidence for Survival from Claimed Memories of Former Incarnations, Part l: Review of the Data. Part 2: Analysis of the Data and Suggestions for Further Investigations," Ian Stevenson, *Journal of the American Society for Psychical Research*, April and October 1960, p. 114.

150. See *You Have Been Here Before* by Edith Fiore.

151. See *Reliving Past Lives: The Evidence Under Hypnosis* by Helen Wambach.

152. See *Coming Back* by Raymond A. Moody, Jr.

153. "A Series of Possibly Paranormal Recurrent Dreams," Ian Stevenson, *Journal of Scientific Exploration*, August 1992, pp. 281-289.

154. *All for the Union: The Civil War Diary and Letters of Elisha Hunt Rhodes*, Robert Hunt Rhodes, pp. 115-116.

155. See *These Honored Dead: The Union Casualties at Gettysburg* by John Busey.

156. See National Archives military records; and *Annual Report of the Adjutant General of the State of Rhode Island and Providence Plantations for the Year 1865* by Brigadier General Elisha Dyer.

14
Paul: Home to Alexandria

157. "In the Grip of the Civil War," Lew Lord, *U.S. News and World Report,* August 15, 1988, p. 52.

158. See *Reliving Past Lives: The Evidence Under Hypnosis* by Helen Wambach.

159. See *Regression Therapy: A Handbook for Professionals, Vols. I and II,* by Winafred Blake Lucas; *Past Lives Therapy* by Morris Netherton; *You Have Been Here Before* by Edith Fiore; and *Past Lives, Future Lives: Accounts of Regressions and Progressions Through Hypnosis* by Bruce Goldberg.

160. *Many Mansions,* Gina Cerminara, p. 57.

161. See *Exploring Reincarnation* by Hans TenDam, p. 121.

162. See *Reincarnation: Claiming Your Past, Creating Your Future* by Lynn Sparrow.

163. See *Russell's Civil War Photographs: 116 Historic Prints* by Andrew Russell.

15
Brian: A Historian's Heart

164. *Civil War Handbook,* William H. Price, p. 24.

165. *New York in the War of the Rebellion: 1861-1865,* Frederick Phisterer, p. 1954.

166. *Ibid.*

167. *Ibid.,* p. 2550.

168. *Ibid.,* p. 2550.

169. *Ibid.,* p. 1954. Also see National Archives military records; and *The Heroes of Albany: A Memorial of the Patriot-Martyrs of the City and County of Albany,* Rufus Clark, pp. 542-544.

Bibliography

Ansari, Masud. *Modern Hypnosis: Theory and Practice* (Washington, D.C.: Mas-Press, 1991).

Baldwin, William. *Spirit Releasement Therapy: A Technique Manual* (Falls Church, Va.: Human Potential Foundation Press, 1992).

Bernstein, Morey. *The Search for Bridey Murphy* (New York, N.Y.: Doubleday, 1978).

Bolduc, Henry. *The Journey Within* (Virginia Beach, Va.: Inner Vision, 1988).

Brown, Louis A. *The Salisbury Prison: A Case Study of Confederate Military Prisons* (Wilmington, N.C.: Broad Foot Pub., 1992).

Busey, John W. *These Honored Dead: The Union Casualties at Gettysburg* (Hightown, N.J.: Longstreet House, 1988).

Casey, Silas. *Infantry Tactics: For the Instruction, Exercise, and Manoeuvres of the Soldier, A Company, Line of Skirmishers, Battalion, Brigade, or Corps D'Armee* (Columbia, S.C.: Steam-Power Presses of Evans and Cogswell, 1864).

Cerminara, Gina. *Many Mansions* (New York, N.Y.: Sloane, 1970).

Cerminara, Gina. *The World Within* (London, Eng.: Daniel, 1973).

Chopra, Deepak, M.D. *Quantum Healing* (New York, N.Y.: Bantam, 1989).

Clark, Rufus W. *The Heroes of Albany: A Memorial of the Patriot-Martyrs of the City and County of Albany* (Albany, N.Y.: S. R. Gray, Pub., 1866).

Crute, Joseph, Jr. *Units of the Confederate Army* (Midlothian, Va.: Derwent Books, 1987).

Driver, Robert, Jr. *The 58th Virginia Regimental History Series* (Lynchburg, Va.: H. E. Howard, Inc., 1990).

Dyer, Brigadier General Elisha. *Annual Report of the Adjutant General of the State of Rhode Island and Providence Plantations for the Year 1865* (2 Vols.). (Providence, R.I.: E.L. Freeman & Son, Printers for the State, 1895).

Ferslow, W. Eugene. "Second Annual Directory of the City of Richmond for 1860," in Dorothy N. Spear (ed.), *Series of Bibliographies of American Directories* (Worcester, Mass.: American Antiquarian Society, 1961).

Fiore, Edith. *The Unquiet Dead* (New York, N.Y.: Ballantine, 1987).

Fiore, Edith. *You Have Been Here Before* (New York, N.Y.: Ballantine, 1978).

Ford, Gary D. "Letters from Today's Civil War." *Southern Living* (March 1993), 94-96.

Geiselman, R. Edward, *et al.* "Eyewitness Memory Enhancement in the Police Interview: Cognitive Retrieval Mnemonics Versus Hypnosis." *Journal of Applied Psychology* (70: 1985), 401-412.

Gilham, William. *Gilham's School of the Soldier and School of the Company; For Infantry and Rifle Drill* (Augusta, Ga.: Bryan and Thompson, 1861).

Goldberg, Bruce. *Past Lives, Future Lives: Accounts of Regressions and Progressions Through Hypnosis* (North Hollywood, Calif.: New Castle, 1982).

Gunn, Ralph White. *The 24th Virginia Regimental History Series* (Lynchburg, Va.: H.E. Howard, Inc., 1987).

Hale, Laura, and Phillips, Stanley. *History of the 49th Virginia Infantry CSA: Extra Billy Smith's Boys* (Lynchburg, Va.: H. E. Howard, Inc., 1981).

Hardee, William Joseph. *Rifle and Light Infantry Tactics: For the Exercise and Manoeuvres of Troops When Acting as Light Infantry and Riflemen* (Louisville, Ky.: J. W. Tompkins, 1861).

Harris, Melvin. "Past-Life Regression: The Grand Illusion," in Robert Basil (ed.), *Not Necessarily the New Age: Critical Essays* (Buffalo, N.Y.: Prometheus Books, 1988).

Hasseltine, William B. *Civil War Prisons: A Study of War Psychology* (New York, N.Y.: Frederick Ungar Publishing Co., 1930).

Head, Joseph, and Cranston, S.L. *Reincarnation in World Thought* (New York, N.Y.: Julian Press, 1967).

Hickman, Irene. *Mind-Probe Hypnosis* (Kirksville, Mo.: Journal Printing, 1983).

Hilgard, E.R. "Divided Consciousness in Hypnosis: The Implications of the Hidden Observer," in E. Fromm and R. E. Shor (eds.), *Hypnosis: Developments in Research and New Perspectives* (New York, N.Y.: Aldine, 1979).

Hodson, Geoffrey. *Reincarnation: Fact or Fallacy?* (Wheaton, Ill.: Theosophical Publishing House, 1972).

Hormuth, Tracy. Interview on Reenactments and Reenactors. (Hormuth, a Park William County, Virginia, Ranger, was organizer of the reenactment at Manassas in 1993.)

Hubbard, L. Ron. *Have You Lived Before This Life?* (Los Angeles, Calif.: Scientology Publications, 1974).

Interment records from the National Cemeteries of Winchester, Culpeper, Spotsylvania, Fredericksburg, Virginia; Antietam Battlefield, Maryland.

Jorgensen, C. Peter. *The Civil War News* (Arlington, Maine: Cutter & Locke, Inc., April 1993).

Jung, Carl G., *et al. Man and His Symbols* (Garden City, N.Y.: Doubleday, 1964).

Kapleau, Philip. *The Wheel of Life and Death* (New York, N.Y.: Doubleday, 1989).

Keating, Rick. *Reenactor's Journal: For Civil War Military and Civilian Reenactors* (Varna, Ill.: Patrick Publishing, 1993).

Keen, Hugh G. *The 43rd Battalion Virginia Cavalry, Mosby's Command* (Lynchburg, Va.: H. E. Howard Publishers, 1993).

Kelsey, Denys, and Grant, Joan. *Many Lifetimes* (London, Eng.: Corgi, 1976).

Krick, Robert E. *The 40th Virginia Regimental History Series* (Lynchburg, Va.: H. E. Howard, Inc., 1985).

Langley, Noel. *Edgar Cayce on Reincarnation* (London, Eng.: Howard Baker, 1969).

Lawrence, Jean-Roche, and Perry, Campbell. "Hypnotically Created Memory Among Highly Hypnotizable Subjects." *Science* (222: 1983), 523-524.

Lord, Lew. "In the Grip of the Civil War." *U.S. News and World Report* (August 15, 1988), 48-59.

Lucas, Winafred Blake. *Regression Therapy: A Handbook for Professionals. Vol. I: Past-Life Therapy. Vol. II: Special Instances of Altered State Work* (Crest Park, Calif.: Deep Forest Press, 1993).

Lynn, Steven Jay, and Nash, Michael R. "Truth in Memory: Ramifications for Psychotherapy and Hypnotherapy." *American Journal of Clinical Hypnosis* (36: 1994), 194-207.

MacMeans, Grant. *Camp Chase Gazette: The Voice of Civil War Reenacting* (Marietta, Ohio: Camp Chase Publishing Co., Inc., April 1993).

Manarin, Louis H., and Wallace, Lee A., Jr. *Richmond Volunteers: The Volunteer Companies of the City of Richmond and Henrico County, Virginia, 1861-65* (Richmond, Va.: Westover Press, 1969).

Military service and pension records, National Archives. Union soldiers: microfilm and individual records; Confederates: on microfilm. Compiled military service records: Home Guard, Record Group 109. Andersonville prisoners of war: Record Group 249.

Moody, Raymond A., Jr. *Coming Back* (New York, N.Y.: Bantam, 1991).

Moody, Raymond A., Jr. *Life After Life* (New York, N.Y.: Bantam, 1975).

Moody, Raymond A., Jr. *The Light Beyond* (New York, N.Y.: Bantam, 1988).

Neill, Michael, and Shaw, Bill. "126 Years After the Real Battle of Cedar Creek, Men in Blue and Grey Fight a Much More Civil War." *People* (November 12, 1990), 173-175.

Netherton, Morris, and Shiffrin, Nancy. *Past Lives Therapy* (New York, N.Y.: Morrow, 1978).

Ohio Roster Commission. *Roster of Ohio Soldiers, 1861-1866: War of the Rebellion* (Cincinnati, Ohio: Ohio Valley Press, 1889).

O'Sullivan, Richard. *The 55th Virginia Regimental History Series* (H.E. Howard, Inc., 1989).

Patton, Robert H. *The Pattons: A Personal History of an American Family* (New York, N.Y.: Crown Publishing, Inc., 1994).

Payne, David G. "Hypermnesia and Reminiscence in Recall: A Historical and Empirical Review." *Psychological Bulletin* (1: 1987), 5-27.

Perry, Campbell, *et al.* "10 Q & A Past-Lives Regression," 50-59.

Phisterer, Frederick. *New York in the War of the Rebellion: 1861-1865* (Albany, N.Y.: J.B. Lyon Co., State Printers, 1909).

Pohanka, Brian. Interviews that included the history of reenacting and historical verification of regression information, 1993-1994.

Rankin, Thomas. *The 37th Virginia Regimental History Series* (Lynchburg, Va.: H.E. Howard, Inc., 1987).

Register, Patricia A., and Kihlstrom, John F. "Hypnotic Effects of Hypermnesia." *International Journal of Clinical and Experimental Hypnosis* (35: 1987), 155-170.

Reidenbaugh, Lowell. *The 33rd Virginia Regimental History Series* (Lynchburg, Va.: H.E. Howard, Inc., 1987).

Reiser, M., and Neilsen, M. "Investigative Hypnosis: A Developing Specialty." *American Journal of Clinical Hypnosis* (23: 1980), 75-84.

Rhodes, Elisha Hunt. *All for the Union: The Civil War Diary and Letters of Elisha Hunt Rhodes.* Robert Hunt Rhodes (ed.). (New York, N.Y.: Orion, 1985).

Riggs, David. *The 7th Virginia Regimental History Series* (Lynchburg, Va.: H.E. Howard, Inc., 1982).

Robinson, John. Interview. History teacher/reenactor: Pre-teens Hooked on History, 1993.

Russell, Andrew J. *Russell's Civil War Photographs: 116 Historic Prints* (New York, N.Y.: Dover Publications, Inc., 1982).

Sheldrake, Rupert. "Can Our Memories Survive the Death of Our Brains?" in Gary Doore (ed.), *What Survives? Contemporary Explorations of Life After Death* (Los Angeles, Calif.: Jeremy Tarcher, Inc., 1991), 111-121.

Sheldrake, Rupert. *The Rebirth of Nature: The Greening of Science and God* (New York, N.Y.: Bantam Books, 1991).

Silverman, Paul S., and Retzlaff, Paul D. "Cognitive Stage Regression Through Hypnosis: Are Earlier Cognitive Stages Retrievable?" *International Journal of Clinical and Experimental Hypnosis* (34: 1986).

Spanos, Nicholas. "Past-Life Hypnotic Regression: A Critical View," in Kendrick Frazier (ed), *The Hundredth Monkey and Other Paradigms of the Paranormal: A Skeptical Inquirer Collection* (Buffalo, N.Y.: Prometheus Books, 1991), 78-84.

Sparrow, Lynn. *Reincarnation: Claiming Your Past, Creating Your Future* (San Francisco, Calif.: Harper & Row, 1988).

Spinhoven, Philip, and Van Wijk, Jorrit. "Hypnotic Age Regression in an Experimental and Clinical Context." *American Journal of Clinical Hypnosis* (35:1, July 1992), 41-45.

Stager, Gordon L., and Lundy, Richard M. "Hypnosis and the Learning and Recall of Visually Presented Material." *International Journal of Clinical and Experimental Hypnosis* (33: 1985), 27-39.

Stalnaker, J.M., and Riddle, E.E. "The Effect of Hypnosis on Long Delayed Recall." *Journal of General Psychology* (6: 1932), 429-440.

Stephens, Elaine. *Whispers of the Mind* (San Francisco, Calif.: Harper & Row, 1989).

Stevenson, Ian. "A Case of the Psychotherapist's Fallacy: Hypnotic Regression to Previous Lives." *American Journal of Clinical Hypnosis* (36:3, January 1994).

Stevenson, Ian. *Children Who Remember Previous Lives: A Question of Reincarnation* (Charlottesville, Va.: University Press of Virginia, 1977).

Stevenson, Ian. "The Evidence for Survival from Claimed Memories of Former Incarnations, Part l: Review of the Data. Part 2: Analysis of the Data and Suggestions for Further Investigations." *Journal of the American Society for Psychical Research* (LIV, April and October 1960), 51-71; 97-117.

Stevenson, Ian. "Reincarnation: Field Studies and Theoretical Issues," in Benjamin Wolman (ed.), *Handbook of Parapsychology* (New York, N.Y.: Van Nostrand Reinhold Co., 1977), 631-663.

Stevenson, Ian. "A Series of Possibly Paranormal Recurrent Dreams." *Journal of Scientific Exploration* (6:3, August 1992), 281-289.

Stevenson, Ian. *Twenty Cases Suggestive of Reincarnation* (Charlottesville, Va.: University Press of Virginia, 1974).

Stevenson, R. Randolph, M.D. *The Southern Side: Or Andersonville Prison* (Baltimore, Md.: Turnbull Brothers, 1876).

Stewart, George R. *Pickett's Charge* (Cambridge, Mass.: Riverside Press, 1959).

Sutphen, Dick. *Past Lives, Future Loves* (New York, N.Y.: Pocket Books, 1976).

Talbot, Michael. *Your Past Lives: A Reincarnation Handbook* (New York, N.Y.: Harmony Books, 1987).

Tarazi, Linda. "An Unusual Case of Hypnotic Regression with Some Unexplained Contents." *Journal of the American Society for Psychical Research* (84, October 1990), 315-335.

TenDam, Hans. *Exploring Reincarnation* (Great Britain: Arkana, 1990).

Van Denburg, Eric J. "Hypnotic Age Regression and the Autokinetic Effect." *American Journal of Clinical Hypnosis* (33: 1991), 51-55.

Walker, Benjamin. "Reincarnation," in Richard Cavendish, *et al.* (eds.), *Man, Myth, and Magic* (New York, N.Y.: Marshall Cavendish, 1983), 2346-2350.

Wallace, Lee A. *The 17th Virginia Regimental History Series* (Lynchburg, Va.: H.E. Howard, Inc., 1990).

Wambach, Helen. *Reliving Past Lives: The Evidence Under Hypnosis* (New York, N.Y.: Harper & Row, 1978).

Weiss, Brian, M.D. *Many Lives, Many Masters* (New York, N.Y.: Simon & Schuster, 1988).

Weiss, Brian, M.D. *Through Time into Healing* (New York, N.Y.: Simon & Schuster, 1993).

Williamson, James J. *Mosby's Rangers* (Alexandria, Va.: Time-Life Books, 1982).

Wilson, Ian. *All in the Mind: Reincarnation, Hypnotic Regression, Stigmata, Multiple Personality, and Other Little-Understood Powers of the Mind* (Garden City, N.Y.: Doubleday, 1941).

Yuille, John C., and McEwan, N. Hope. "Use of Hypnosis as an Aid to Eyewitness Memory." *Journal of Applied Psychology* (70, May 1985), 398-400.

For Further Reading

Bache, Christopher M. *Lifecycles: Reincarnation and the Web of Life* (New York, N.Y.: Parean House, 1991).

Blavatsky, H.P. *The Secret Doctrine: The Synthesis of Science, Religion, and Philosophy,* Vols. 1 and 2 (Pasadena, Calif.: Theosophical University Press, 1963).

Brennan, Barbara Ann. *Hands of Light* (New York, N.Y.: Bantam, 1987).

Cohen, Daniel. *The Mysteries of Reincarnation* (New York, N.Y.: Dodd, Mead & Co., 1975).

Cranston, S.L., and Williams, C. *Reincarnation: A New Horizon in Science, Religion, and Society* (New York, N.Y.: Julian Press, 1984).

Dethlefsen, Thorwald. *Voices from Other Lives* (New York, N.Y.: Evans, 1977).

Dossey, Larry. *Recovering the Soul: A Scientific and Spiritual Search* (New York, N.Y.: Bantam, 1989).

Gardner, Martin. *Science: Good, Bad, and Bogus* (Buffalo, N.Y.: Prometheus Books, 1981).

Geiselman, R. Edward. "Hypnosis and Memory." *Encyclopedia of Learning and Memory* (New York, N.Y.: Macmillan Publishing Co., 1992), 255-258.

Head, Joseph, and Cranston, S.L. *Reincarnation: The Phoenix Fire Mystery* (New York, N.Y.: Julian Press, 1977).

Hilgard, E.R. *Divided Consciousness: Multiple Controls in Human Thought and Action* (New York, N.Y.: Wiley, 1977).

Holzer, Hans. *Life Beyond Life: The Evidence for Reincarnation* (West Nyack, N.Y.: Parker, 1985).

Iverson, Jeffrey. *In Search of the Dead* (San Francisco, Calif.: HarperCollins Pub., 1992).

Kramer, Carol, and Bulmhorst, David. "Secrets of Life, Death, and Rebirth: An Interview with Sogyal Rinpoche." *Body, Mind, Spirit* (March/April 1993), 44-48.

Lenz, Frederick. *Lifetimes: True Accounts of Reincarnation* (New York, N.Y.: Ballantine, 1986).

Monroe, Robert A. *Journeys Out of the Body* (New York, N.Y.: Doubleday, 1977).

Montgomery, Ruth. *Here and Hereafter* (New York, N.Y.: Howard MacCann, 1968).

Montgomery, Ruth. *Threshold to Tomorrow* (New York, N.Y.: Putnam, 1982).

Murrey, Gregory J., *et al.* "Hypnotically Created Pseudomemories: Further Investigation into the 'Memory Distortion or Response Bias' Question." *Journal of Abnormal Psychology* (101:1; February 1992), 75-77.

Osis, Karlis. *At the Hour of Death* (New York, N.Y.: Avon, 1977).

Porter, M. J. "Past-Life Therapy with Brian Weiss." *Body, Mind, Spirit* (March/April 1993), 49-51.

Rieder, Marge. *Mission to Millboro* (Nevada City, Calif.: Blue Dolphin Publishing, Inc., 1993).

Rinpoche, Sogyal. *The Tibetan Book of Living and Dying* (San Francisco, Calif.: Harper, 1992).

Rogo, D. Scott. *The Search for Yesterday: A Critical Examination of the Evidence of Reincarnation* (Englewood Cliffs, N.J.: Prentice Hall, 1985).

Sagan, Carl. *The Dragons of Eden: Speculations on the Evolution of Human Intelligence* (New York, N.Y.: Ballantine, 1977).

Schlotterbeck, Karl. *Living Your Past Lives: The Psychology of Past-Life Regression* (New York, N.Y.: Ballantine, 1987).

Sheehan, Peter W., and Tilden, Jan. "Real and Simulated Occurrences of Memory Distortion in Hypnosis." *Journal of Abnormal Psychology* (93; 1984), 47-57.

Spanos, Nicholas, *et al.* "When Seeing Is Not Believing: The Effects of Contextual Variables on the Reports of Hypnotic Hallucinators." *Imagination, Cognition, and Personality* (2; 1983), 195-209.

Stearn, Jess. *The Search for the Girl with the Blue Eyes: A Venture into Reincarnation* (Garden City, N.Y.: Doubleday & Co., 1968).

Tebbetts, Charles. *Miracles on Demand: The Radical Short-Term Hypnotherapy* (Royal, Ariz.: Living Life Publications, 1985).

Thurston, Mark. *Soul Purpose: Discovering and Fulfilling Your Destiny* (San Francisco, Calif.: Harper & Row, 1984).

Reenactment Events and Involvement

For information on upcoming reenactments or how to join a re-enactment unit, call the *Civil War News* at 1-800-222-1861 for your free issue. Also, feel free to talk to reenactors at events.

Preservation
Founded in 1987 by a group of historians deeply concerned over the irresponsible development and eradication of America's Civil War battlefields, the Association for the Preservation of Civil War Sites (APCWS) is a membership-driven organization of more than 10,000 individuals. For more information on how you can join the fight to save America's hallowed ground, contact the APCWS at:

> APCWS
> Elizabeth Hager Center
> 14 N. Potomac St., Suite 201
> Hagerstown, MD 21740

It is my privilege to donate a portion of my royalties to the APCWS for the preservation of Civil War battlesites.

About the Author

Barbara Lane, a clinical hypnotherapist in private practice, was trained by some of the foremost regression therapists in the United States. She is a member of the Association for Past-Life Research and Therapies.

In her practice, Ms. Lane combines alternative and traditional healing techniques. She is a Reiki master, and her work incorporates the mind/body connection. She has career experience in social work as case manager of a homeless shelter and as a crisis counselor.

Ms. Lane's background is in teaching, management, public relations, and as an international flight attendant. She also served as anchor and reporter of an award-winning newscast in California and has produced, reported, and directed for television.

Currently working on her Ph.D., Ms. Lane received her M.A. in metaphysics from Westbrook University, New Mexico; a B. A. in history from Mercy College, Michigan; and an A. A. in telecommunications from Cuesta College, California. She is presently researching other historical time periods and their corresponding past-life links.

A native of Michigan, Ms. Lane is comfortable living on both coasts. Her interests include travel, ancient cultures, and the arts.

For information on speaking engagements or private sessions, Ms. Lane can be contacted by writing to: P.O. Box 25502, Alexandria, VA 22313.